WITHDRAWN

# Fundamentals of Motor Vehicle Technology

## WORKBOOK

Trevor Catt
Richard Miller

## 2

LRC Stoke Park
GUILDFORD COLLEGE
D1078839

Nelson Thornes
a Wolters Kluwer business

153023
629.287 CAT

Text © Trevor Catt and Richard Miller 2006

The right of Trevor Catt and Richard Miller to be identified as authors of this work has been asserted by them in accordance with the Copyright Designs and Patents Act 1988.

All rights reserved. No part of this publication may be reproduced or transmitted in any form or by any means, electronic or mechanical, including photocopy, recording or any other information storage and retrieval system, without permission in writing from the publisher or under licence from the Copyright Licensing Agency Limited, of 90 Tottenham Court Road, London W1T 4LP.

Any person who commits any unauthorised act in relation to this publication may be liable to criminal prosecution and civil claims for damages.

Published in 2006 by:
Nelson Thornes Ltd
Delta Place
27 Bath Road
CHELTENHAM
GL53 7TH
United Kingdom

06 07 08 09 10 / 10 9 8 7 6 5 4 3 2 1

A catalogue record for this book is available from the British Library.

ISBN 0 7487 9600 2

Page make-up by GreenGate Publishing Services, Tonbridge, Kent

Printed and bound in Croatia by Zrinski

# CONTENTS

# INTRODUCTION TO THE INDUSTRY

## The motor industry

### A way forward

Did you know your industry, the motor industry, is worth £130 billion per year and employs hundreds of thousands of people in the UK?

Did you know that there are career opportunities that go beyond the workshop?

The motor industry is growing and the career opportunities available to skilled young people are incredibly varied. The qualifications you gain can be used to take you beyond your local garage. Your skills as a technician can be used in the armed forces, roadside assistance and recovery, or in motorsport, for example – and there are many more opportunities available to you!

Automotive Skills, the Sector Skills Council for the retail motor industry, works closely with employers to help promote all the different career paths on offer. Automotive Skills also influences your training to ensure that you are equipped with the appropriate skills required to do your job and to enable you to fulfil your career ambitions and learning potential.

Read on to find out more about the different careers available for motivated young people, like yourself, who want to be part of this exciting and challenging industry.

## Routefinder

### Your future direction

The motor industry is made up of a number of 'sub-sectors' or distinct areas of business. Here's a brief introduction to each, linked to further information on the Automotive Skills careers website. Although your training will lead you to work on the technical side of things, you may be interested in a career change at some point in the future – plus you'll probably find yourself coming into close and regular contact with people working in these sub-sectors, so it's good to know what they're up to.

### Vehicle maintenance, repair and fast-fit

Every vehicle needs to be maintained regularly. But sometimes they may break down and will need to be repaired – quickly and to a high standard. This is where you are most likely to start in the industry – employers of all sizes need technicians, so you should have no shortage of options. There will be different specialisms to suit as well, whether you're interested in cars, motorbikes or trucks, auto electrics, diagnostics, or exhaust and tyre fitting – even motorsport!

### Vehicle body repair and refinishing

Thousands of vehicles are involved in scrapes every day of the week and many drivers are likely to need their car, van or motorcycle repaired at least once. Working in vehicle body repair and refinishing involves removing dents and bumps, and restoring the paintwork, as well as repairing the electrical and mechanical parts so that they are in sound working order.

### Vehicle parts

There are lots of people who are fascinated by vehicles but who don't necessarily feel they would enjoy the hands-on technical aspects. Vehicle parts operatives play a vital role in ensuring that technicians have the components they need to maintain and repair vehicles – using sophisticated computer systems and often working to tight deadlines.

### Roadside assistance and recovery

Vehicles today are pretty reliable but from time to time, inevitably, things do go wrong. That is why a key role in the motor industry is played by technicians whose job it is to go out on the road and to solve a problem where a vehicle has broken down, or to recover the vehicle and take it and its passengers to their destination. Jobs are offered to technicians who have gained several years' experience in the workshop, and have excellent customer service skills – so if you're good with people as well as your hands, there could be a future here.

### Vehicle sales

For most people, buying a vehicle is the second most expensive purchase they make (after buying a home). That's why it's important that they make the right choice. The job of vehicle sales is to help the customer make a decision with which they will be satisfied – not just for a day but for the lifetime of the vehicle, so that they come back again in the future.

### Vehicle rental and leasing

This area focuses on providing customers and clients with vehicles on a non-permanent basis whether that be for a few days or weeks – that's vehicle rental – or longer term, which is known as leasing. In both of these areas, staff are more likely to be involved in the financial, legal, insurance, customer service and administrative part of the business, instead of working directly on vehicles.

## Products and resources

### What next?

There is a wide range of materials and resources available which show just how challenging and exciting the retail motor industry can be.

### Careers information folder

This folder consists of six inserts, each profiling a different part of the motor industry. It is an excellent introduction to the key career options.

### *Career Driven* magazine

This is a careers and lifestyle magazine full of case studies, celebrity profiles, motoring news and guidance on how to make your way in the motor industry.

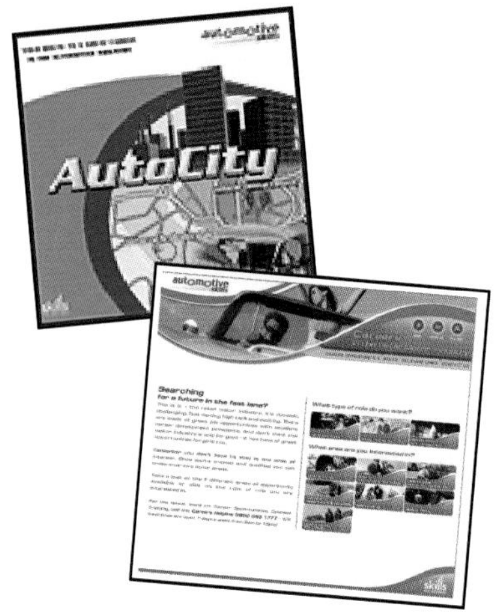


### *AutoCity™*

This interactive, game-based careers CD is produced by Automotive Skills. Travel around AutoCity™ and find out all the latest careers information from a whole range of different employers.

### Automotive Skills – careers web portal

The portal is packed with everything you need to know about getting on in the motor industry – and it is linked to all the key careers and industry organisations. Try our course search, which is powered by learndirect.

### www.automotiveskills.org.uk/careers

If you wish to order any of the above products and materials, or if you wish to sign up for careers information updates, please contact us at careers@automotiveskills.org.uk.

## Careers Helpline

**Want to know more about any of these areas?**
Visit our careers website at www.automotiveskills.org.uk/careers, or call our free Careers Helpline on 0800 093 1777 for more information.

## Acknowledgements

The authors would like to thank their friends, family and colleagues for all the support they have given during the compilation of this book.

We should like to thank the following companies for permission to make use of copyright and other material:

Robert Bosch Ltd
Jaguar Cars Ltd

Although many of the drawings in this book are based on commercial components, they are mainly intended to illustrate principles of motor vehicle technology. For this reason, and because component design changes so rapidly, no drawing is claimed to be up to date. Students should refer to manufacturers' publications for the latest information.

Every effort has been made to trace the copyright holders but if any have been inadvertently overlooked the publishers will be pleased to make the necessary arrangement at the first opportunity.

Cover image courtesy of Honda.

### Reviewers

Christian Wilkins MSc, BSc, PGCE, MILT, MIMI
Kingston and Merton College (CoVE), United Kingdom

Graham R. Haydon-Hill BSc, FIMI
Automotive Study Centre, Grantham, United Kingdom

# HOW TO USE THIS WORKBOOK

Welcome to the *Fundamentals of Motor Vehicle Technology Workbook 2*, which has been specially designed to encourage you to work independently and help you through your course with ease. You can complete the questions, exercises and activities directly into the workbook and refer back to your answers when it's time to revise! Some of the research tasks and mini projects will require you to use additional paper in order to complete them.

You will find some text within each chapter that talks about basic principles; this will help you to recap and ensure that you have a full understanding of these. Other topics are intended as introductions and will be fully investigated when you progress to Workbook 3.

Here are the features you will notice as you work through the book:

**Essential knowledge** – a list of topics you will need to know before completing each chapter. *Hillier's Fundamentals of Motor Vehicle Technology Book 1* is an excellent resource to refer to. Your tutor can advise you about other resources that are available.

**Q** – these boxes contain straightforward questions for you to answer.

**E** – these boxes contain a variety of exercises for you to complete, including missing words, sketching, labelling, research and calculation tasks.

**Discussion points** – these encourage you to discuss different issues with your fellow students.

**Practical activities** – These activities, at the end of the chapter, will help you to put the theory you have learnt into practice.

**Mini projects** – you will find a selection of mini projects at the end of each chapter which involve you researching and investigating various topics. These will encourage you to learn and discover more about new and emerging technology.

**Safety notes** – these brightly coloured boxes are intended to draw your attention to essential health and safety information.

**Environmental notes** – these boxes highlight important environmental issues that you must consider.

**Check boxes** appear in the margin so you can keep a record of what you have learnt and monitor your own progress.

Wishing you lots of success for the future!

# CHAPTER 1

# ENGINES

You will need to read and research vehicle technology covering the following:

- The internal-combustion reciprocating engine
- Single-cylinder and multi-cylinder engines
- Crankshafts
- Connecting rods
- Pistons, piston rings and combustion chambers
- Intake, exhaust valves and valve springs
- Valve operating mechanisms
- Intake manifolds
- Air cleaners and filters
- Exhaust systems, silencers and catalytic converters
- The engine lubrication system

Note: some of this chapter refers to basic principles to ensure a full understanding.

Over time, motor vehicles have evolved from horseless carriages to the high performance cars that we now have. Coal powered, steam-driven vehicles have given way to modern cars powered by petrol and diesel engines. Amongst the limitations of steam were large water tanks, coal tenders and the long delay needed to heat the steam up to its operating temperature.

Designers and inventors knew about alternative fuels and different ways of releasing energy, but simple problems such as igniting fuel in a chamber took many years to be solved successfully.

Two types of internal-combustion engine (ICE) developed alongside each other: petrol (spark ignition) and diesel (compression ignition) engines. Both of these have their advantages and disadvantages.

Other types of engine, such as gas, electric and hybrid, can be found in some modern vehicles. There is an activity at the end of this chapter on researching further information about these systems.

**discussion point**

**Test your knowledge of the four-stroke cycle for both petrol and diesel engines by discussing their operation with a partner. Prove your understanding by presenting your ideas to the group, using sketches to help you if necessary.**

E In the table below, enter the correct cylinder phases for the firing order of 1–2–4–3.

| Cylinder no. | 1 | 2 | 3 | 4 |
|---|---|---|---|---|
| 1st stroke | | | | |
| 2nd stroke | | | | |
| 3rd stroke | | | | |
| 4th stroke | | | | |

## The internal-combustion reciprocating engine

### Compression ratio

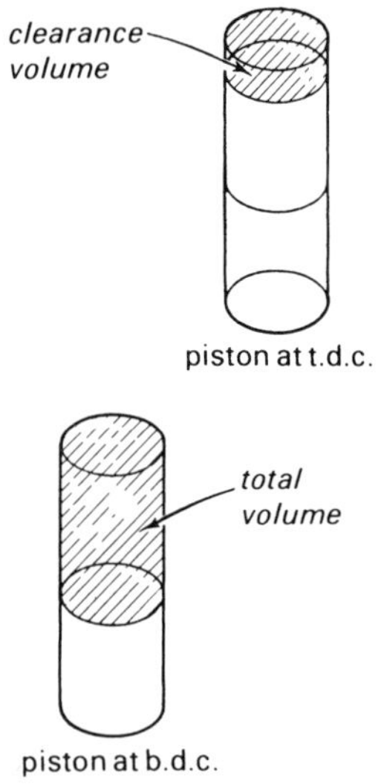


Q Look at the diagram (left). Can you complete the formula for calculating compression ratios below?

Compression ratio =

=                +

=                +

E Calculate what the compression ratio would be if the swept volume is 100 $cm^3$ and the clearance volume is 10 $cm^3$.

E Research and define the terms 'torque' and 'power' in relation to the output of an engine. Sketch a torque and power curve graph for a petrol engine with fixed valve timing. Compare your graph with one showing the torque curve for an engine with variable valve timing. Explain the differences in torque output.

### The main components of a reciprocating engine

E Describe what is meant by the following terms:

Bore

Stroke

**Flywheel**

A flywheel has many purposes, such as a mounting surface for a clutch to operate on, maintaining rotational force between power strokes and mounting starter motor ring-gear.

E Manufacturers are moving away from the conventional construction of flywheels. Through research, identify and sketch a dual-mass flywheel and briefly explain its function and operation.

## Single-cylinder and multi-cylinder engines

### Cylinder arrangements

Vehicles can be equipped with a wide range of engine configurations, such as single-cylinder or multi-cylinders,'V' (or 'vee') formation, opposed, in-line, etc. Space within the vehicle's engine bay often determines the choice of engine.

**Cylinder numbering**

**discussion point**

Test your knowledge of engine arrangements by discussing with a partner the advantages and disadvantages of single-cylinder and multi-cylinder engines. Write down your list of advantages and disadvantages, including any sketches that you think might help when you present your ideas to the rest of the group.

## Crankshafts

E

Check your knowledge by completing the diagram (using numbers and arrows), showing the different parts of the crankshaft.

1 Crankpin
2 Web
3 Flying web
4 Balance weight
5 Flywheel mounting flange
6 Pulley mounting
7 Spigot bearing
8 Oil ways

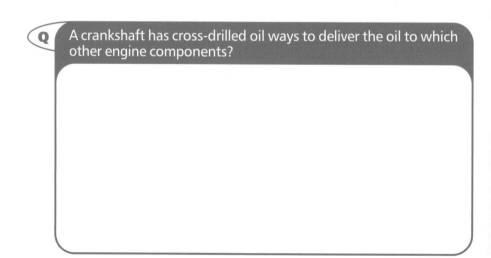

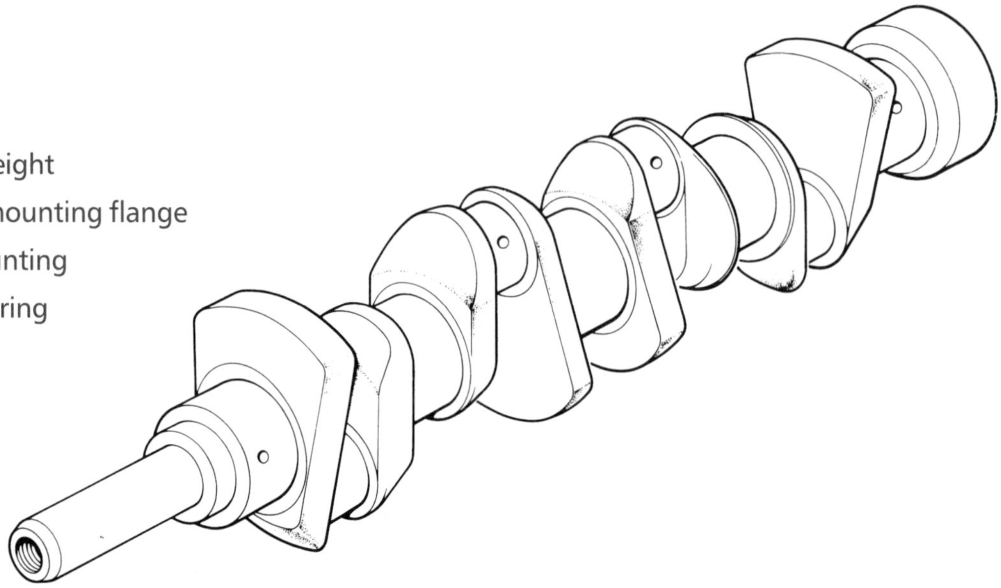

Q What is meant by the term 'crank radius'?

Q What is meant by the term 'balance masses'?

**Oil ways**

To provide lubrication to the various parts of an engine it is necessary to have a network of oil ways to deliver oil to other moving parts. These oil ways can be thought of as being similar to the arteries in a body.

Q A crankshaft has cross-drilled oil ways to deliver the oil to which other engine components?

### Crankshaft oil retainers (seals)

E

Draw a lip type seal and a scroll type oil retainer, showing the direction of oil flow. Label the parts as necessary.

## Connecting rods

A connecting rod serves to attach the piston to the crankshaft and connects reciprocating motion of the piston to rotational movement of the crankshaft.

E

Label the diagram and sketch in the correct location of the big-end bearings. List and explain the forces that the connecting rod is subjected to.

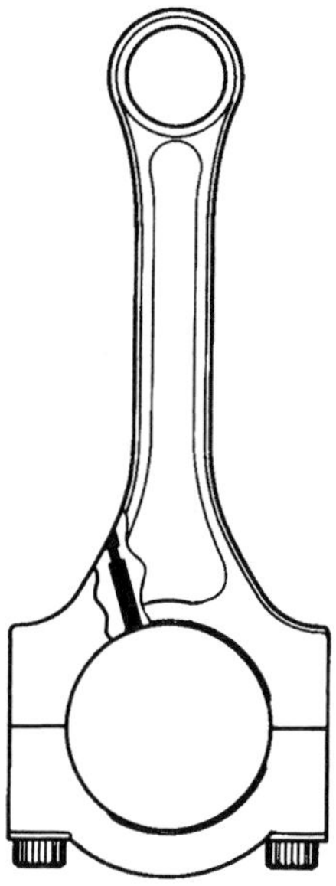

Q What are the terms fully floating and semi-floating in relation to the small end?

Q How are the big-end bearings lubricated?

Q How are the small-end bearings lubricated?

## Pistons, piston rings and combustion chambers

### Pistons

E Label the parts in the diagram and make sketches of domed and concave piston crowns. Explain the reasons for the different shapes

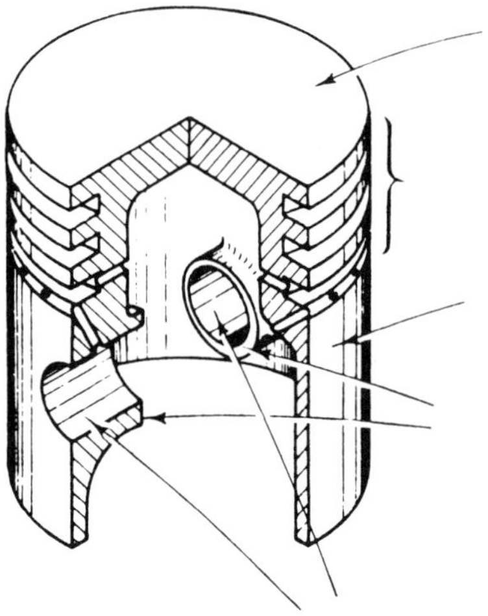

E On the power stroke the piston is forced over to one side of the cylinder. Label the diagram showing the 'thrust side'.

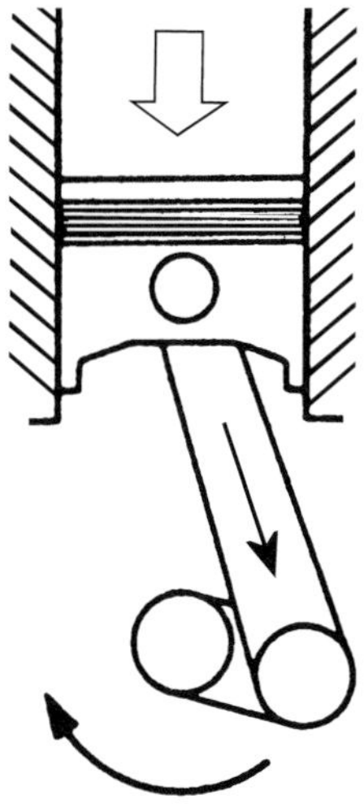

E Fill in the spaces in the description below to describe 'piston slap'.

Large __________, especially when the engine is __________, allow excessive side-to-side movement of the __________. This movement is usually at its __________ when the __________ passes the top and bottom __________ centres (when the connecting-rod angle changes), and this causes a __________ called piston __________, which is objectionable and can result in __________ wear of the piston and __________ wall.

piston | cylinder | slap | dead | greatest | clearances | premature | crankpin | cold | noise

Various materials are used in the construction of a piston to cater for expansion.

## Combustion and combustion chambers

E Sketch a graph showing cylinder pressure relative to crankshaft rotation for a typical petrol engine.

## Combustion chambers

E

All manufacturers strive to make their engines as efficient as possible. But what is meant by the terms volumetric efficiency, thermal efficiency and mechanical efficiency? Complete the table below. Also state briefly what you consider is the important point about each of these efficiencies.

| Term | Definition | Explanation |
|---|---|---|
| Volumetric efficiency | | |
| Thermal efficiency | | |
| Mechanical efficiency | | |

E

Research the preferred valve arrangement and combustion chamber shape to give a modern engine good economy, power and clean running. Sketch the layout and combustion chamber shape, and explain why this design is so effective.

## Combustion chambers – diesel

### Types of combustion chambers

There are two main classes of combustion chamber shapes known as direct injection and indirect injection.

We will look first the direct injection system. As the diagram shows, the injector sits almost centrally above the combustion chamber.

**Q** What two clear design differences are there compared with a petrol engine?

**Q** What effect will a small combustion chamber have on the compression ratio?

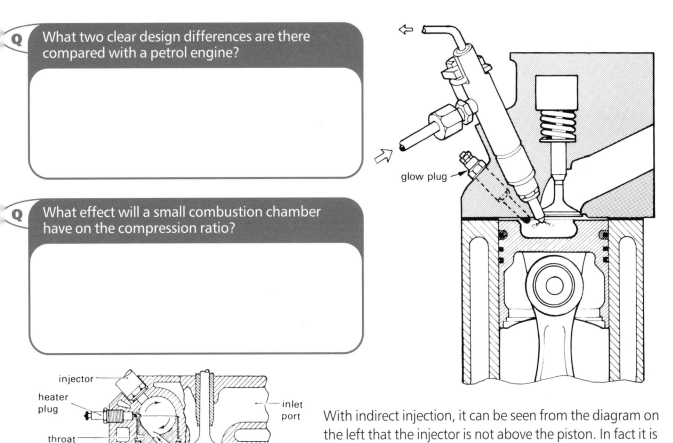

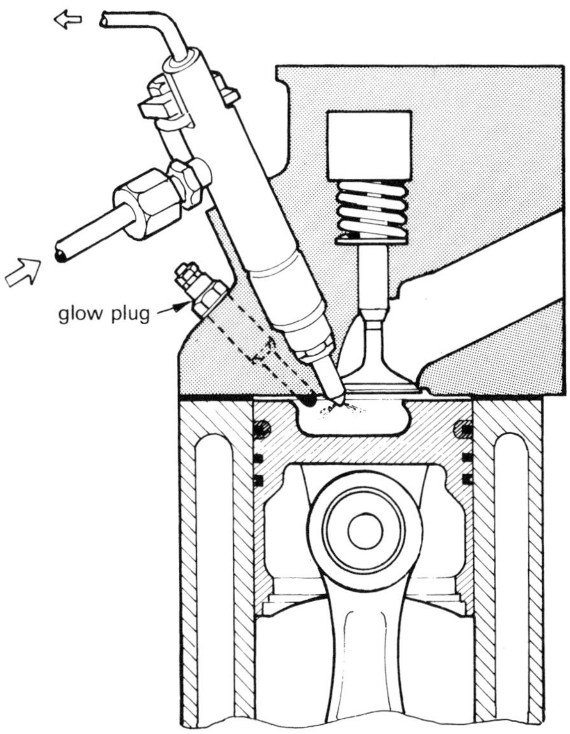


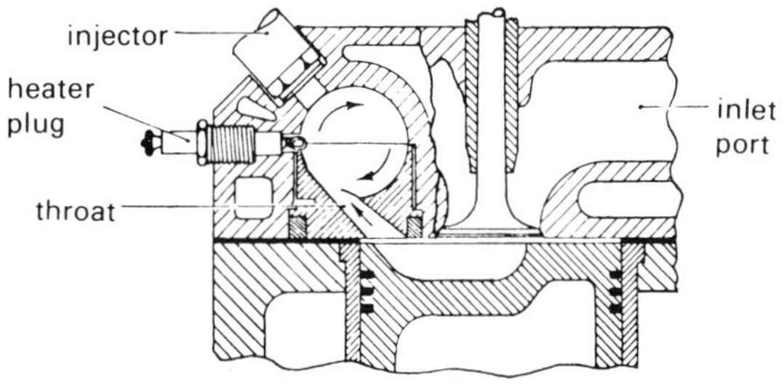


With indirect injection, it can be seen from the diagram on the left that the injector is not above the piston. In fact it is not even in the same combustion chamber; this additional chamber is called a swirl chamber, an ante-chamber or a pre-chamber.

**E** **Complete the description of the operating cycle of the indirect injection system using the missing words from the list below.**

The air is pumped through the hot __________ into the chamber during __________, so by the end of this __________ the ante-chamber contains very __________ air in a high state of __________. Fuel injected into this fast moving __________ mass is quickly __________ into a very fine state. This atomisation is very effective, even though the fuel is __________ in the form of a 'soft' spray by a pintle or single holed nozzle set at a comparatively low __________ (100 bar). After combustion has been initiated in the ante-chamber, burning fuel, together with the unburnt and partially burnt __________ is carried into the piston __________ in the main __________. When the injection period is increased to produce higher engine power, most of the fuel that is __________ towards the end of the spraying period does not ignite until it mixes with the air in the __________ chamber.

atomised | pressure | cavity | compression | throat | main | air | hot | swirl | injected | chamber | ignite | stroke | fuel

**discussion point**

Discuss with the group cold starting methods used on diesel systems. Compile information about at least two types. This may require some research.

## Piston rings

E

Explain why is it important to have correct piston-ring gaps, and suggest a typical sized gap. Sketch different types of oil control and compression rings. Describe their applications and the material that they are made from.

## Intake, exhaust valves and valve springs

The air and fuel mixture enters the cylinder via the intake ports and after combustion the burnt gases exit through the exhaust ports.

These ports must be opened only for the period when the intake mixture is being drawn in or when the exhaust gases are being expelled. All other times they must be closed. A valve is therefore fitted to each port.

**discussion point**

You are rebuilding a cylinder head. Discuss in a small group or with a partner the procedure that you must follow to ensure a gas-tight seal between the valve face and the valve seat. Come to a conclusion and write down your ideas, including any sketches that you think might help when you present your ideas to the rest of the group.

E

Check your knowledge by labelling the diagram showing the various components of the poppet valve arrangement.

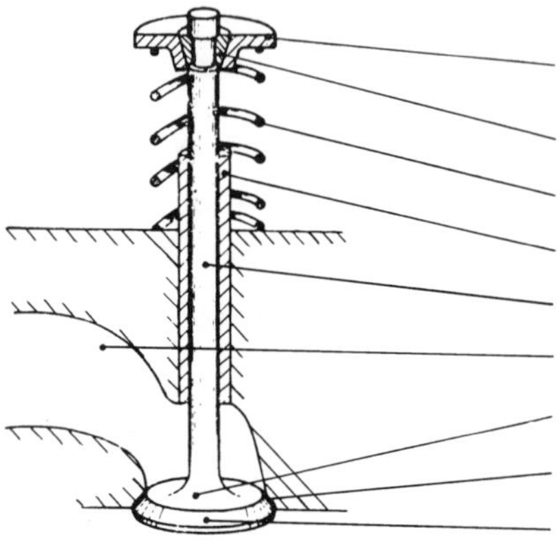

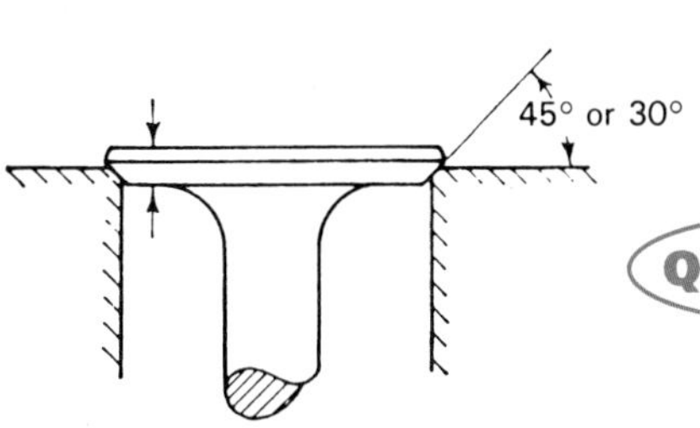


The diagram on the left shows the typical angles used for matching valve faces and seats.

**Q** Why is the seating narrower than the face?

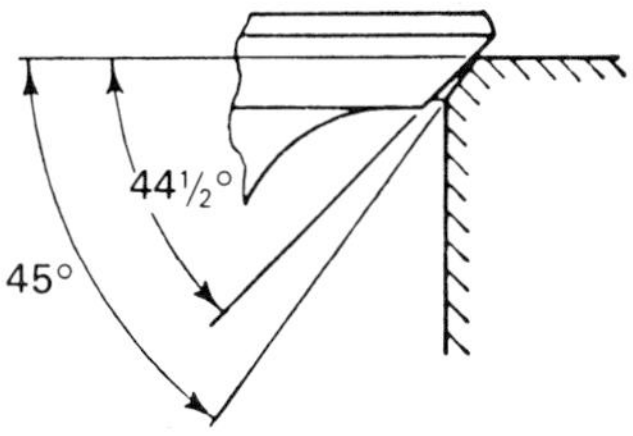


**Q** The diagram on the left shows the valve face and seat in more detail. Sometimes the valve face is ground to an angle of approximately ¼° less than the seat angle. What are the three reasons why this is done?

## Valve seats

The valve seat has to be made of a material that can withstand the impact of the closing valve, will not wear or corrode and can withstand the high temperatures during engine operation.

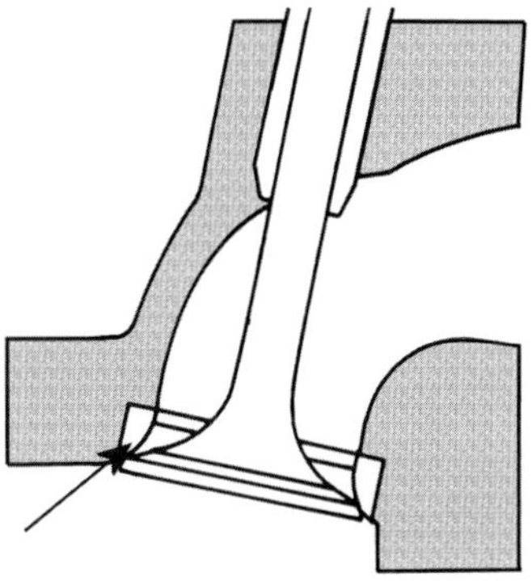

**Q** The drawing to the left shows an arrow pointing to a component. What is the component called and how is it held in the cylinder head?

**Q** How is a valve seat formed in a cast-iron cylinder head?

## Valve guides

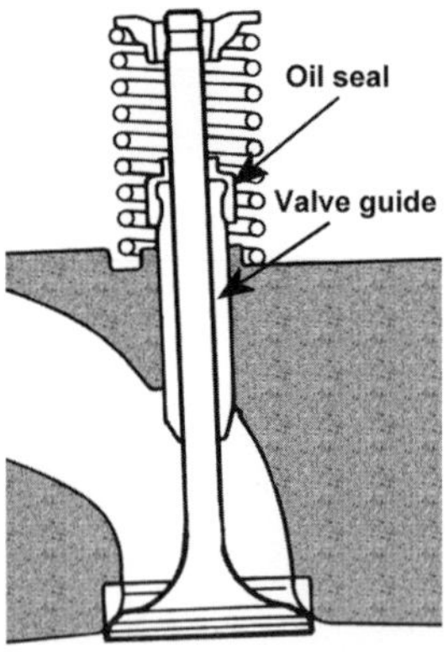


The valve slides in a hole in the cylinder or cylinder head called the 'valve guide'. The guide must be perfectly true with the seating, and a small operating clearance is allowed between the valve stem and the guide.

**Q** Why is this clearance built into the design of a valve guide?

**Q** What problems would be caused by an excessive clearance between the guide and the valve?

**Q** The valve guide is normally a replaceable sleeve (permitting easy renewal when worn) but in a cast-iron cylinder head the guide can be machined into the integral head casting. Which process can be used to remedy the problem of oil burning with a worn integral guide?

**discussion point**

Discuss with a partner why valve guide oil seals are normally fitted to inlet valves. Think about the faults that can occur if the seals or guides are worn excessively. Come to a conclusion and write down your ideas, including any sketches that you think might help when you present your ideas to the rest of the group.

**Q** Why are valve guide oil seals not normally fitted to the exhaust valves?

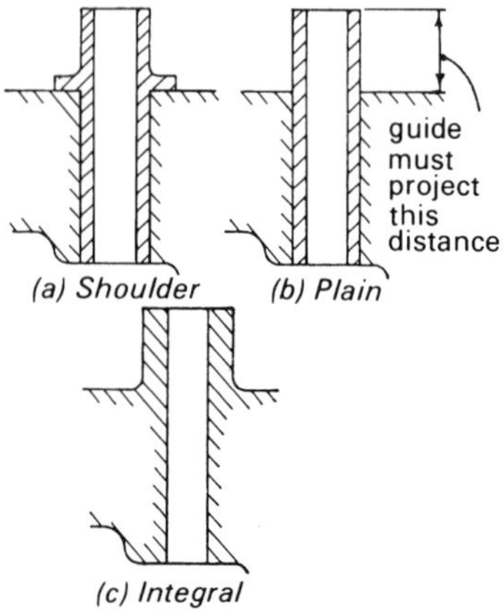


The diagram on the left shows three different types of valve guides.

**Q** Why does the guide protrude from the cylinder head?

## The valve spring

**discussion point**

Discuss with a partner the factors that need to be taken into account when determining the strength of a valve spring. Come to a conclusion and write down your ideas, including any sketches that you think might help when you present your ideas to the rest of the group.

E

Fill in the missing phrases from the list below to describe three ways in which 'surging' and 'valve bounce' can be overcome.

Helical or ____________ to 'surging' at certain engine speeds, when the centre coils vibrate in a ____________ stem. In ____________ this can lead to breakage of the springs, and can also allow the valves to bounce off their seating after closing. There are three ways ____________ can be overcome by using ____________ of spring. The springs are designed so that, when the ____________, they are compressed until adjacent coils ____________, so preventing the build up of excessive surging. The coils are ____________ at one end than the other. Springs of this kind must be fitted with the 'close' coils nearest the cylinder head. ____________ are used, one inside the other. This does not prevent surging, but the two springs ____________ at the same engine speed, and 'valve bounce' will be prevented. Also, if one ____________, the second spring will maintain pressure on the spring attachment and prevent the valve ____________ the cylinder.

two (or occasionally three) springs
different types
spaced closer together
direction parallel to the valve
extreme cases
spring should break
almost touch
'surging' and 'valve bounce'
valve is fully open
coil springs are liable
dropping into
will not both surge

Q

Explain what the diagram opposite is showing and sketch a typical tool used to carry out this operation.

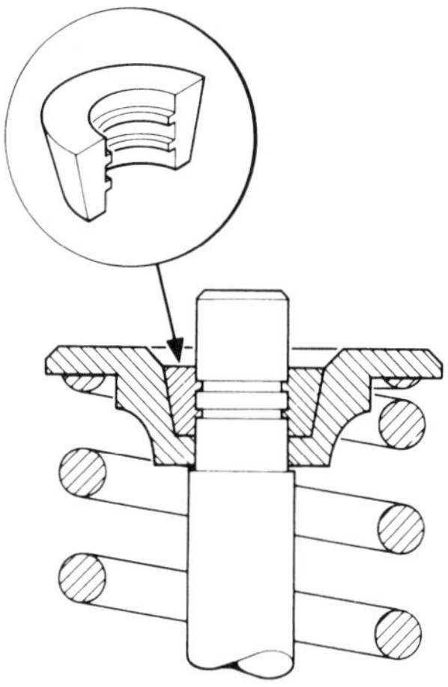

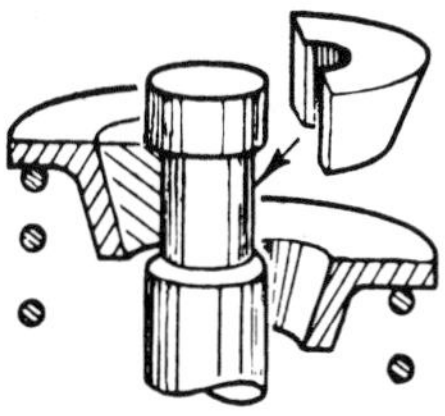

## Valve materials

### Exhaust valve

The exhaust valve head is exposed to the full heat of the burning gas during combustion, and when the hot gases are released from the cylinder they sweep past the exhaust valve head.

**Q** Under full power conditions what is the estimated temperature that an exhaust valve reaches?

**Q** What materials are used for the construction of exhaust valves?

**Q** The exhaust valve is cooled by passing on the heat in two directions. What are the two directions?

**Q** Sodium-filled valves are sometimes used in high performance engines to dissipate the heat generated. How do these valves do this?

**discussion point**

Discuss in a small group the advantages and disadvantages of using aluminium-coated valves. Come to a conclusion and write down your ideas, including any sketches that you think might help when you present your ideas to the rest of the group.

### Valve clearance

**discussion point**

With a partner, discuss the factors that must be taken into account when checking valve clearances. Come to a conclusion and write down your ideas, including any sketches that you think might help when you present your ideas to the rest of the group.

Q What problem can exist if the clearances are too large?

Q What problem can exist if the clearances are too small?

Q What potential engine damage can result from a clearance that is too small?

Q How would you ensure that you have correctly adjusted the valve clearances?

Q At which position on the cam lobe should you measure the valve clearances?

**Valve rotation**

E The diagram shows one method of enabling valve rotation. Indicate what this method is on the diagram and explain why valve rotation is important.

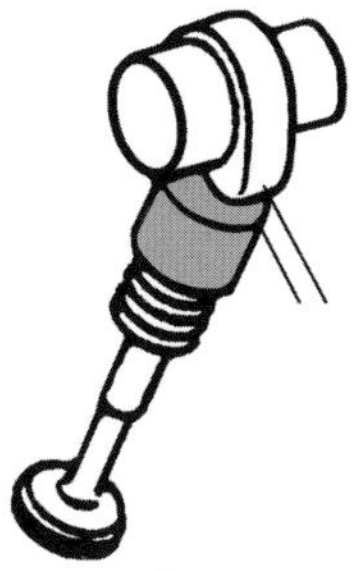

# Valve operating mechanisms

## Cams and camshafts

### Overhead valve (OHV) engines with pushrods

E

Check your knowledge by describing the layout and advantages of an overhead valve engine with pushrods. Label the diagram to show the individual components and show the motion of the moving parts.

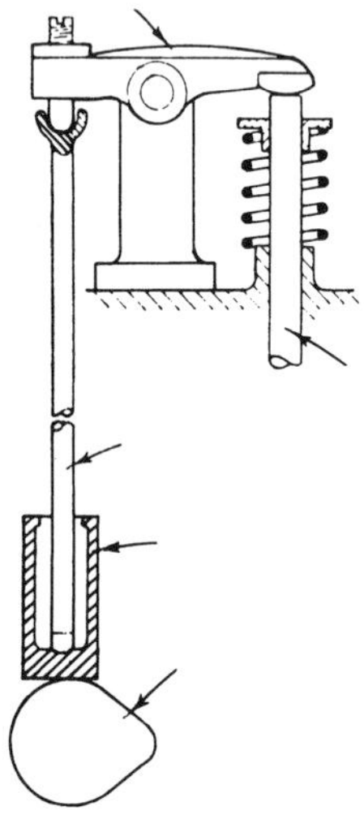

### Overhead camshafts (OHC)

E

The diagram shows a commonly used simple overhead-camshaft system using a rocker. Label the individual components and describe the advantages of using an overhead-camshaft layout by making a comparison with an overhead-valve layout. Explain how this set-up can be adjusted.

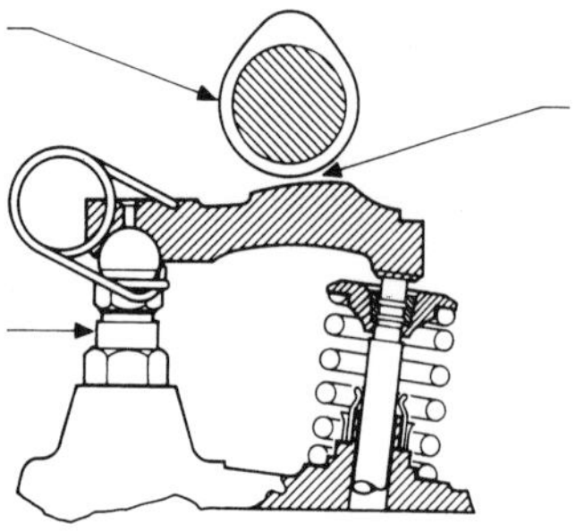

## Cam follower and tappets

### Overhead-camshaft cam followers

E

Label the diagram and explain the differences between this and the layout of the diagram on the previous page.

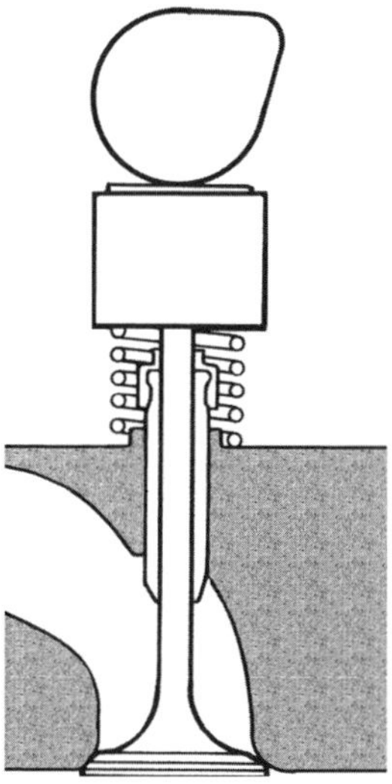

E

Describe the purpose of a cam follower shim.

Q

What course of action would you take if the working clearance was not correct on a shim-type layout?

## Hydraulic cam followers

E

Label the various components of the hydraulic cam follower as shown in the diagram. Describe how it operates and suggest advantages over other types of cam follower.

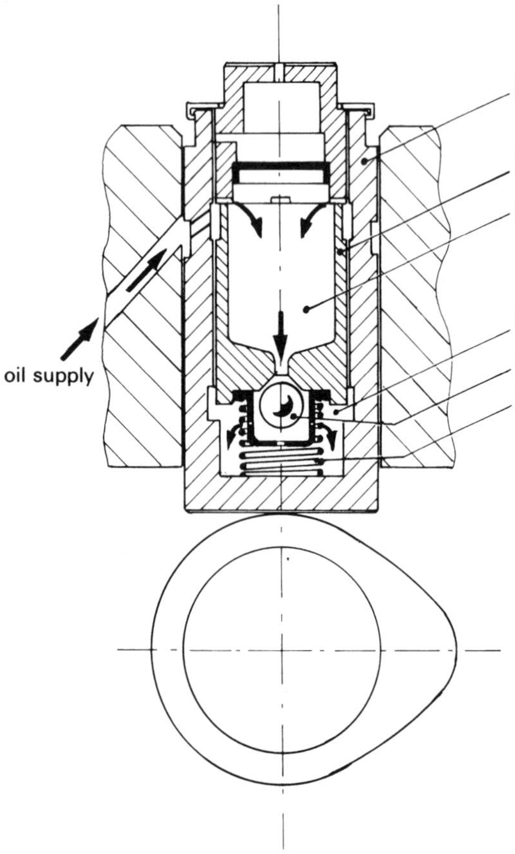


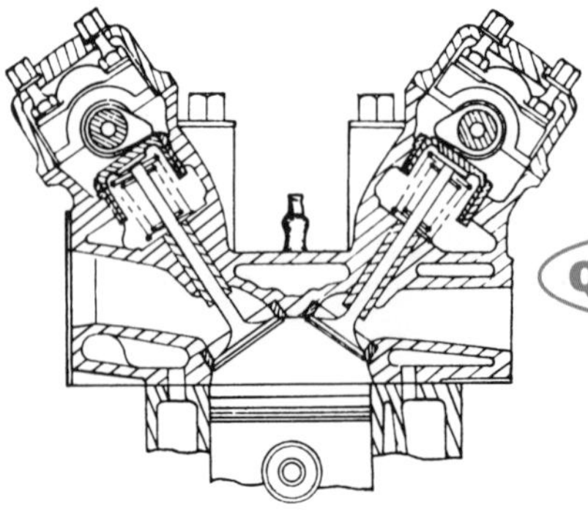

When the valves are arranged in an inclined manner, it is often preferable to operate the valves using a camshaft situated directly over each row of valves, as shown in the diagram on the left.

Q

What is this camshaft layout known as and how does it operate in simple terms?

discussion point

Discuss in a small group the advantages of the DOHC layout. Come to a conclusion and write down your ideas, including any sketches that you think might help when you present your ideas to the rest of the group.

**Q** Which type of cam follower is more commonly used in DOHC engines?

**Q** In an engine working on the four-stroke cycle, how many times must each valve be opened for every two revolutions of the crankshaft?

## Camshaft drives

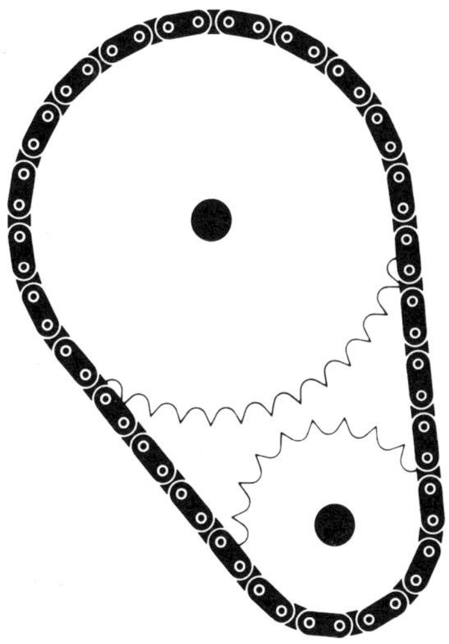

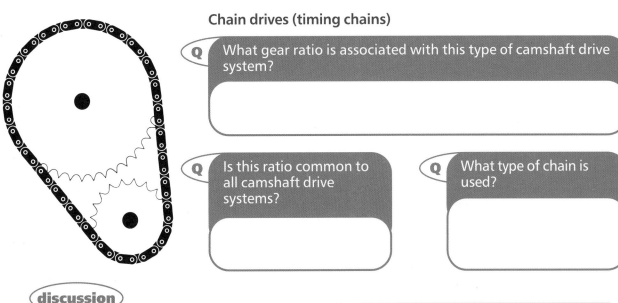

### Chain drives (timing chains)

**Q** What gear ratio is associated with this type of camshaft drive system?

**Q** Is this ratio common to all camshaft drive systems?

**Q** What type of chain is used?

**discussion point**

Discuss in a small group how camshaft drive component wear will cause the chain to lengthen and result in excessive noise (rattle). How can this problem be overcome? Come to a conclusion and write down your ideas, including any sketches that you think might help when you present your ideas to the rest of the group.

### Hydraulic adjustment for timing chains

The diagram below shows a hydraulic type of automatic adjuster, which is used in conjunction with a fixed slipper made of a plastic material; the slipper damps chain 'flutter'.

**E** Label the components in the diagram and describe the basic operation of the hydraulic timing chain tensioner.

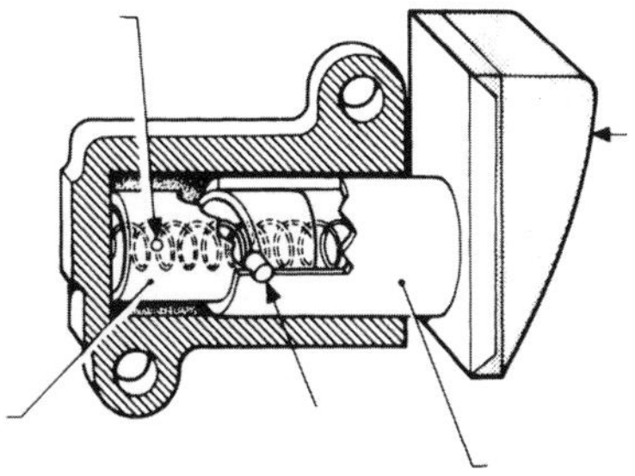

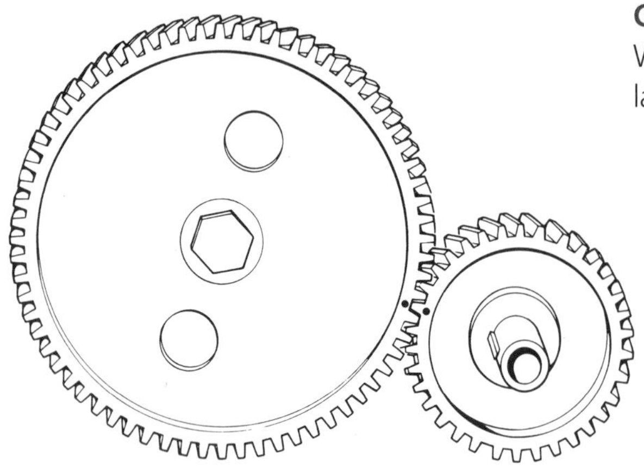

## Gear drives

When the camshaft is fitted close to the crankshaft a gear layout similar to that in the left-hand diagram can be used.

**Q** Which materials can be used for the construction of the gearwheels?

**Q** Which type of gear design can be used to reduce noise?

## Belt drives

Many modern overhead camshaft engines use a timing belt to drive the camshaft or camshafts. The belt is notched to form equally spaced teeth, which maintain the correct valve timing. An example is shown in the diagram.

**discussion point**

With a partner, discuss and think of reasons why a timing belt is superior to a timing chain. Write down your reasons, including any sketches that you think might help when you present your conclusions to the group.

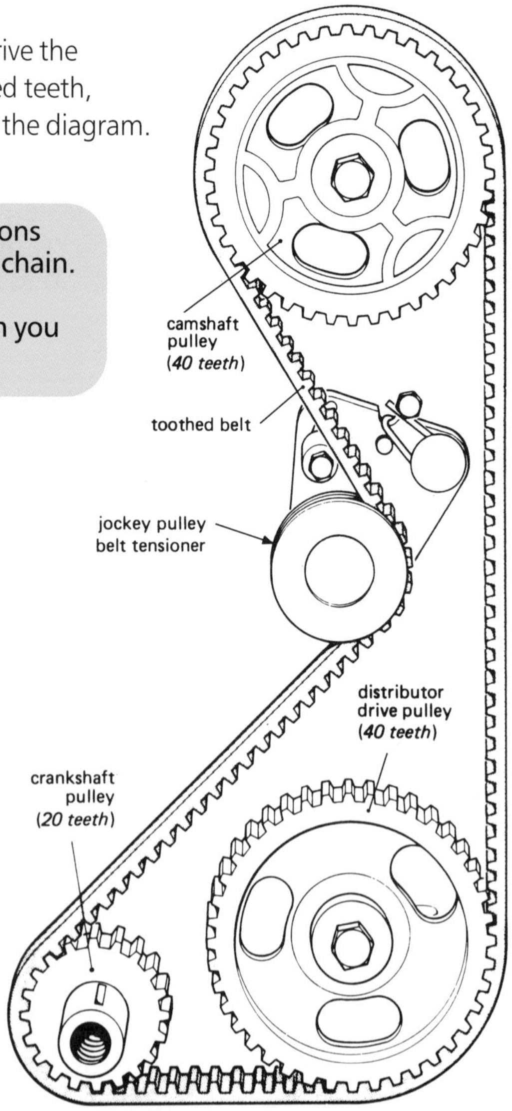


**Q** What is one reason why a belt can fail prematurely?

**Q** Which other components can a timing belt drive?

**Q** What materials are used for the construction of a timing belt?

**Q** Why is it important to ensure that the engine is timed correctly after fitting a new belt and before starting the engine?

**Note:** A broken timing belt can cause internal engine damage if the piston were to strike an open valve.

Sometimes an arrow printed on the timing belt indicates the direction of rotation. If a timing belt is to be removed and refitted during engine repairs, the direction of rotation should be noted before the belt is removed.

The timing belt should always be replaced at the correct manufacturer service intervals. Always ensure that the manufacturer's instructions are followed regarding timing alignment marks. Failure to follow instructions exactly can risk setting the camshaft(s) in the wrong position, which can lead to bent valves or piston damage.

## Valve and ignition timing

**Note:** To carry out the next task it will be useful to have a pencil, eraser, protractor and a workshop manual.

On the two blank circles on the left draw a valve timing diagram using the valve degrees given. Remember that the DOR (direction of rotation) is clockwise. This can be a group/class effort, but in the space on the right, you will have to use a workshop manual and draw your own diagram from the data given in it.

Also on your drawings arrow the approximate point where the spark will fire at idle and add an arrow at the point where maximum advance occurs.

Inlet valve opens 10° before top dead centre (BTDC); inlet valve closes 28° after bottom dead centre (ABDC); exhaust valve opens 28° before bottom dead centre (BBDC); exhaust valve closes 10° after top dead centre (ATDC).

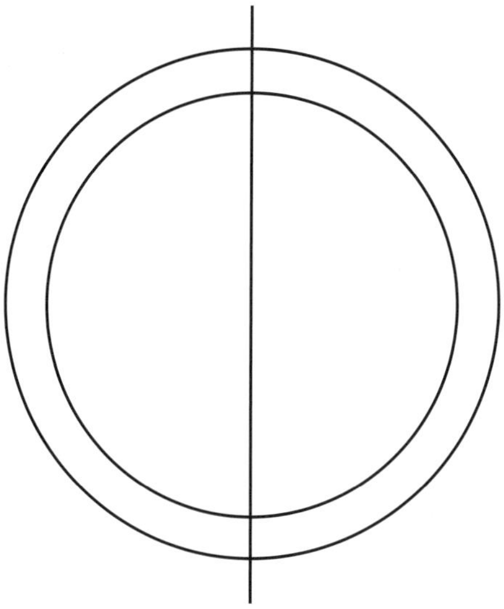

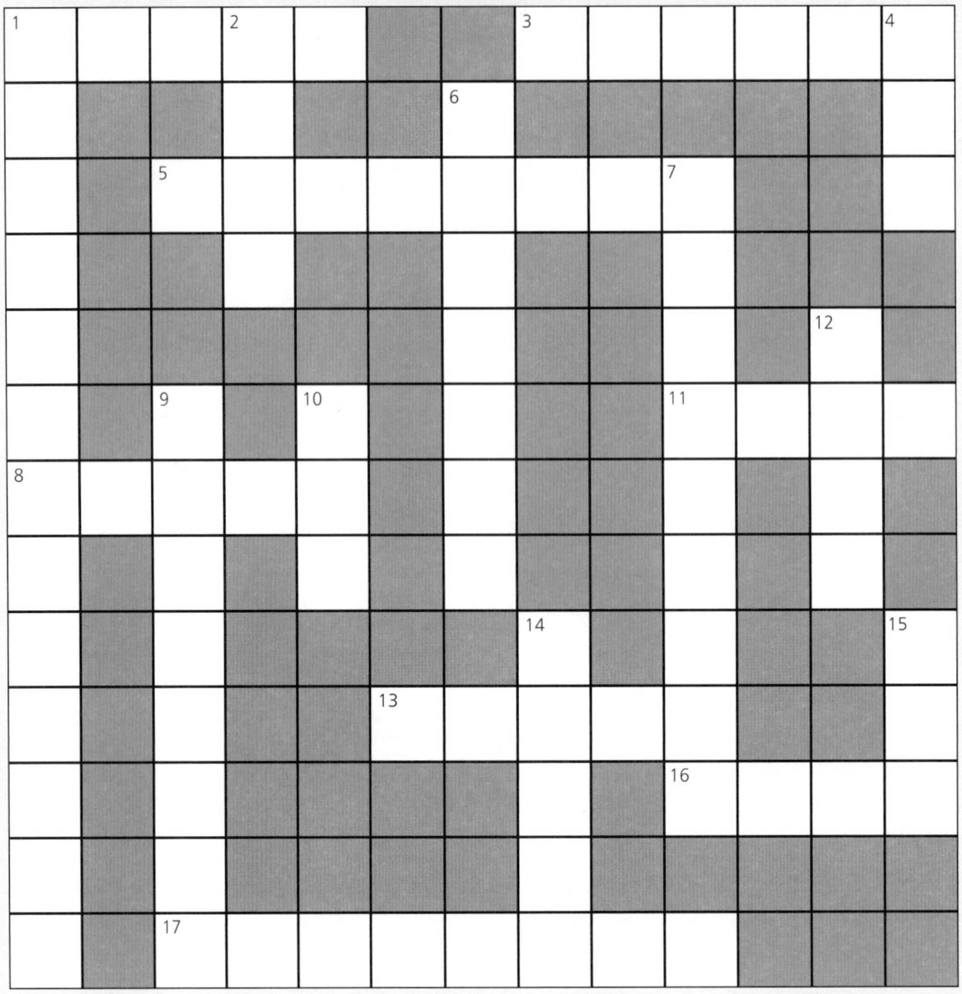


**Across**

**1** Type of bearing found in a crankshaft
**3** Side of a piston that is subjected to greater force
**5** Opens valves
**8** Components that support both inlet and exhaust valves
**11** Part of a valve
**13** Allows mixture into the cylinder
**16** Type of gear found on a flywheel
**17** Normally fitted on the front of a camshaft

**Down**

**2** The term when the inlet valve is open before TDC
**4** Highest point of piston travel (initials)
**6** Place where combustion takes place
**7** Normally used in a valve train
**9** Method of retaining gudgeon pins
**10** Stops rings turning on two-stroke pistons
**12** Connects crankshaft and camshaft
**14** Engine mountings are normally connected to this
**15** The term when the inlet valve is open after BDC

## Intake manifolds

E

Sketch one basic manifold with good unrestricted gas flow and even distribution of fuel/air charge, and one with poor gas flow and uneven distribution of fuel/air charge.

| Good gas flow | Poor gas flow |
| --- | --- |
| | |

E

Research and identify the shape of intake manifold fitted to modern vehicles with fuel injection. Sketch the different types you have found and explain the reason for their shape. It would be good to consider variable intake tracts.

## Air cleaners and filters

Engines always have some form of air-intake filtration system fitted. Abrasive particles can be carried in large quantities in the air.

Q

Test your knowledge and see if you can remember the three purposes of an air cleaner.

E

Describe why an air cleaner element has a concertina shape. Sketch some of the different external shapes of cleaner elements. List the applications that oil-bath air cleaners are used for. Explain why some air cleaners have automatic hot-air intake control.

**discussion point**

In a small group, consider alternative forms of filtration found on vehicles. Discuss how manufacturers can resolve problems where vehicles are used in high-dust conditions such as the desert. Come to a conclusion and write down your ideas, including any sketches that you think might help when you present your ideas to the rest of the group.

## Exhaust systems, silencers and catalytic converters

E

Research and discover the features of the following types of silencer: capacity, absorption and composite. Use sketches to help you to explain their operation.

E

Sketch an exhaust system and a cross section of a catalytic converter. Describe how the catalytic converter works. Show on your sketch the position of the lambda sensor.

E

Sketch two different multi-cylinder exhaust manifold systems. Explain how gas flow can be improved through the use of different designs.

## The engine lubrication system

**Q** What is meant by the term 'viscosity' and how is it measured?

**Q** What is meant by the term 'chemically engineered' when considering synthetic oils?

**E** If an adequate cooling system is provided, why does oil need to act as a coolant and how is the heat removed?

During its journey around an __________ the oil touches very hot surfaces that the __________ does not contact. The underside of the __________ and the lower parts of the bore are examples. As the oil touches these surfaces it collects __________ directly. This heat can be removed in a number of ways. A small oil cooler, where the oil passes through a __________ fed by the oil pump and set in the main cool airstream, is efficient at removing heat but could overcool in __________. Alternatively, a heat __________ can be used. Here, coolant in the cooling system can warm the oil quickly to reach running temperature. Then, when the temperature of the oil is above that of the coolant, heat is __________ back to the coolant to maintain a __________ temperature. Another option is to make the sump or oil __________ from a good heat conductor such as steel or aluminium and placed it in the cool air flow.

engine coolant pistons heat regulated

radiator winter exchanger transferred reservoir

E

Draw a comprehensive diagram of an engine lubrication system. This can be in block form but must show the direction of the oil flow and at least 10 of the main components. The use of a workshop manual or any technical literature is acceptable but must be documented. Your tutor may require you to add additional supporting information from any practical workshop tasks. State whether it is a full-flow or a bypass system.

Engine make/model:

Engine size:

Manuals/technical literature used:

E

Sketch two different types of oil pump. Label the parts and briefly explain how they work. Suggest a procedure for checking the pump for wear.

## The oil filter

E

Label the components of the oil filter. Explain what happens when/if the filter becomes blocked and what effect this may have on engine wear.

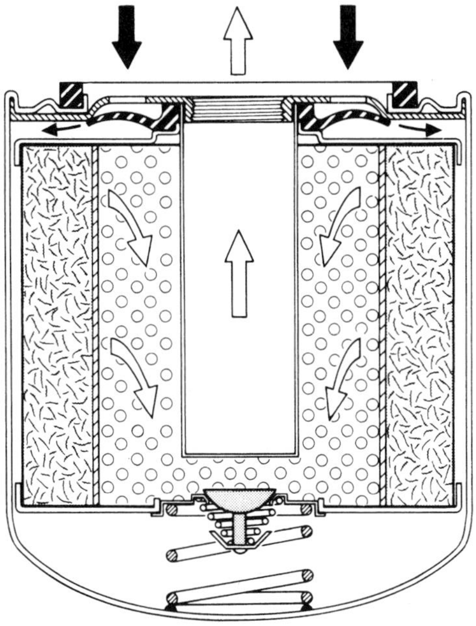

E

Research and discover the purpose of an oil pressure switch and pressure relief valve. Use sketches to help you to explain the operation of each.

***Environmental Note:* The Environmental Protection Act and local by-laws require you to dispose of hazardous waste through an approved collector. You must not allow the waste to enter the environment, that is, not into the drains or into landfill sites.**

## Crankcase ventilation

The fumes that accumulate in the crankcase are the most toxic the engine produces. This is because the blow-by of combustion gas down the sides of the pistons is only partly burnt. Why? The gas that escapes would be the last of the mixture to be burnt (end gas), but, as the cylinder pressure rises, it forces the end gas down past the piston before it can be burnt or the gas is only partly burnt. In the past this gas was vented to the atmosphere, but in keeping with modern trends it is now recycled.

E

**Research how a crankcase ventilation system works. Support your answer with a diagram, showing the flow around the system.**

Test your knowledge with this wordsearch. Can you find these words associated with engines in the grid? They have been written forwards, backwards, upwards, downwards and diagonally, but always in a straight line.

| | | | | | | | | | | | | |
|---|---|---|---|---|---|---|---|---|---|---|---|---|
| C | R | A | N | K | S | H | A | F | T | H | J | T |
| D | A | K | U | Y | P | Q | L | L | L | E | H | S |
| F | C | M | U | I | M | Y | M | E | Q | R | O | O |
| I | J | G | S | A | W | C | X | C | E | O | T | V |
| R | X | T | M | H | H | H | J | N | R | B | T | E |
| I | O | C | E | S | A | P | D | I | R | S | O | R |
| N | W | E | F | U | D | F | V | A | L | V | E | L |
| G | L | H | S | D | L | L | T | E | L | N | I | A |
| O | A | T | T | O | N | Y | Z | P | Z | G | Y | P |
| R | G | W | A | G | F | L | M | W | G | E | T | M |
| D | H | T | O | E | J | U | T | E | K | S | A | G |
| E | A | N | O | I | S | S | E | R | P | M | O | C |
| R | R | E | H | S | A | W | T | S | U | R | H | T |

Crankshaft
Piston
Thrust washer
Sump
Lobe

Overlap
Exhaust
End float
Flywheel
Seat

Bore
Otto
Firing order
Gasket
Key

Inlet
Compression
Shell
Valve
Lag

It is very easy to develop a narrow outlook on how a vehicle can be powered: petrol or diesel, four, six or eight cylinders. Most manufacturers follow a standard tried and tested format of vehicle layout, engine configuration and of course, fuel type.

It is easy to see why. To set up an engine plant to build engines for a high volume family car costs billions of pounds. To build an engine that customers might not want, or one that is too radical and different from normal engines would be a huge financial risk.

## mini projects

Agree the following with your tutor:

- which projects to do in which order
- the format and quantity of content
- the time frame for completion.

1 There has always been considerable development in motor manufacturing. Now, with high fuel prices, ever stricter emissions and new technologies there has been an evolution towards hybrid vehicles.

Research and list alternative engine designs and systems. State how manufacturers have used these systems of propulsion in the past or how they are currently testing and using them. Give a brief description of the function and operation of these systems and state what their advantages and disadvantages are for use in cars and trucks.

Consider: the Wankel engine (from the NSU Spider and R080 to today's Mazda RX-8); dual fuels (conversion problems, engine component considerations such as valves, duty on fuels, safety); hybrid vehicles (including fuel cell technology and future trends).

2 Carry out research on supercharging and turbocharging engines. Through your research explain, using diagrams, how superchargers and turbochargers improve the performance of naturally aspirated engines.

Consider: intercoolers, lubrication and lubricants, Rootes blowers, vane compressors and variable geometry turbochargers.

3 Research different types and grades of engine oil, to include synthetic types, used in a modern motor vehicle. From your research identify and compare the requirements and features of a multigrade mineral oil and a synthetic type. Describe typical applications and advantages/disadvantages of both types.

A lubricant manufacturer's specification chart or book would be useful for this exercise.

4 Research and identify the layout and components of both wet- and dry-sump lubrication systems. Create diagrams of the layouts and compare and explain any differences between the two systems.

## Practical activities

**practical activity 1**

1 Using a suitable vehicle and following manufacturer's procedures drain the engine oil into a suitable container and remove the oil filter. Dispose of the waste products in line with COSHH regulations.

2 Record the following manufacturer's data:

| Oil capacity in litres (inc. filter) | Recommended grade of oil | Sump plug torque setting |
|---|---|---|
| | | |
| | | |
| | | |
| | | |

3 Fit a new oil filter and replace the sump plug using the correct torque setting.

4 Measure out the correct amount of oil and refill the sump.

5 Run the engine and check for leaks (ensuring the oil pressure warning light goes out).

6 Re-check the oil level and top up if necessary.

7 Carry out an oil pressure test and record your results in the chart below.

| Manufacturer's specified oil pressure | Recorded oil pressure |
|---|---|
| | |
| | |
| | |
| | |

**practical activity 2**

Dismantle an engine that is safely fitted to a stand. During the dismantling process ensure that everything is set out so that it can be rebuilt to an operating standard. Inspect and measure the following components for wear and record your findings on a separate sheet. Compare your measurements with manufacturer's specifications and explain whether the components are serviceable or not:

Cylinder bores

Pistons

Piston rings

Oil pump

Crankshaft journals

Cylinder head (for distortion)

# CHAPTER 2

# TRANSMISSION SYSTEMS

### *Essential knowledge*

You will need to read and research vehicle technology covering the following:

- Transmitting the driving thrust
- Clutches
- Gearboxes
- Rear axle construction
- Propeller shafts and drive shafts
- Universal and constant-velocity joints
- Final drive gears
- The differential

Note: some of this chapter refers to basic principles to ensure a full understanding.

## Transmitting the driving thrust

Beware! A practical example of torque reaction

Isaac Newton stated in his third law of motion that 'for every action there is an equal and opposite reaction'.

**Q** In the drawing here, if the driving wheel were locked into the ground, what could happen to the tractor if the driver used all the tractor's power to pull forward?

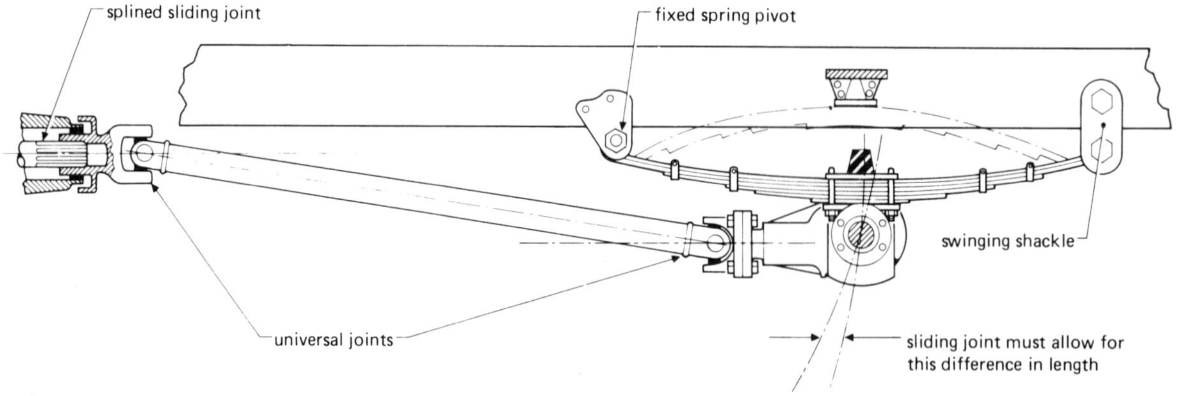


In the diagram we can see the layout of a rear-wheel drive system known as the 'Hotchkiss' (open type) drive.

When the vehicle is being driven the torque reaction will deflect the rear springs.

E

Draw a simple diagram of how the springs above will deflect when the vehicle is:

a under acceleration

b under braking.

Use arrows to show the torque reaction.

Q

You can see from the diagram on the previous page that the driving thrust is transferred to the vehicle frame. Which components transmit this driving thrust?

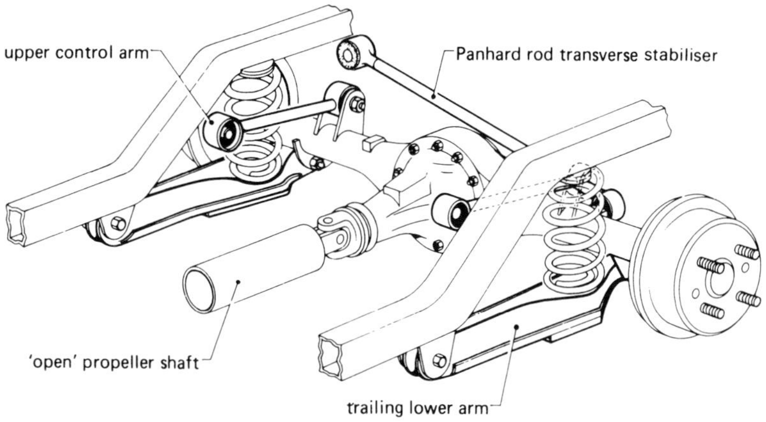


For various reasons the leaf spring has fallen out of favour with manufacturers. A later design is the four-link drive system.

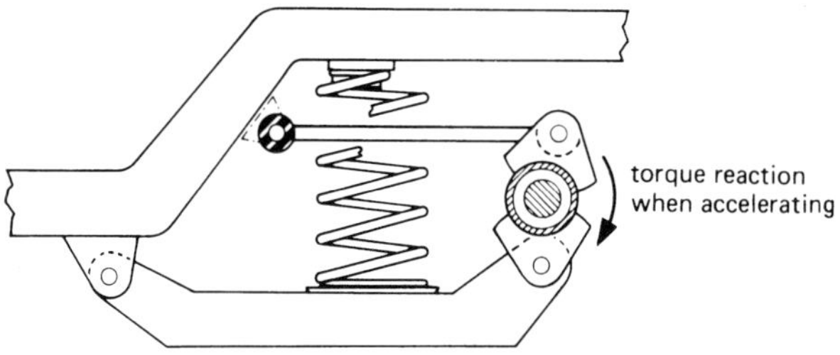


It is very important to familiarise yourself with the reaction of various suspension systems to the transmission of drive.

**discussion point**

Look at the diagram above of the four-link drive system. Discuss with a partner what is different about it compared with the Hotchkiss system. Write down your conclusions, including any sketches that you think might help, and be ready to present your ideas to the rest of the group.

# Clutches

## Single plate clutch

### Single-plate clutch arrangements

The single-plate clutch is relatively simple, smooth in operation and has the advantage of producing quick engagement and disengagement.

This style of clutch is not now used, but it is shown in diagrams because it illustrates the basic operating principles and components.

### Clutch springs

The coil springs shown in the diagram above make operation heavy, since the springs become stiffer the more they are deflected. To overcome this stiffness most cars are fitted with a diaphragm spring clutch.

**discussion point**

Test your knowledge by discussing with a partner the purposes of a clutch. Referring to the diagram on the previous page, list the advantages that a diaphragm spring offers compared with a coil spring. Write down your list of advantages, including any sketches that you think might help when you present your list to the rest of the group.

### Pressure plate construction

This cutaway diagram represents a diaphragm clutch.

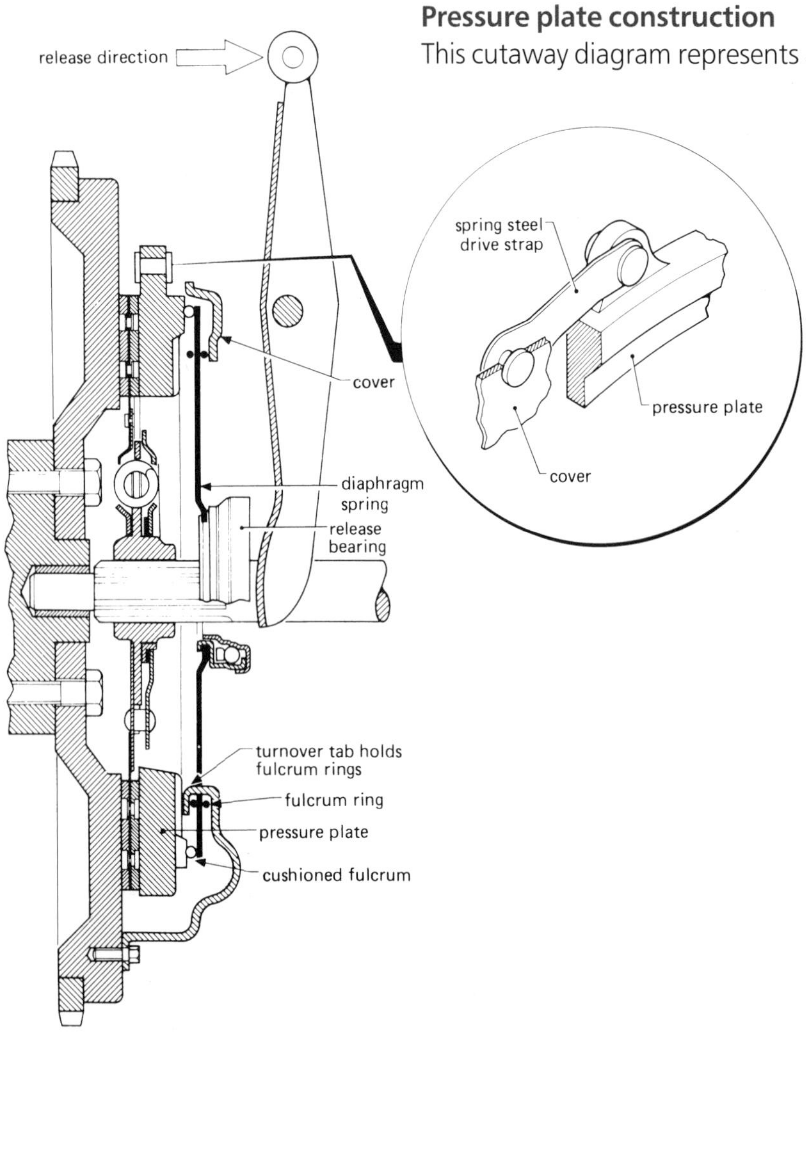

**Q** When you are fitting a new clutch assembly, you have to follow a particular procedure. What is this procedure?

**Q** Look at the diagram on page 36. Which component pivots on the fulcrum ring?

**Q** In the diagram on page 36, what is a strap drive and what is its purpose?

## The driven plate

**discussion point**

Look at the diagram or a physical example of a clutch driven plate and discuss in a small group the purpose of the design features built into it. Write down your ideas, including any sketches that you think might help when you present your conclusions to the rest of the group.

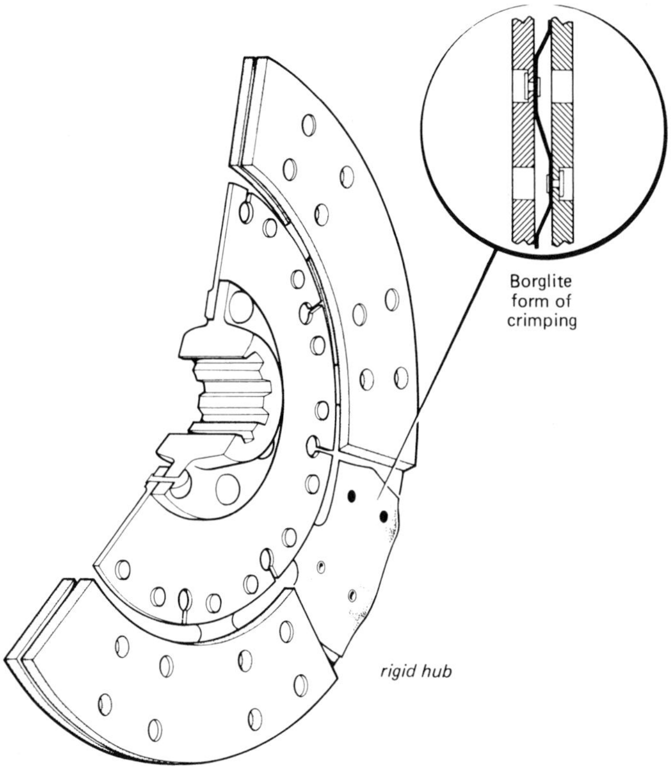


*rigid hub*

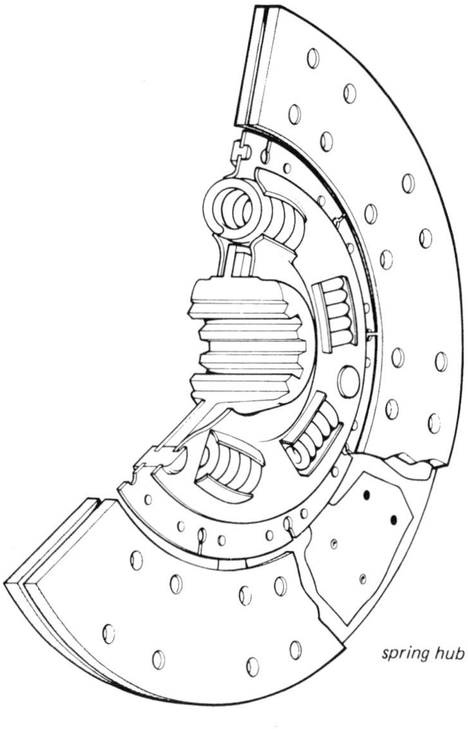

*spring hub*

E

Using the missing words on the right, describe why the springs are fitted and what the friction reduces.

oscillation
hub
shock
dampens
torsional
vibration
friction
driven

The outer part of the ___________ plate is separate or independent from the ___________ and fitted with springs to absorb ___________ shocks. The ___________ between the inner and outer components ___________ the spring ___________ as it absorbs the ___________, which reduces engine ___________.

E

Research and find out what is meant by the term 'mean effective radius'. Report on how this affects the amount of torque a clutch can transmit. Also, note other factors that affect torque transmission capabilities of clutches.

### Clutch alignment

Q

Which component is used to align accurately the cover plate to the flywheel?

### Release bearing

Q

What is the purpose of the release bearing?

Q

What should exist between the release bearing and the fingers of the diaphragm spring?

Using the missing words from the list below, complete the following description of the effect of excessive or insufficient clearance in the clutch mechanism.

rotate | low | slipping | wear | disengage | clearance | contact | high | release

Excessive __________ would make the bite point very __________. In extreme conditions the clutch might not fully __________.

Insufficient clearance would make the bite point very __________, which can cause the __________ bearing to partly stay in __________ with the clutch. This will cause it to continuously __________ and prematurely __________. In extreme cases the clutch would be partly held on and __________ could occur, similar to the bad driving habit of resting your foot on the clutch pedal.

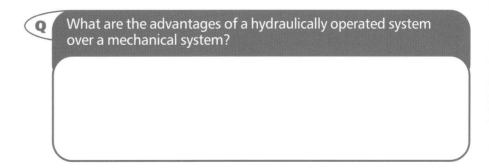

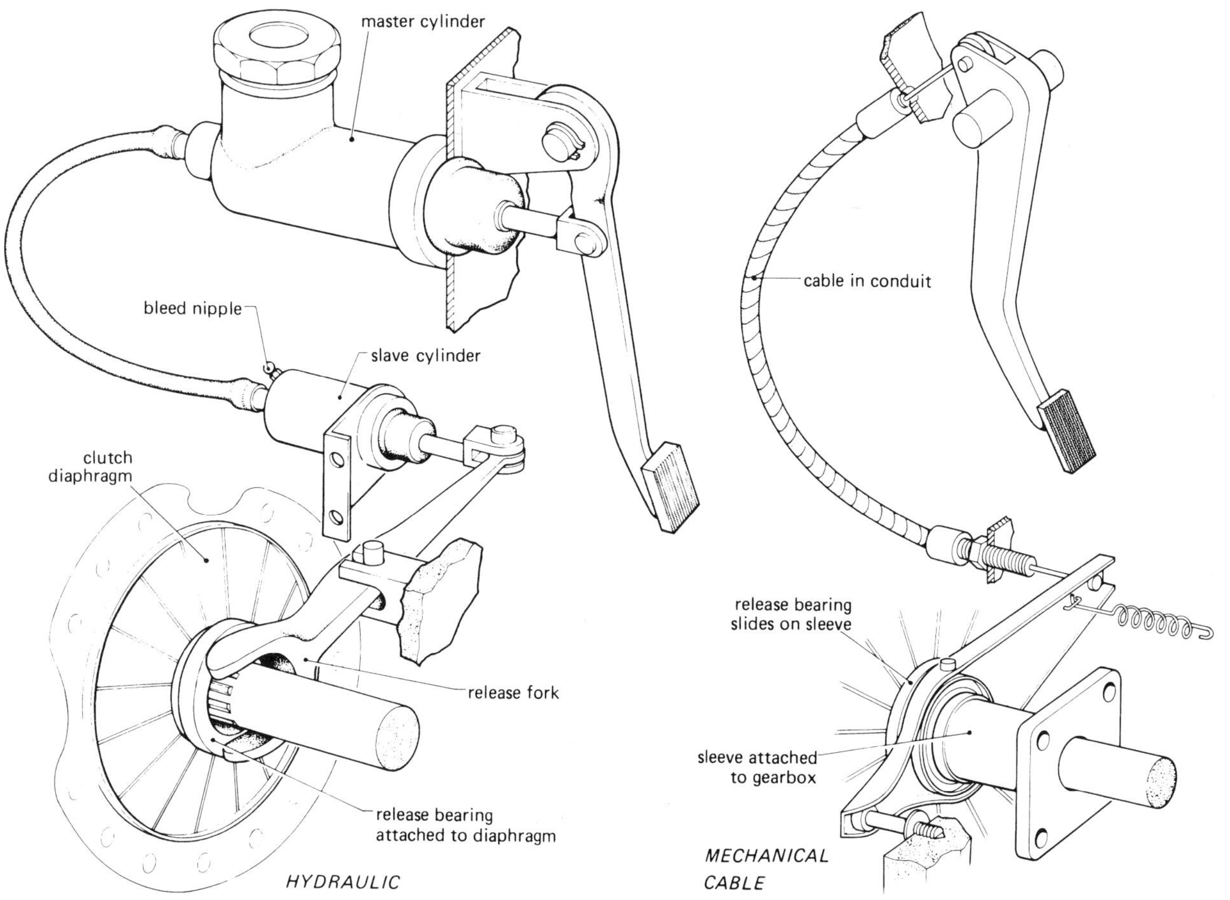


In the diagram above, we can see the two methods of operating the clutch mechanism.

**Q** What are the advantages of a hydraulically operated system over a mechanical system?

**discussion point**

In a small group, discuss a hydraulic clutch system and the effect worn slave cylinder seals might have. What symptoms could worn master cylinder seals produce when a clutch is operated? Write down your ideas, including any sketches that you think might help when you present your conclusions to the rest of the group.

**Q** If the strands of a cable clutch system started to fray and unwind, what might the symptoms be?

### Clutch adjustment systems

In the previous diagram of clutch operating systems, the cable system has an adjusting nut and thread.

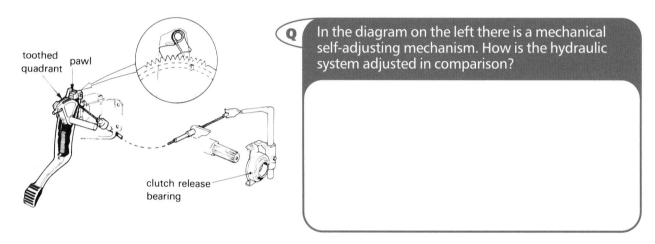

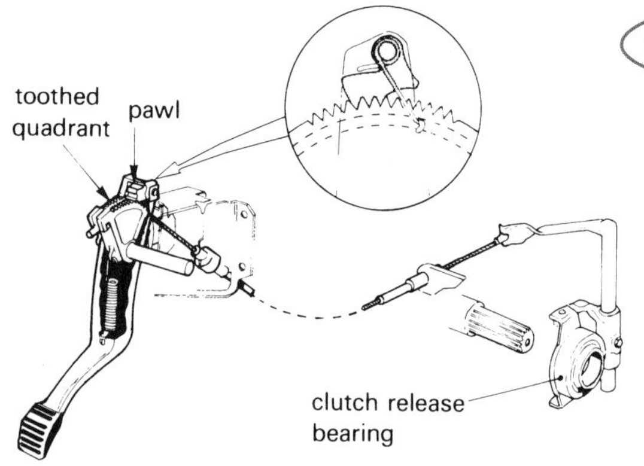


**Q** In the diagram on the left there is a mechanical self-adjusting mechanism. How is the hydraulic system adjusted in comparison?

## Multi-plate clutches

The diagram (left) shows a multi-plate clutch. The system is not dissimilar to the previous clutch systems you have looked at.

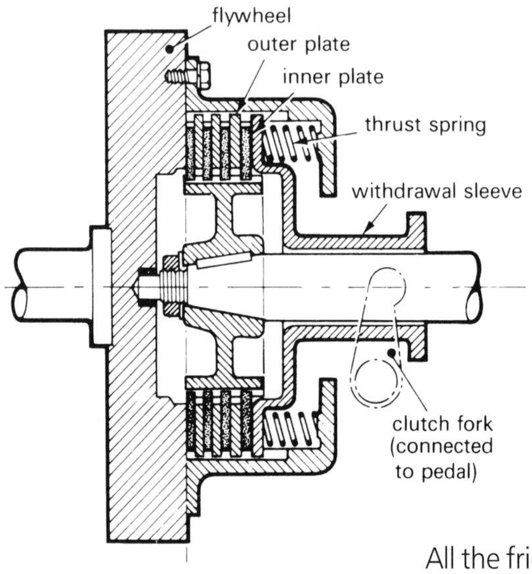


**Q** What are the differences in design?

All the friction pairs grip only when one set of springs is applied. This single set of springs applies equal pressure to every pair of friction surfaces, so it has considerable torque transmitting properties for a small compact unit.

**Q** Where is the multi-plate type of clutch commonly used?

**discussion point**

A customer reports that when his car is driving uphill it seems to be losing speed and the engine revolutions increase. Discuss with a partner:

- the questions that you would ask the customer
- the initial diagnostic checks that you would carry out
- the equipment you could use for diagnosis
- the conclusions and outcomes that you would expect to find from these symptoms.

Write down your list of questions, checks, equipment and conclusions and be ready to present your list to your group.

**discussion point**

Discuss with a partner common faults that will occur on a clutch. Write down your list of faults, including any sketches that you think might help when you present your list to the rest of the group.

**E** Referring to a maintenance schedule, list necessary maintenance tasks to be carried out on a clutch operating system.

## Gearboxes

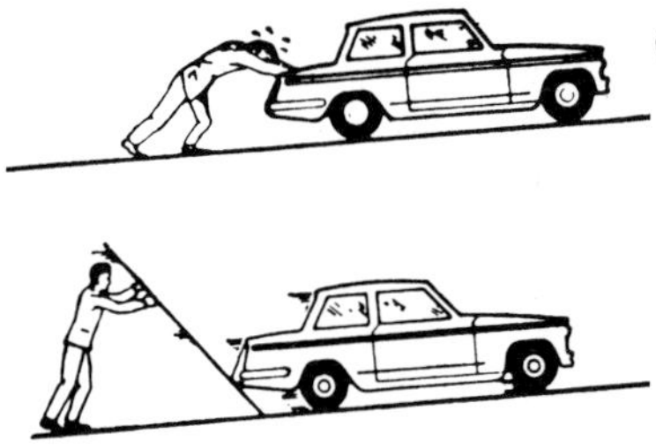

**E** Describe what the diagrams represent.

**discussion point**

Try to work out, through discussion with a member of your group, why a gearbox is necessary. Write down your thoughts, including any sketches that you think might help, then compare your ideas with the whole group so that you can form a list of reasons.

## The correct gear ratios

High vehicle speeds, good acceleration and economy throughout the whole speed range demand a gearing system that allows the engine to operate at the speeds at which it develops its best performance. Maximum engine power, torque and economy occur at different engine speeds, so the task of matching the gear ratios is difficult, especially when variable operating conditions and driver demands have to be taken into account.

**Q** Four forward gears are sufficient for most driving conditions, so why do most modern cars have a fifth gear fitted as standard?

**Q** Which of the gear ratios below is likely to be a high gear?

a 1:1 b 2:1 c 3:1 d 4:1

## Maximum vehicle speed

**Q** Which two other factors determine the overall gear ratio and hence maximum speed of a vehicle?

### Calculating gear ratios

It is important to know which gear is being driven and which gear is doing the driving. This might be satisfactory for two gear wheels but in a gearbox there is a compound gear train (a number of gears linked by a common shaft). This sounds complicated? It is not really: it is just a case of putting numbers to the gears and using the formula driven gear over driver gear.

**E** Find out the formula for calculating gear ratios. Using a gearbox identify the ratios for first and third gears using the formula to make the calculation.

## Different types of gears

E Various types of gearing are used in motor vehicles. Sketch and label the four most common types.

**discussion point**

Helical gears are generally not used in motorsport gearboxes. Discuss with a member of your group why you think this might be. Consider why helical gears are commonly used in road vehicle gearboxes. Present your ideas to the group.

Gears take considerable loads and general driving wear.

**Q** To resist this wear, which one of the following processes do manufacturers use?

a Case softening
b Case hardening
c Hard softening
d Hard casening.

E Using the missing words from the list below, complete the description of the two main groups of gearboxes and their differences.

gearbox | ratios | reverse | selection | automatically | automatic | forward | control

**Manual:** the driver of the vehicle has full ___________ of the ___________ of the available gear ___________ via a gear selection lever.

**Automatic:** the term ___________ gearbox refers to systems in which the gears are ___________ changed by the ___________ itself once the driver has made the initial selection of ___________ 'D', ___________ 'R' or any other driving options.

## Gearbox operation

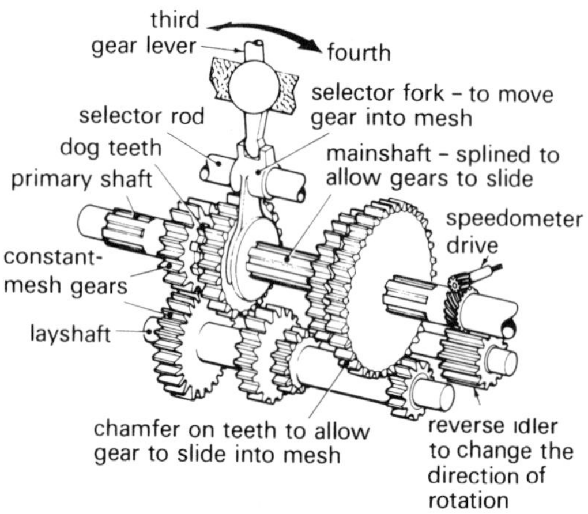


### The sliding-mesh gearbox

The sliding-mesh gearbox is seldom used. However, technicians should have an understanding of its operating principles.

**Q** What type of gears are used in the diagram on the left?

**E** Link the alternative names for the first motion shaft, countershaft and third motion shaft.

| | |
|---|---|
| First motion shaft | Mainshaft |
| Counter shaft | Primary shaft |
| Third motion shaft | Layshaft |

### Primary shaft

**Q** What is the primary shaft's main function?

### Layshaft (rear-wheel drive only)

**Q** What is the function of the layshaft?

### Mainshaft

**discussion point** With reference to the above diagram, discuss with a friend how the gears engage and disengage. Come to a conclusion and write it down, including any sketches that you think might help when you present your conclusion to the rest of the group.

Gears are engaged and disengaged by the driver via the gear lever and selector mechanism.

**Q** Which type of gearbox is shown in the diagram at the top of the next page?

E Name the components numbered 1 to 5 in the diagram.

1

2

3

4

5

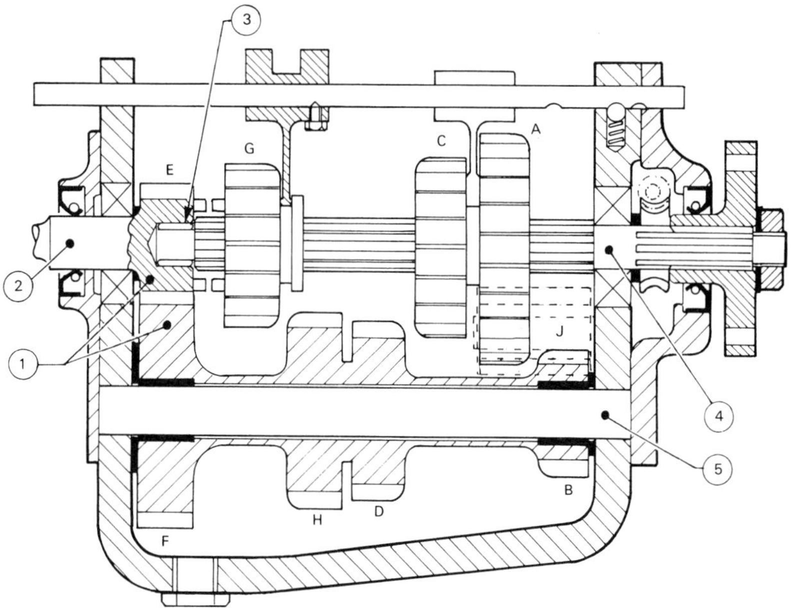


Q How is the main shaft supported at its front end?

Q Although this is a sliding-mesh gearbox, two gears are in constant mesh. Which two are they?

E Referring to the letters in the diagram above, complete the table below, explaining which gears will be meshed and how the drive will pass through the gear box. The first one has been done for you.

| | | |
|---|---|---|
| First gear | E to F, F to B, B to A | Primary shaft to layshaft cluster, layshaft cluster to first gear on mainshaft |
| Second gear | | |
| Third gear | | |
| Top gear | | |

discussion point

**Neutral gear**

With neutral engaged, the driver does not have to hold down the clutch to disconnect the engine power from the driven wheels. Discuss with a partner why this is. When you have decided why, write down your conclusion, including any sketches that might help when you present your ideas to the rest of the group.

**Q** With the engine running and neutral selected, which components in the gearbox will be rotating? (Give the component names and their letters from the diagram.)

### Reverse gear

**Q** Reverse is always a very low gear and, as its name suggest, it is for reversing the vehicle. To produce a reverse gear the output has to be in the opposite direction to all the forward gears (output is on the output or mainshaft). How is this reversal obtained?

**E** Consider two gears rotating. If the driver gear is rotating clockwise then the driven gear is rotating anti-clockwise. Add another gear to the sequence and it will rotate clockwise.

Make this clear by drawing two and then three circles touching.

Look at the diagram of the sliding-mesh gearbox. It can be seen that a gear (letter 'J') is added to rotate the mainshaft in the opposite direction when reverse gear is selected.

**Q** Does the idler gear used for reverse make a difference to the output ratio?

**Q** How will the drive pass through the gearbox? (Give the component names and their letters.)

Q

What are the gear ratios of the following:

a a driving gear A with 20 teeth and a driven gear B with 45 teeth

b a driving gear A with 28 teeth and a driven gear B with 50 teeth

c a driving gear A with 32 teeth and a driven gear B with 54 teeth?

Q

What is the compound gear ratio for a set of gears with the following number of teeth?

Gear E has 20 teeth, gear F has 40 teeth, gear H has 27 teeth and gear G has 33 teeth.

## Selector mechanism

In the illustration here you can see two small boxed diagrams of the selector forks. Now look at the previous diagram of the sliding-mesh type gearbox, where you can see clearly the selector forks and rods.

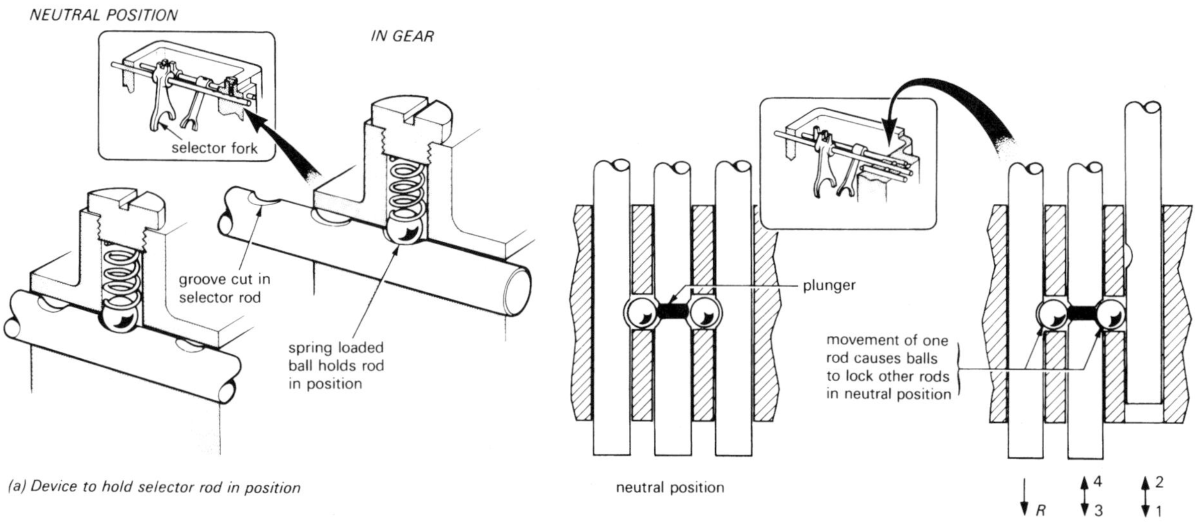


*(a) Device to hold selector rod in position*

*(b) Ball and plunger type of interlocking mechanism prevents two gears engaging at the same time*

E

Complete the following description of a selector mechanism using the missing phrases from the list below.

There are two important features in this selector mechanism, the ___________. The detent holds the ___________ in the required position, preventing ___________ or disengagement due to vibration. The interlock, prevents the engagement of ___________. If two gears were to be selected, the ___________ and shaft rotation would be impossible.

- two gears simultaneously
- gearbox would lock up
- two different ratios
- detent and the interlock
- unintentional gear engagement

Q What would be the effect of a broken or weakened selector lock spring?

Q What would happen if a technician is dismantling a gearbox and leaves out the interlock plunger on reassembly?

### Lubrication

*Safety Note:* **Take care when checking a gearbox oil level. The oil can be very hot and if the car has just been on a long run it will froth up, so it will spill out as you remove the plug. Give it a short time to cool.**

Q At what level is the oil in the gearbox usually set and why?

Q What is an alternative way in which the components in a gearbox can be lubricated instead of being splash fed?

## Constant-mesh and synchromesh gearboxes

The sliding-mesh gearbox previously described is now rarely used but is useful for gaining an understanding of how gearboxes work. Many of the design features and principles used now have evolved from these earlier systems.

**discussion point** Discuss with a partner the two main disadvantages of the sliding-mesh gearbox. Prepare to present your ideas to the rest of the group.

### Constant-mesh gearbox

At a first glance at the diagram on the next page, the gearbox looks the same as a sliding-mesh gearbox and many of the components are the same. The input (primary shaft), layshaft and the output (mainshaft) are common to both gearbox types.

Q A constant-mesh gearbox has all of its forward gears meshed at the same time, so why does it not 'lock up'?

Q The constant-mesh gearbox provided an improvement over the noisy spur gears of the sliding-mesh system, but double de-clutching was the only way to avoid the teeth on the dog clutches from grating. Which system was introduced to overcome gear selection faults?

E Label the diagram of the constant mesh gearbox below.

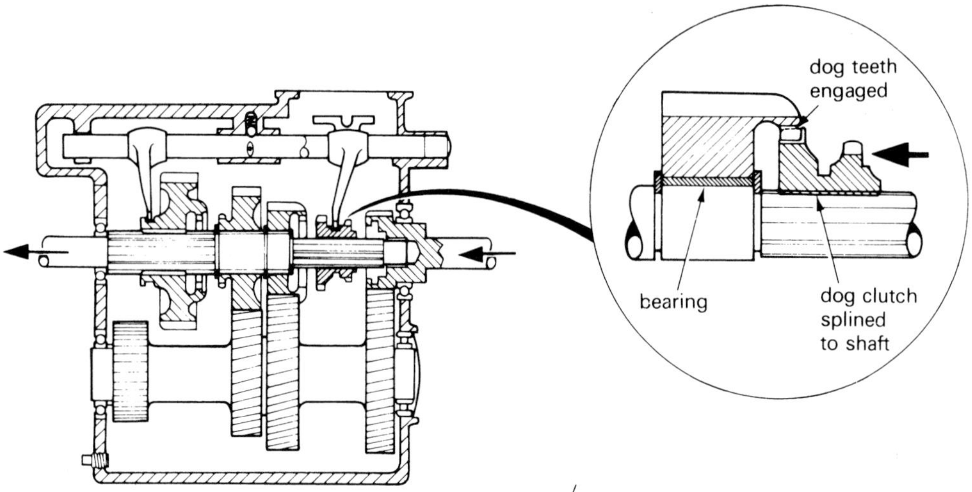


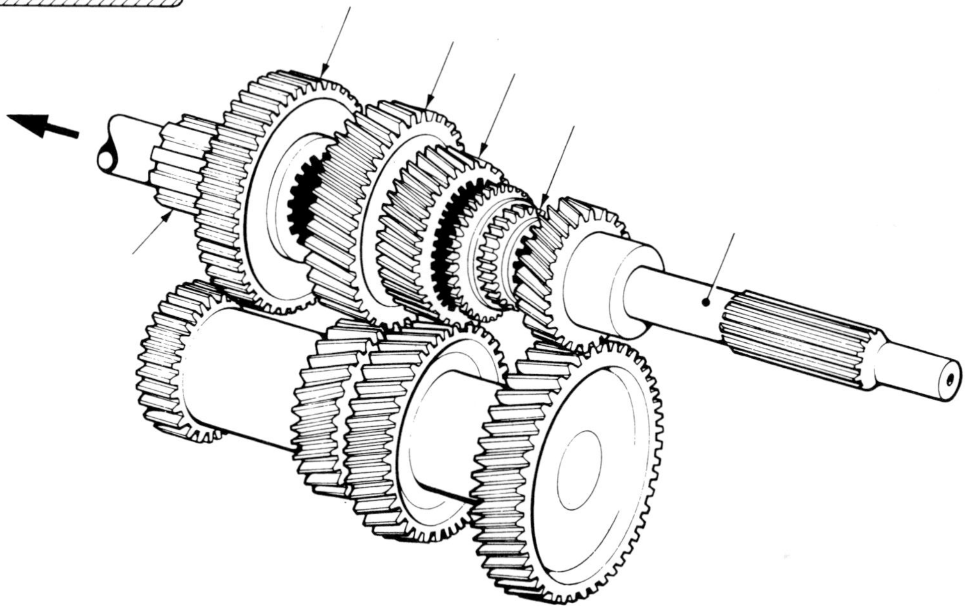

## Synchromesh (constant load type)

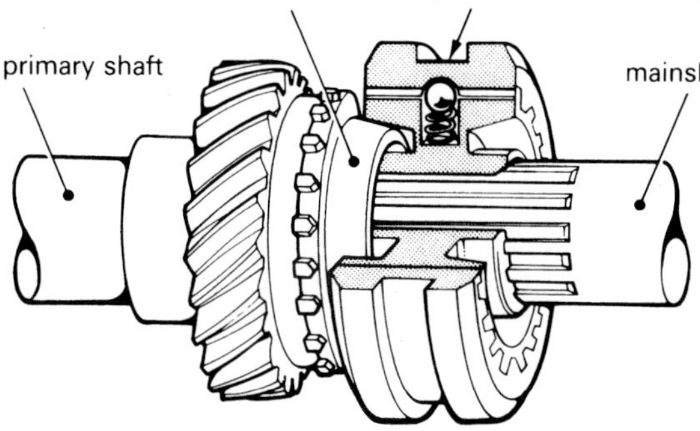


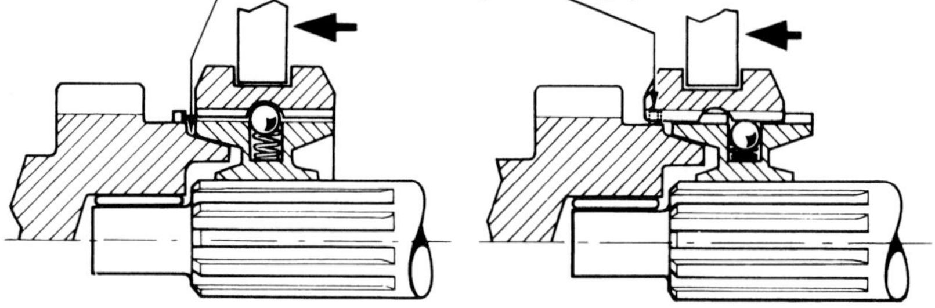

discussion point

With reference to the diagrams on the previous page, discuss with a partner how synchromesh works. Record your thoughts, include any sketches that you think might help when you present your ideas to the rest of the group.

Baulk ring synchromesh

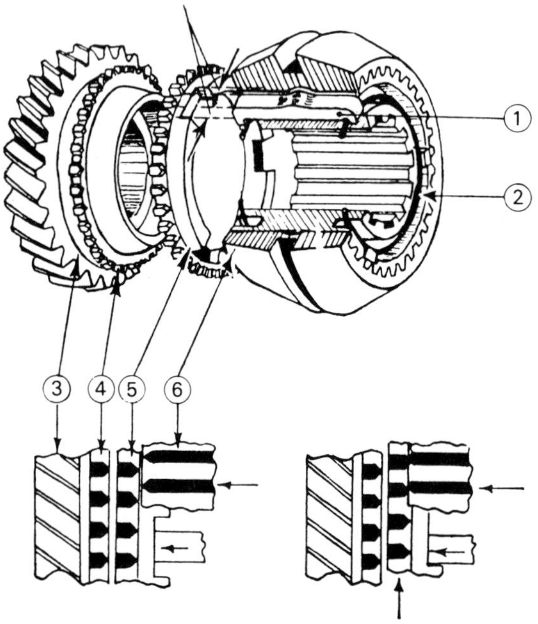


E Name all the parts in the diagram opposite.

1

2

3

4

5

6

Q What is an alternative name for the shifting plates?

Q What material is the baulk ring made from?

Q How does the chamfer on the baulk ring teeth affect engagement?

Q Why is there a small clearance around the shifting plates?

**Rear-wheel drive gearboxes**

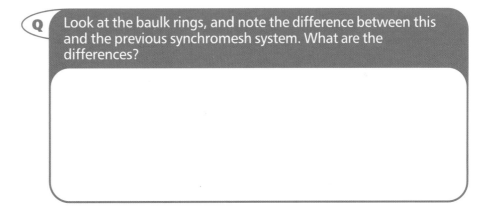

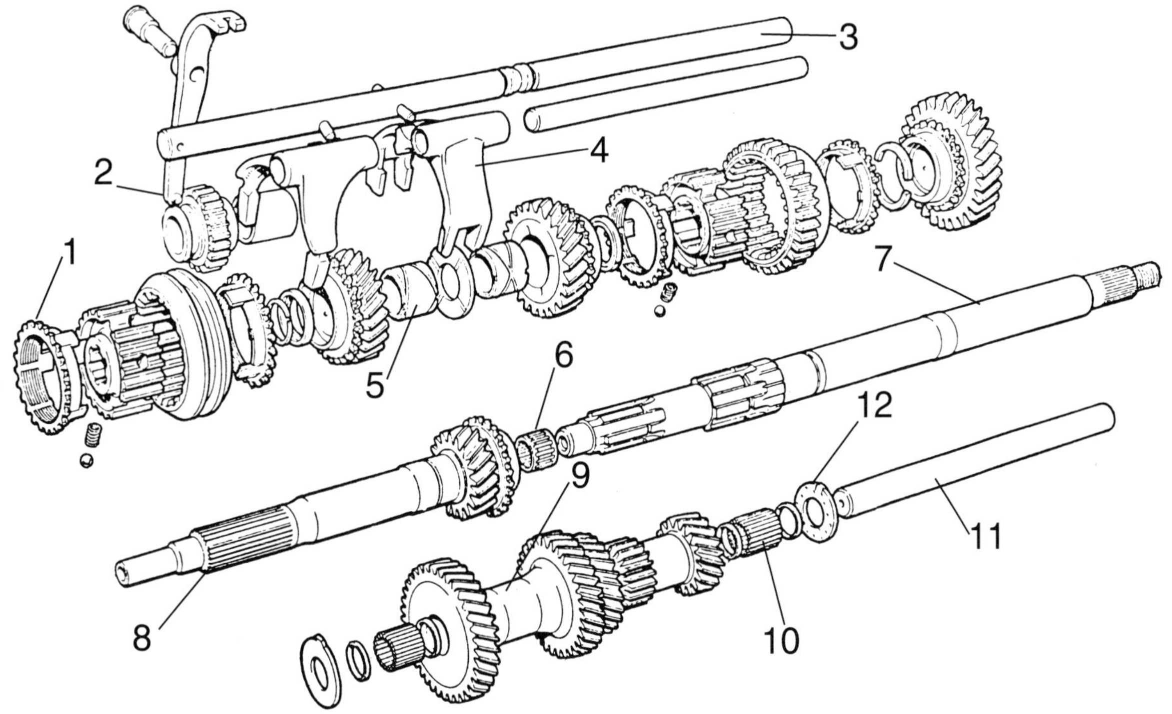


The diagram above shows an exploded view of a four-speed and reverse gearbox.

**Q** Look at the baulk rings, and note the difference between this and the previous synchromesh system. What are the differences?

**E** Look at the diagram above. Try to name the numbered parts.

| | |
|---|---|
| 1 | 7 |
| 2 | 8 |
| 3 | 9 |
| 4 | 10 |
| 5 | 11 |
| 6 | 12 |

**discussion point**

Discuss with a partner the gearbox below. Decide between you how many gears there are and how fourth gear is obtained. Record your thoughts and be prepared to present them to the group.

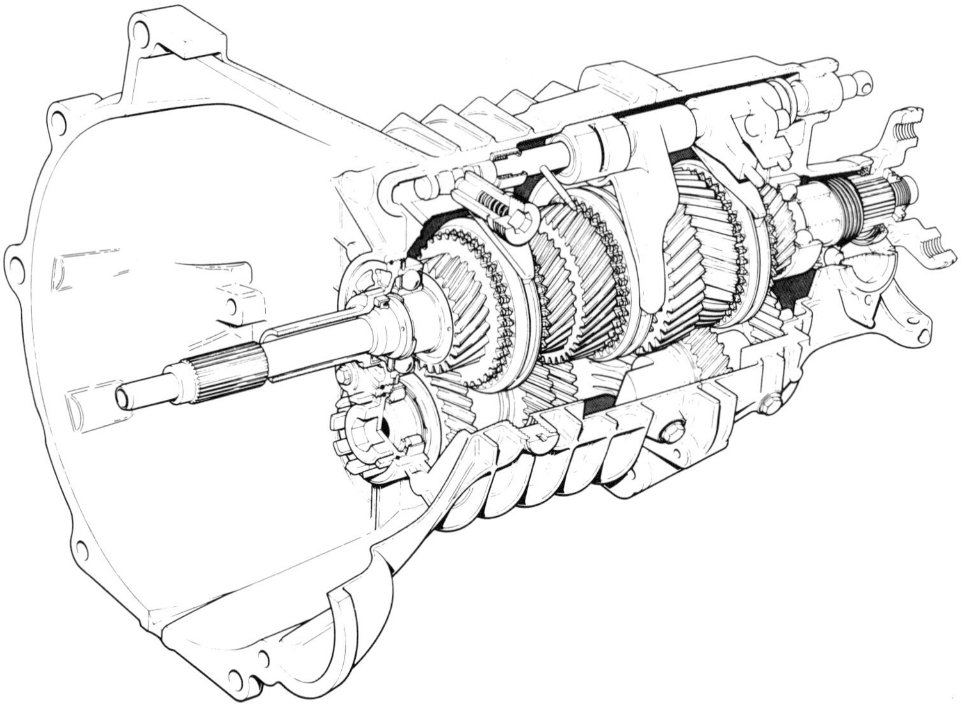

## Front-wheel drive gearboxes

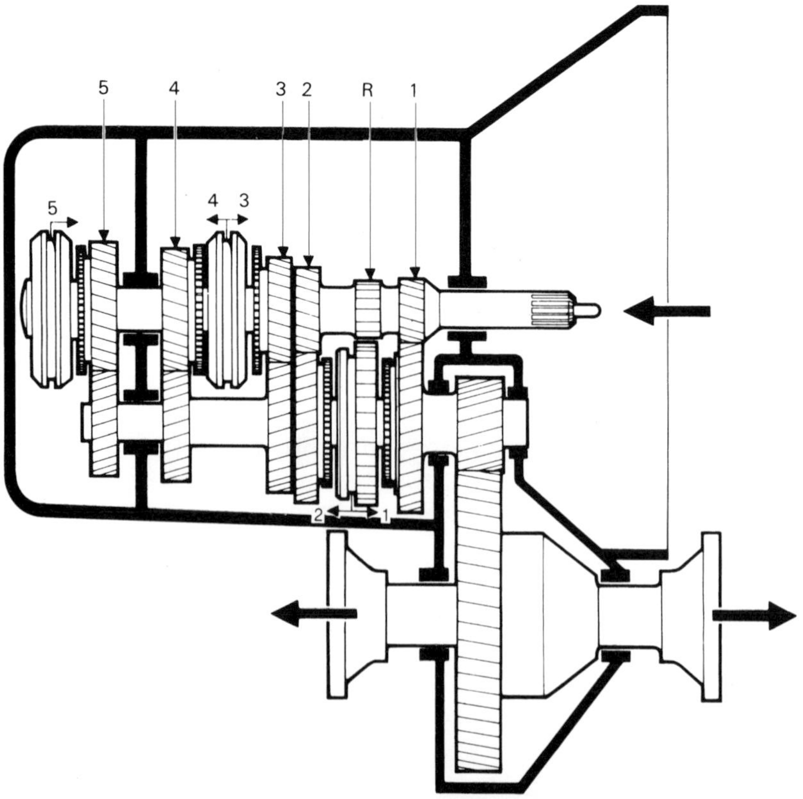


**discussion point**

With reference to the diagram above, discuss with a member of your group the differences between this gearbox and the rear-wheel drive gearbox in the previous section. Make a list of differences that you can see. Between you label the main parts on the diagram. On completion be prepared to let the rest of the group know what you have discovered and what you have named the parts.

Q

Why is it not necessary for the input shaft to locate into a spigot bearing in the flywheel?

E

Complete the table below stating the faults in a manual gearbox that could give rise to the symptoms listed.

| Symptom | Fault |
|---|---|
| Gear whine | |
| Knocking or ticking | |
| Jumping out of gear | |
| Gear fails to select | |

**discussion point**

A customer's speedometer has stopped working. Discuss with a friend which components might be at fault. Make a list and be prepared to present your ideas to the group. You might like to use diagrams to help you.

## Automatic gearboxes

**discussion point**

Discuss in a small group what you think are the advantages and disadvantages of an automatic gearbox. Write down your ideas to present to the group.

### Planetary gearing

The term planetary gearing refers to the way that the gears rotate around a central gear, the sun wheel, in exactly the same way as the planets in our solar system rotate around the Sun.

Q

What is an epicycle?

E Label the main components on the diagram below and state the purpose of the brake band.

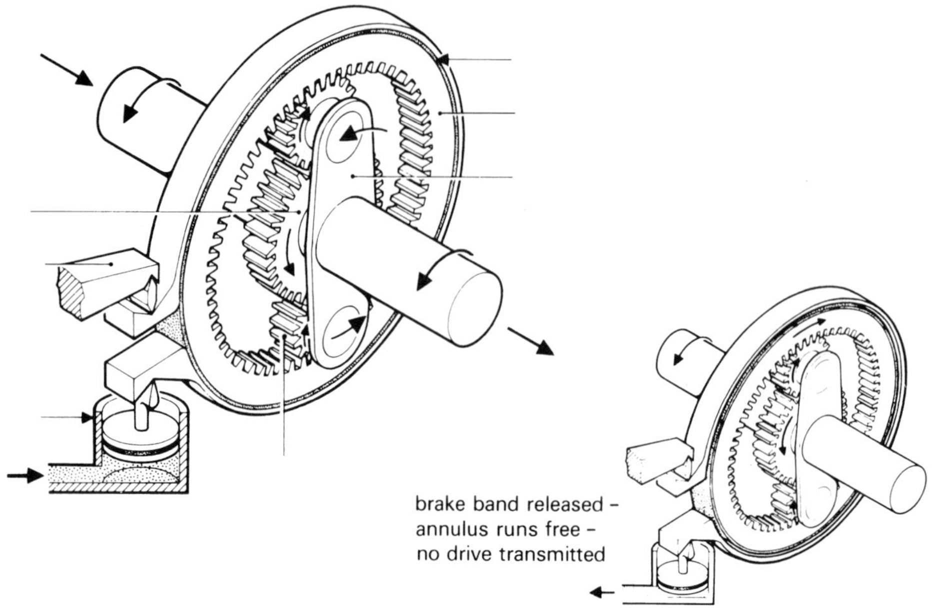


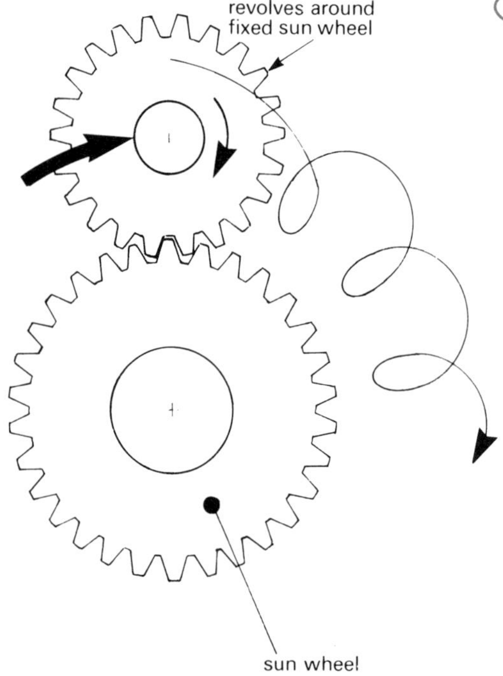


Q A sun wheel has 40 teeth, a planet wheel has 20 teeth. Both wheels are meshed and the planet is at the top (12 o'clock). How many times will the planet rotate to complete one full rotation of the sun wheel?

**Note: If your answer is incorrect you might be struggling to understand, so keep thinking. Perhaps some sketches will help.**

Another form of planetary gearing is shown below.

Where the planet moves inside an internal gear it is called an annulus.

**discussion point**

If the annulus is held stationary and the input drive is via the sun wheel, the output will be via the planet wheels and the carrier. Will the planet wheels rotate faster than the sun wheel and in which direction they will rotate? Write down your conclusions, including any sketches that you think might help when you present your ideas to other members of your group.

E Find the centre of the figure below and draw a circle where a sun wheel would go. You will then have the basis of an epicyclic gear train.

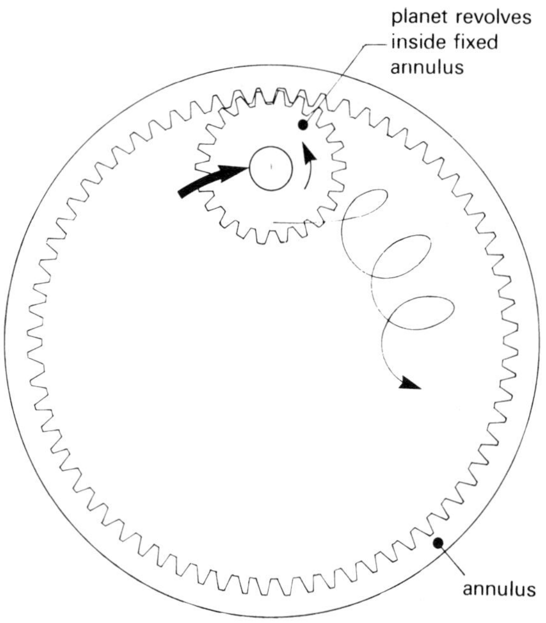


## Principles of the fluid coupling flywheel

Look at this diagram showing a very simple way of transferring energy and motion to another member (the plate left in b). Automatic gearboxes rely on this principle but use a torque converter instead.

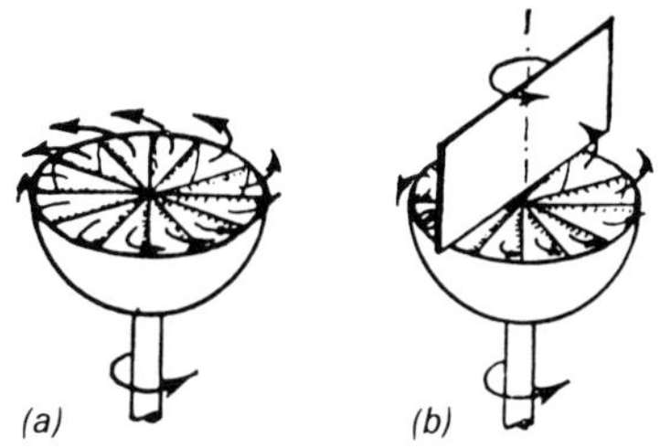


Q What does a torque converter do over and above a basic fluid flywheel?

E Use the phrases to complete the following description of how a gearbox makes effective use of engine power.

An automatic gearbox provides a number of ______________ to allow the effective use of ______________. The power from the engine is transmitted to the ______________ by the use of a ______________, which in the case of most modern vehicles is a torque converter. However, other than selecting the direction of travel, the driver does not need to ______________ gears.

automatic gearbox
gear ratios
engine power
fluid coupling
manually select

Q What control does the driver have over the transmission?

Q Which systems work together to operate a modern automatic gearbox when the driver selects drive?

*Safety Note:* ***For safety reasons, the selector mechanism incorporates an inhibitor switch.***

**Driver selection system**

The selector system is usually floor mounted in the console in front of the park brake or located on the steering column.

Q How does the inhibitor switch work?

E The table below has been jumbled. Match the description of the gear selection to the appropriate gear position (P, R, N, D, 2, 1).

| | |
|---|---|
| Second gear '2' | Normal automatic mode – the gearbox selects the appropriate gear. |
| Neutral 'N' | A parking pawl, mounted to the gearbox casing is engaged with a special gear on the output shaft; when selected it locks the output shaft stationary. |
| Drive 'D' | This allows only for the selection of the lowest gear, first. There will be no freewheel action and on overrun there will be engine braking. |
| First gear '1' | This allows only automatic selection from first up to second and back down to first. No higher gear can be selected and there is engine braking on overrun. |
| Park 'P' | Rearward movement is achieved by only one gear. |
| Reverse 'R' | There is no drive – the engine is not connected mechanically or hydraulically. |

Automatic gearboxes use multi-plate clutches.

**Label the main components of the diagram.**

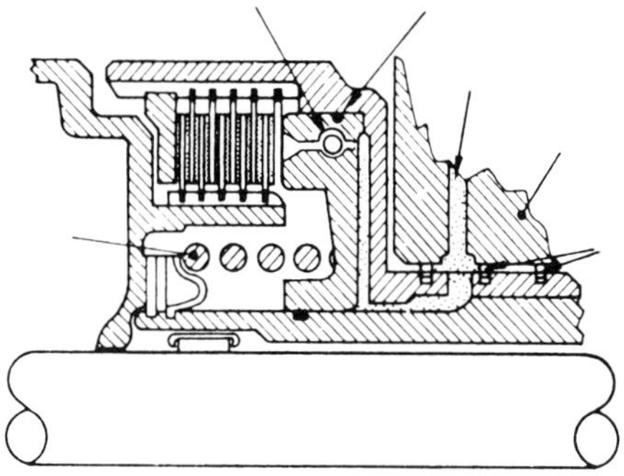

**What would be the symptoms of clutch slip in an automatic gearbox?**

## Automatic transmission fluid

*Safety Note:* **Automatic gearbox fluids can reach very high temperatures, way beyond the boiling point of water. There are large quantities of fluid in a gearbox, which will take a considerable time to cool down.**

The fluid in an automatic gearbox must be capable of performing many functions:

- it serves to operate the torque converter
- it actuates the clutches and brakes through hydraulic pressure
- it lubricates the various gears and bearing surfaces
- it acts as a coolant to the internal components.

Modern fluids, such as Dextron II which is made to General Motors' specification, have special qualities. These qualities are introduced through the use of additives.

**Research and describe a method of checking an automatic transmission oil level.**

**Link the following phrases with lines in pencil to complete statements describing the qualities of modern fluids and the problems they prevent.**

| | |
|---|---|
| The fluid does not cause oxidisation | to avoid grab or slip in extreme conditions. |
| Anti-foaming agents keep the fluid | by excessive heat. |
| The viscosity is not adversely affected | when it is used at high oil temperatures. |
| The fluid has a stable friction value over varying conditions | in liquid form. |

**Q** Which automatic gearbox components might require adjustment during a service? Describe typical maintenance checks.

Electronically controlled systems are now standard for automatic gearboxes; these will be covered in Workbook 3.

## Rear axle construction

### Dead and live axles

**Q** Although most modern vehicles have independent rear suspension, some vehicles might still be fitted with a solid axle. Solid axles are often referred to as being 'dead' or 'live'. What is the fundamental difference between the two?

### Axle shaft

The axle shaft transmits the drive from the differential sun wheel to the rear hub.

The various types of axle shaft and hub assemblies can be compared by considering the stresses and forces imparted on the shaft.

**E** Draw lines in pencil to match the different types of stress with their causes.

| | |
|---|---|
| Bending stress | is due to the weight of the vehicle. |
| Tensile and compressive stress | is due to cornering forces. |
| Shear stress | is due to driving and braking stress. |
| Torsional stress | is due to the weight of the vehicle. |

In the diagram below there are three different layouts for axle shafts. Label each of them correctly.

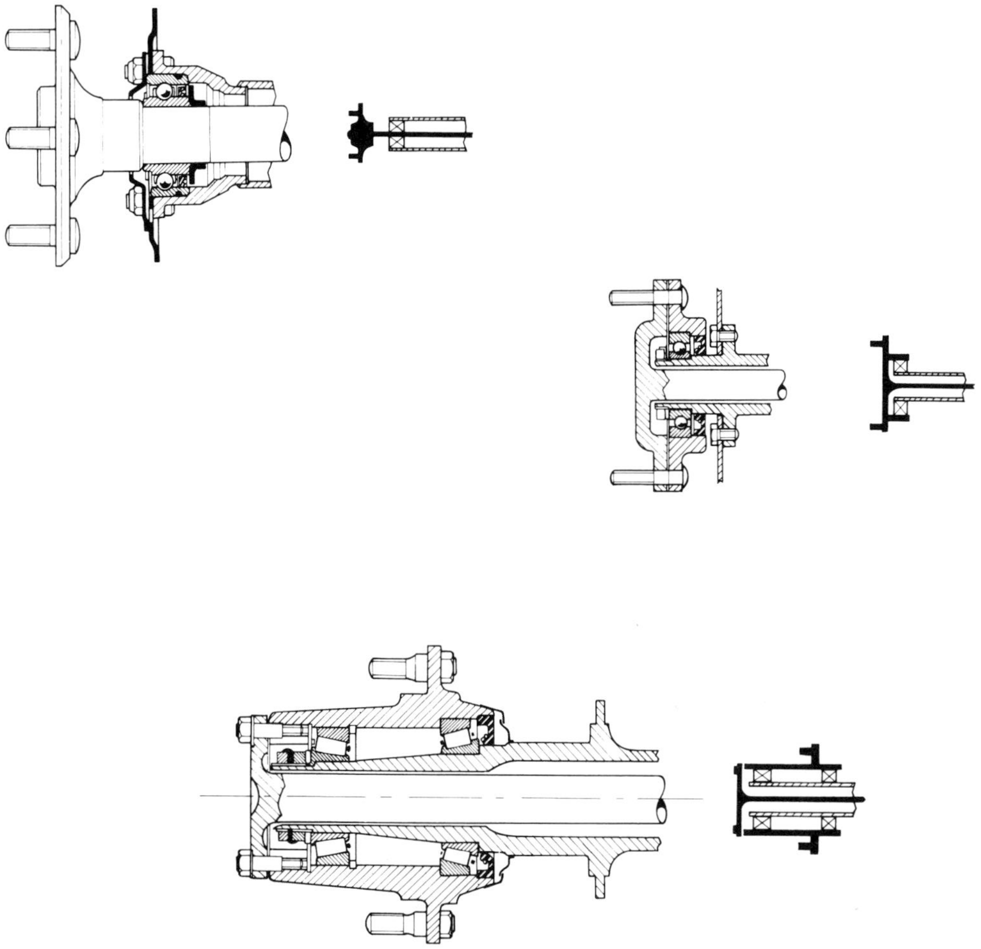

Below are three axle types. Complete the table stating which forces act on each type of axle shaft and the bearings.

| | |
|---|---|
| Semi-floating | |
| Three-quarter floating | |
| Fully-floating | |

## Axle shaft material

A tough, hard material must be used to withstand the various stresses, resist spline wear and provide good resistance to fatigue.

Q What type of material are the axle shafts made from?

## Propeller shafts and driveshafts

Q Describe the purpose of a propshaft.

Q Explain why a propshaft is of tubular construction.

Q What type of vehicle layout are propshafts used for?

Q How are the propshafts balanced?

Q What advantages are there to using a split propshaft over a single propshaft assembly?

## Universal and constant-velocity joints

The universal joint (UJ) allows the drive of a shaft to be transmitted through moderate angles.

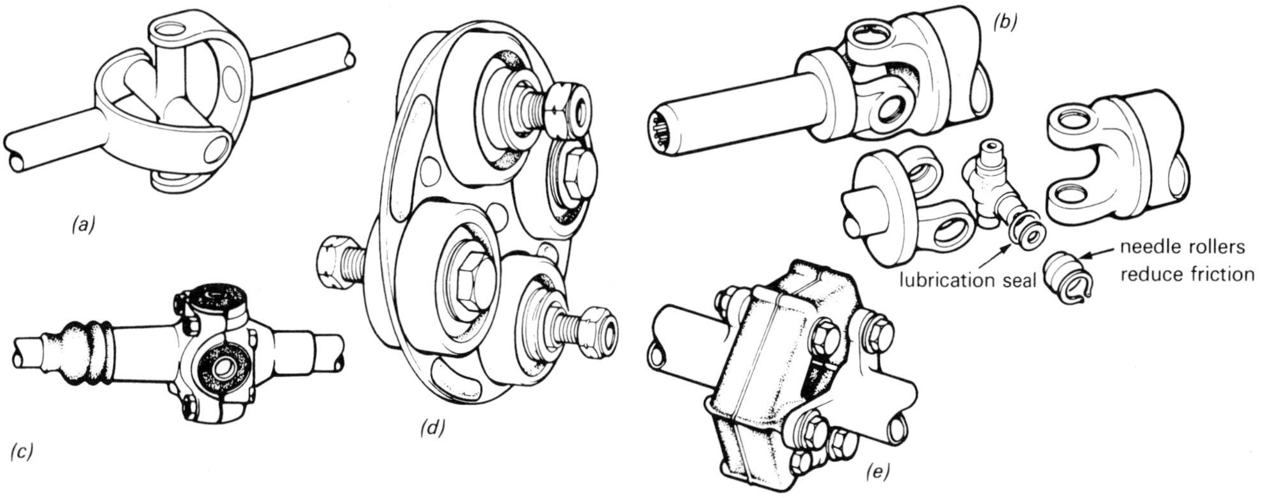


E

**Look at the diagrams of the various universal joints in the diagram above, and using the letters identify the types.**

Hooke-type joint

Hardy Spicer joint

Cross-type joint

Layrub

Doughnut

## Speed variation of a Hooke-type coupling

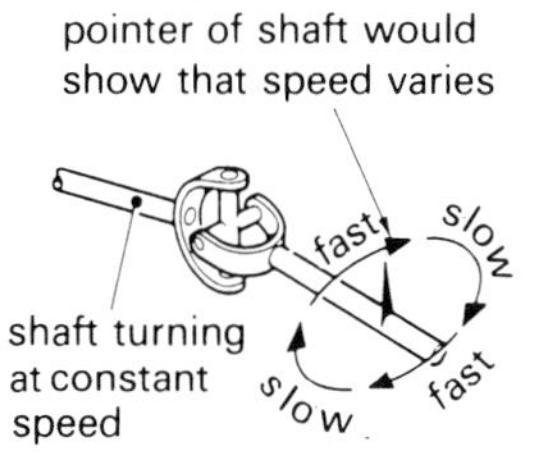


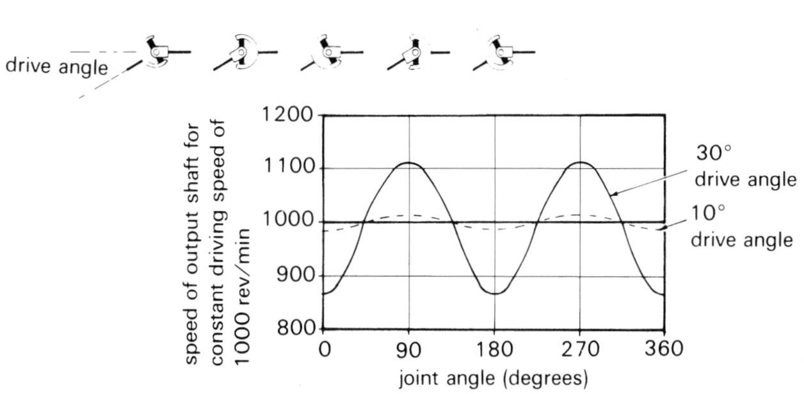


E

**Look at the graph above and explain why the output speed of a Hooke-type joint is not constant. Look at a physical example and see how an increased angle affects the output speed.**

E

Using the missing words from the list below, complete the following statement describing how vibration at high drive angles is overcome.

One method of achieving a __________ speed output from the __________ shaft is to mount two Hooke-type __________ back to back or positioned in a certain way at each end of the propeller __________ . In both configurations the relative __________ of each coupling must be arranged so that each __________ change of one coupling is __________ by the other.

propeller
constant
shaft
speed
couplings
positions
counteracted

## Constant-velocity joints (CV)

Q

Describe what is meant by the term constant velocity.

E

Label the main components on the diagram of the constant-velocity joint below.

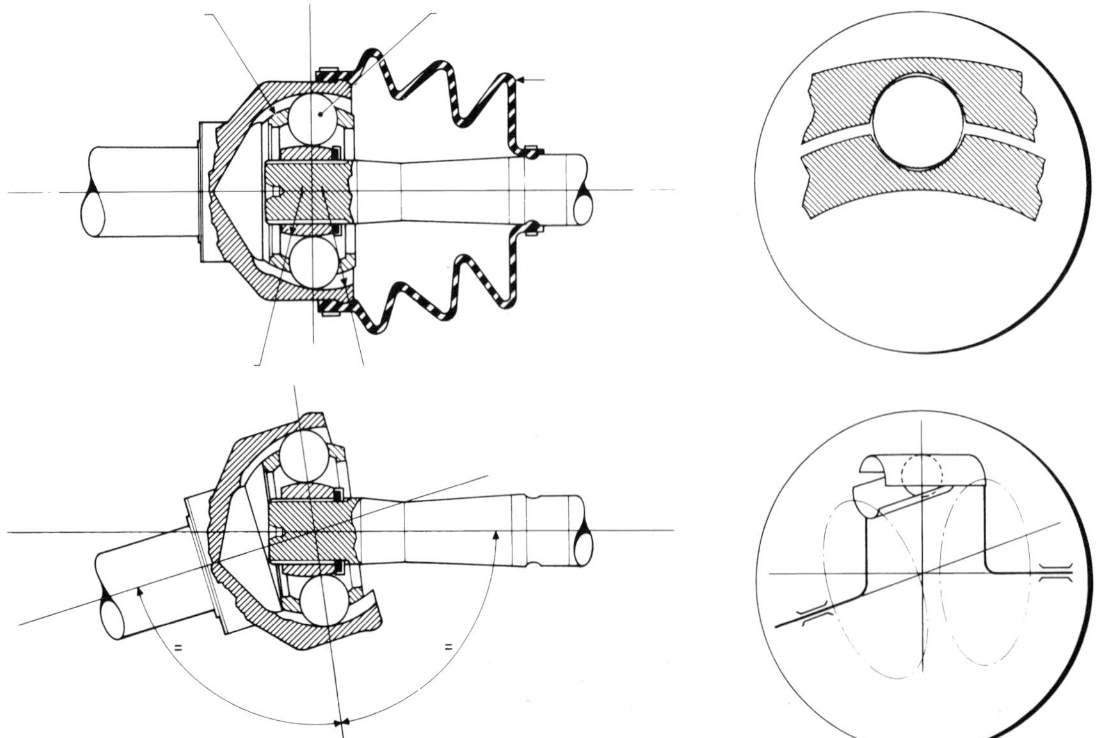

Q What is different between the output of a CV joint and that of a Hooke-type coupling?

Q Why do front-wheel drive cars need to use a constant-velocity joint?

Q What is a plunge constant-velocity joint?

**A review of the term 'constant velocity'**
Constant velocity means that the shaft rotates at a steady, continuous or constant speed, with one end turning at the same speed as the other, all of the time, even when a tight angle is applied.

E Draw a simple sketch of a Tracta or a Tripode joint.

**Q** What is the most common fault that causes premature wear in a CV joint?

**Q** What symptom might occur during a road test that could indicate that the CV joints have excessive wear?

**E** Research and describe typical maintenance methods for driveshafts and/or propshafts.

## Final drive gears

**Q** What is the purpose of final drive gears?

## Straight bevel

Label the crown wheel and pinion on the diagram and describe the features of this type of final drive gear.

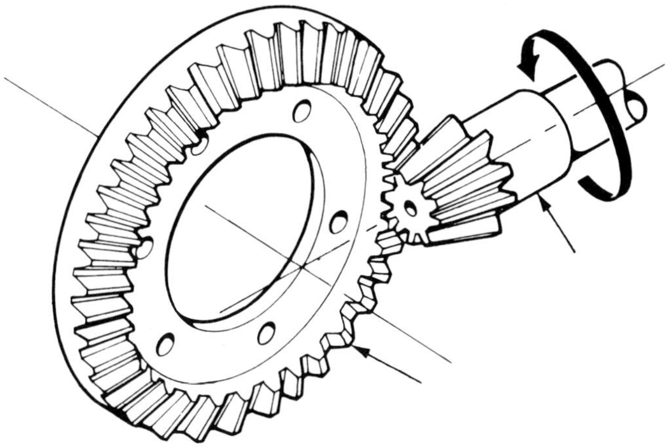

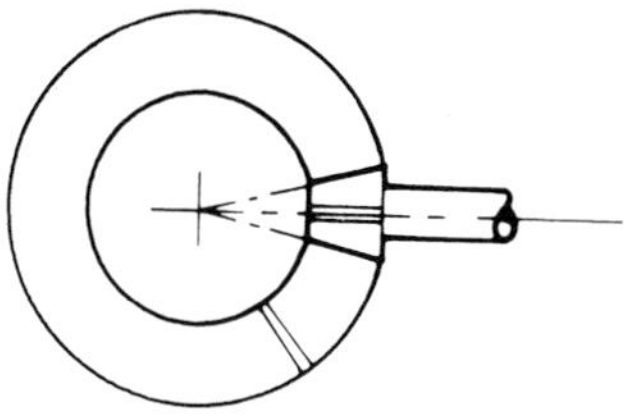

*straight bevel*

## Spiral bevel

Label the crown wheel and pinion on the diagram. Compare this type and the straight bevel and report on your findings.

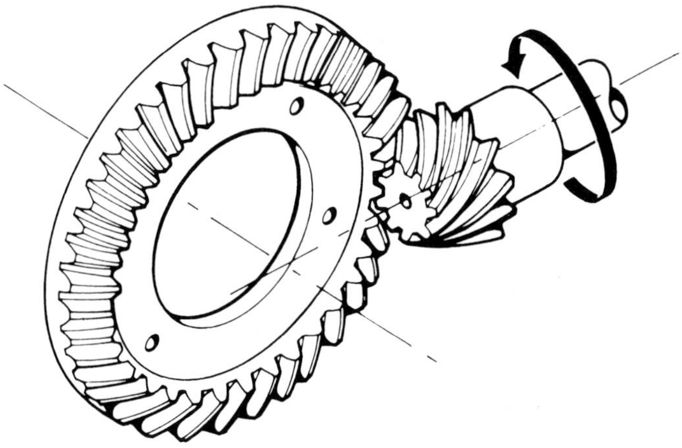

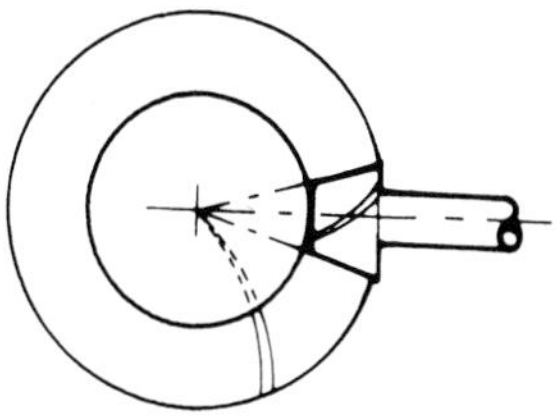

*spiral bevel*

A straight bevel gear is relatively inexpensive to produce and mechanically efficient (it has low friction). A disadvantage is its excessive noise, which is unacceptable to vehicle occupants.

**Q** How is the noise caused?

## Hypoid bevel

**E** Label the crown wheel and pinion on the diagrams below. Suggest what typical vehicle applications the different pinion offset positions may suit.

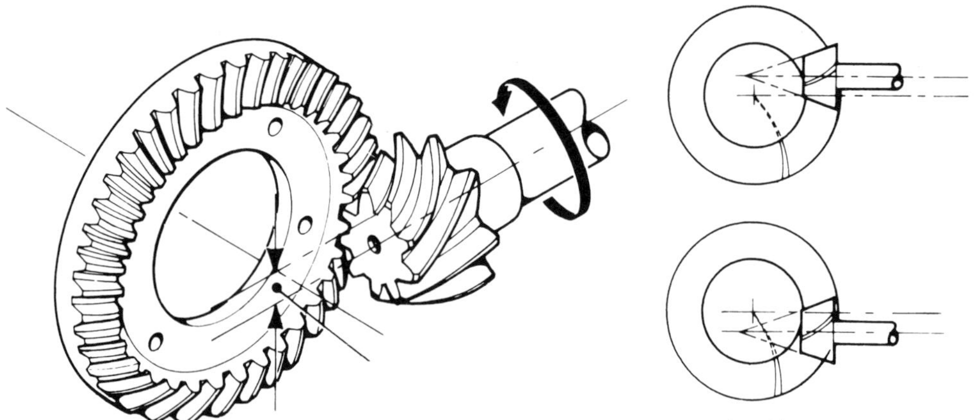

*hypoid*

**discussion point** Hypoid gears are commonly used in final drives. Discuss with a member of your group why you think this might be. Consider the advantages in terms of tooth design of offsetting the centre line of the pinion. Present your ideas to the group.

**Q** The sliding action of the gears creates a higher pressure on the surfaces of the teeth. This high pressure could break down the lubricant, allowing the surfaces of the teeth to rub together. What was developed to avoid this problem?

**E** Identify the service procedures and type of oil required for the final drive of a vehicle of your choice.

# The differential

## Purpose of a differential

**discussion point**

If both driving wheels were connected by a solid driving shaft, the two wheels would rotate at exactly the same speed all the time. What problems would this cause with the vehicle? Develop some conclusions with a partner, including any sketches, and be ready to present your ideas to the rest of the group.

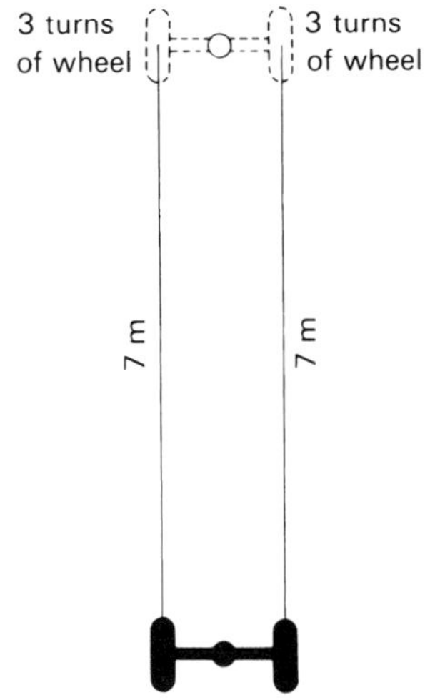


travelling straight ahead

both wheels turn at same speed

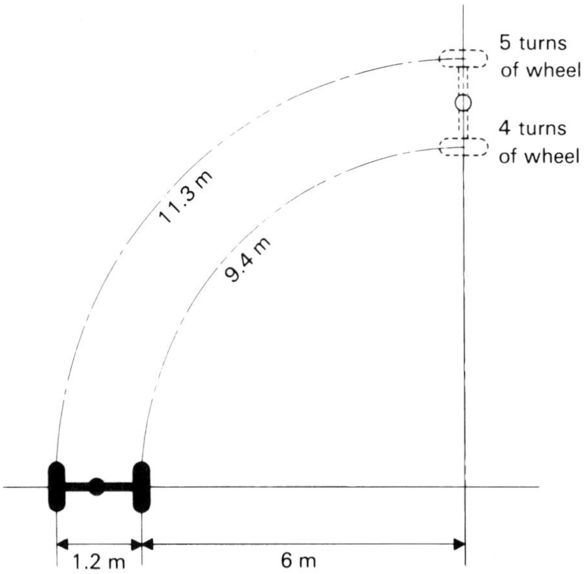


cornering

inner wheel turns more slowly than outer wheel

In the diagram at the left you can see that when a vehicle travels in a straight line, both wheels cover the same distance.

However, you can also see from the diagram on the right that when a vehicle turns a corner, one wheel (the inner wheel) follows a much shorter arc so one wheel has to travel faster and further than the other.

**discussion point**

Pass a physical example of a differential around your group and discuss its operation. Look carefully at the way the gears work together and gain a full understanding of how the unit works so that you are able to explain this to the group if you are asked to.

## Principle of operation

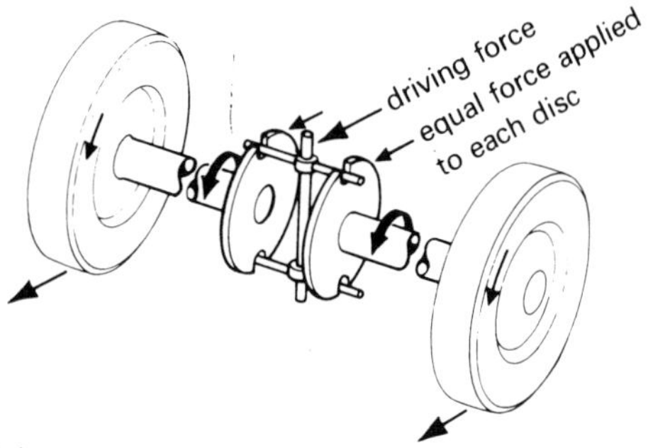


(a)

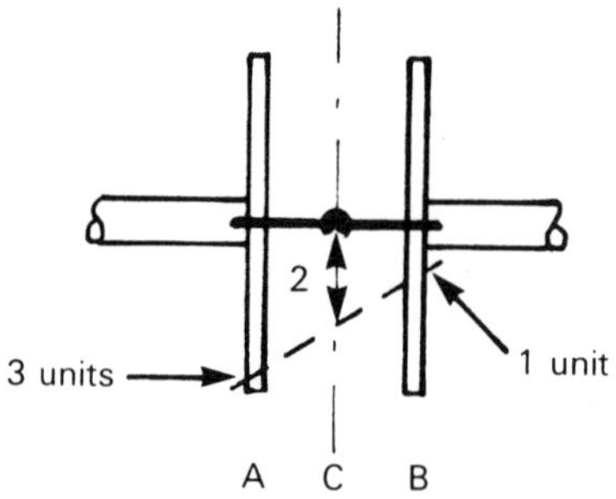


(b)

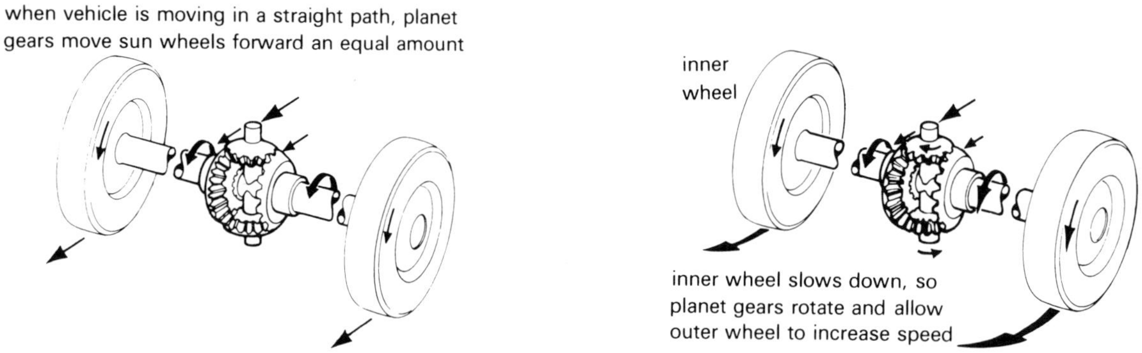

when vehicle is moving in a straight path, planet gears move sun wheels forward an equal amount
inner wheel
inner wheel slows down, so planet gears rotate and allow outer wheel to increase speed


(c)

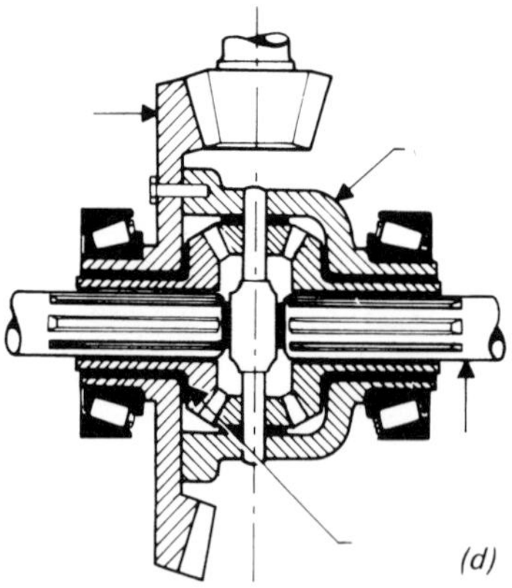

(d)

E On the above diagram (d), using a coloured pen or highlighter, draw the power flow from the pinion through to the drive shafts and label all the parts.

## Differential lock

The differential enables each wheel to be driven independently via the cage, cross-shaft, planets and sun wheels. This works well under normal driving conditions, with a moderate driving style and where the road surface is good.

Q What type of driving conditions would a differential lock improve, and how would this be operated by the driver?

Q Look at the diagram on the right. Which two components are locked together to stop the differential operating?

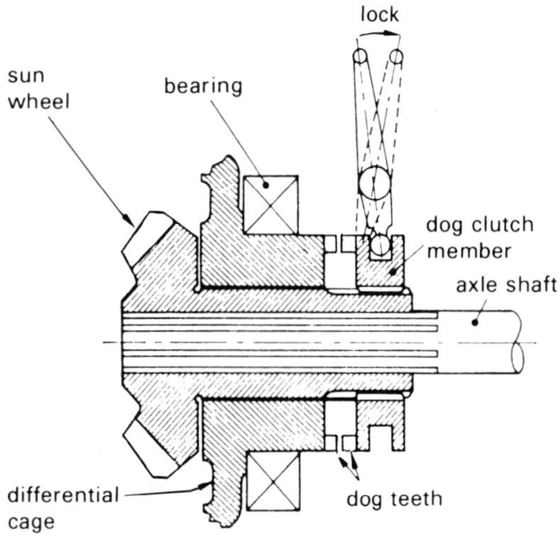


## Four-wheel drive systems

A four-wheel drive vehicle can transmit drive to all four wheels. They are often referred to as 4 × 4 (four by four) vehicles.

**discussion point** Discuss with the group the disadvantages of a two wheel drive vehicle compared with a four wheel drive system. Record the findings of the group.

### Selectable four-wheel drive

Q Why should a selectable four-wheel drive system not be used in four-wheel drive mode on good road surfaces?

### Permanent four-wheel drive

Q To enable a four-wheel drive system to be used on hard surfaces an extra component has to be added into the drive train. What is this extra component?

Most vehicles now have front-wheel drive. If a manufacturer wants a four-wheel drive vehicle in its model range then it will usually have to derive the vehicle from an existing front-wheel drive arrangement.

E **In the box below draw a four-wheel drive arrangement derived from a front-wheel drive vehicle.**

Four-wheel drive systems will be looked at in detail in Workbook 3.

**mini projects**

Agree the following with your tutor:

- the format and quantity of content
- the timeframe for completion.

Carry out research and identify any differences between the gear ratios of five- and six-speed gearboxes and explain why a number of vehicle manufacturers are now fitting six-speed gearboxes. Choose examples that are fitted to either front-wheel drive or rear-wheel drive vehicles and use diagrams to help with your explanations. On one of your diagrams identify the location of the speedometer drive and reverse light switch. Explain how the reverse light switch works when reverse gear is selected. For one of your chosen vehicles calculate the overall gear ratios for each forward gear.

# Practical activities

**practical activity 1**

Look at three to four different makes of vehicle and describe accurately how manufacturers introduce an extra action (gate lock) to engage reverse gear. Here is an example:

| Make | Model | Action |
|---|---|---|
| Renault | 5 | The gear lever needs to be lifted over a gate and spring to the left and forward. |

**practical activity 2**

Using a final drive assembly from a rear-wheel drive layout vehicle, carry out the following tasks:

1 Dismantle the final drive gears.

2 Dismantle the differential gears.

3 Identify the crown wheel and pinion and sketch them.

4 Identify the sun and planet gears.

5 Identify the crown wheel and pinion, and differential bearings.

6 Calculate the final drive gear ratio.

$$\text{Formula: } \frac{\text{No of teeth on the driven gear}}{\text{No of teeth on the driving gear}} = \ :1$$

7 Reassemble the complete unit, taking care to ensure that everything is in place and it is in operational condition.

**practical activity 3**

Find out and record the following manufacturer's data for a front-wheel drive vehicle and carry out a service inspection of a front-wheel drive vehicle's transmission system.

| Gearbox oil type and grade | Gearbox oil capacity | Hub nut torque type | Hydraulic clutch fluid (if applicable) |
|---|---|---|---|
| | | | |

**practical activity 4**

Dismantle a front-wheel drive gearbox. Carefully assess the condition of all of the components. Record your findings and create a report that clearly states the condition of the gearbox. Reassemble the gearbox to an operational standard. (Note that most of the learning process here occurs during reassembly; the activity will not be considered successful if the gearbox does not work afterwards.)

# CHAPTER 3

# STEERING AND SUSPENSION SYSTEMS

*Essential knowledge*

You will need to read and research vehicle technology covering the following:

- Steering systems
- Power-assisted steering
- Steering and wheel alignment
- Suspension

Note: some of this chapter refers to basic principles to ensure a full understanding.

## Steering systems

### Basic principles of a steering system

**discussion point**

What basic operations must a steering system enable the driver to carry out? Come to a conclusion and write down your ideas, including any sketches that might help when you present your conclusions to the rest of the group.

E

On the diagrams below state the differences you can see and indicate which one has the Ackermann layout.

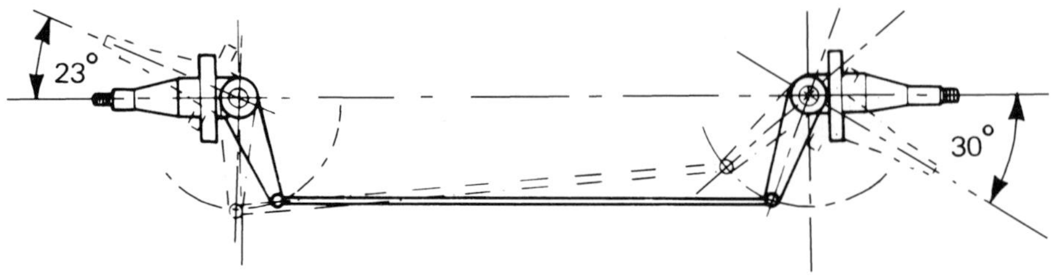

**discussion point**

Test your knowledge and discuss with a partner what the term 'Ackermann principle' refers to. Record your thoughts and be prepared to present them to the group.

## Oversteer and understeer

### Slip angle

**discussion point**

Through discussion and research find out what the terms 'slip angle' and 'self-aligning' torque mean and how they affect a vehicle when it is cornering. Set out your ideas in the form of notes and diagrams and be prepared to let the rest of the group know what you have discovered.

**Q** In the previous task you would have identified some steering conditions. Which one is considered to be safer and why?

## Steering mechanism

Complete the table below by considering vehicles that you may have worked on and are familiar with. State whether they have a steering box or a rack and pinion system.

| Vehicle type | System used | Vehicle type | System used |
|---|---|---|---|

## Camber, castor and swivel-axis inclination

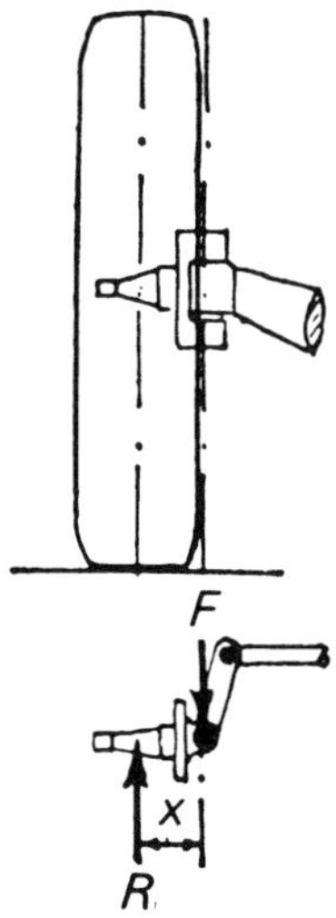


### Centre-point steering

**Q** What are the disadvantages of the steering assembly layout in the diagram to the left?

**discussion point**

Discuss with a partner what would happen if the resistance 'R' was seriously increased, possibly by the blow-out of a tyre? Write down your suggestions and conclusion. Include any sketches that you think might help when you present your ideas to the rest of the group.

**Q** To overcome some of the problems posed above, the wheel and kingpin can be arranged so that the offset distance *X* is reduced. What happens when the offset is eliminated and what is this arrangement called?

**E** State the factors that make it possible to have centre-point steering. Sketch the layout of an assembly with centre-point steering.

**Q** Sketch a steering assembly layout with positive camber and one with negative camber. Describe what the advantages of negative camber are, along with any disadvantages there may be.

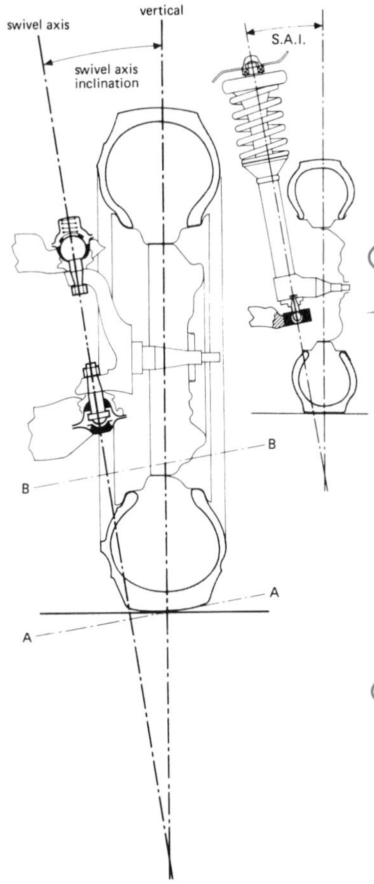


**Note:** Too much negative or positive camber to a wheel could increase wear on either the outer or inner edges of the tyre tread. See the tyre section for wear patterns.

### Kingpin inclination (KPI) or swivel axis inclination (SAI)

**discussion point**

Discuss with a partner the effect of a bent lower suspension link on SAI and camber angles. When you have written down your ideas and come to a conclusion, add any sketches that you think might help when presenting your ideas to other members of the group.

Look at the diagram on the left. When the wheel is steered or turned around the swivel axis, it will have a tendency to move downwards. As this is not possible, the vehicle will be lifted.

**Q** How will this lifting action benefit the steering operation?

### Dished wheels

It would seem simple to obtain the correct offset by having a large dish in the wheel.

### Negative offset (negative scrub radius)

**Q** Describe what is meant by the term negative offset.

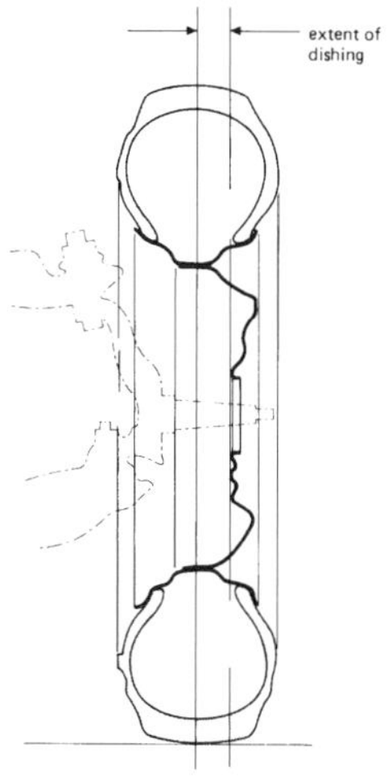

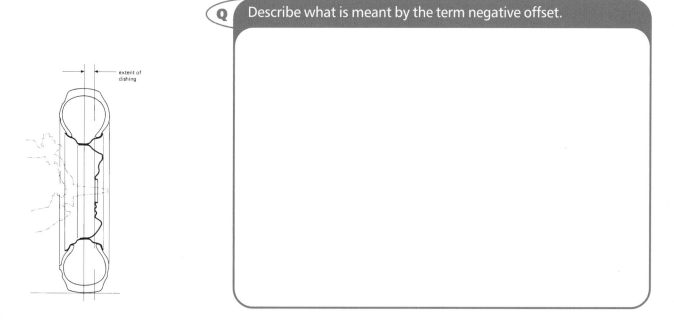

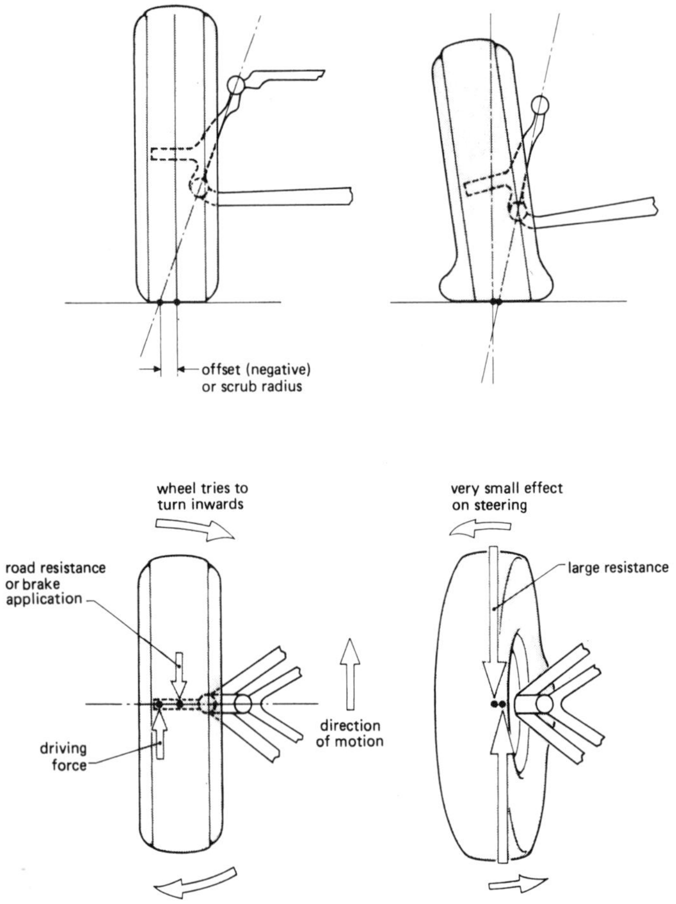


E

Look at both of the diagrams on this page. Compare the left-hand drawings in both. The intersection or crossover point is above the surface of the road (in the negative offset drawing). Now compare the right-hand drawings in both diagrams. Which is preferable?

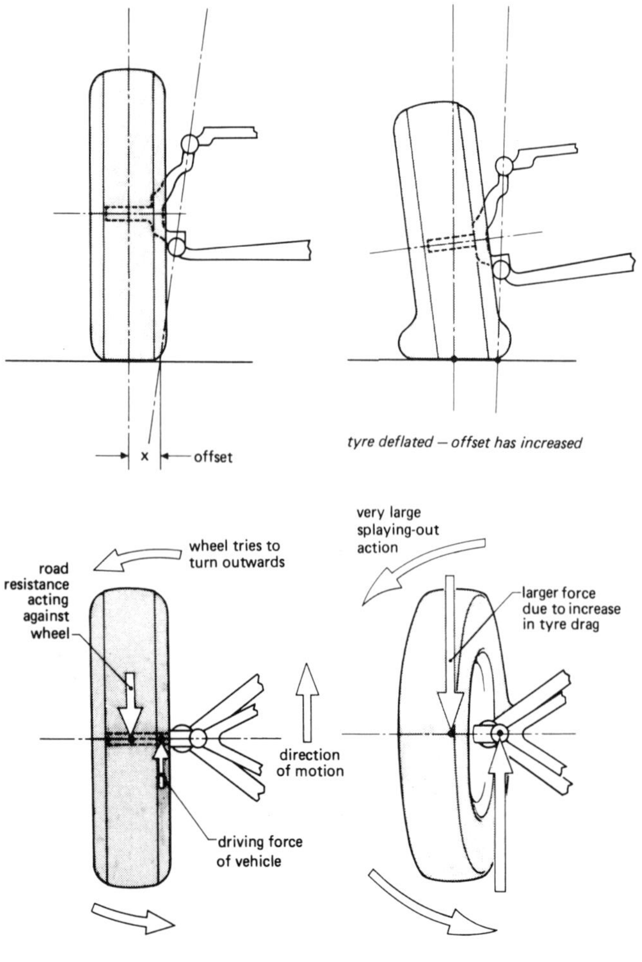


Q

How is vehicle safety affected by building in negative offset?

## Castor angle

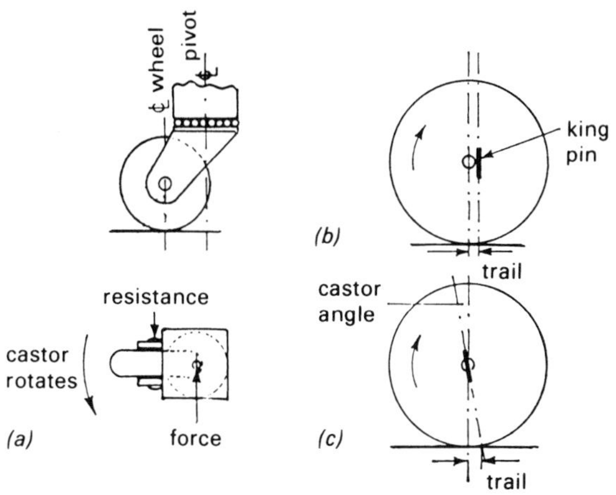


In the diagram on the left, wheels (a) and (b) are travelling from left to right and wheel (c) is travelling from right to left. In (a) the normal shopping trolley wheel is trailing the pivot point.

In diagram (b), the kingpin is mounted in front of the stub axle, giving a trailing effect.

In diagram (c), note the direction of travel: the wheel is still trailing.

All three are referred to as positive castor (trailing).

E

**Through research find out what are the benefits of building in a degree of castor angle.**

E

**Label the diagram showing castor angle and state whether the angle is positive or negative.**

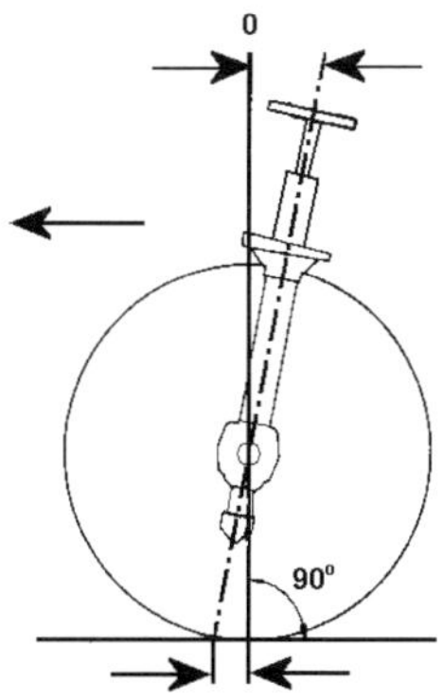


Q

**What will be the result of too much castor angle?**

### Toe in/toe out – wheel alignment

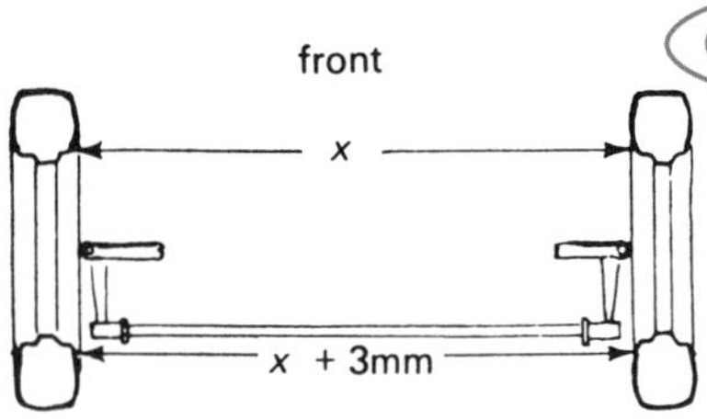


*(a) Wheel alignment*

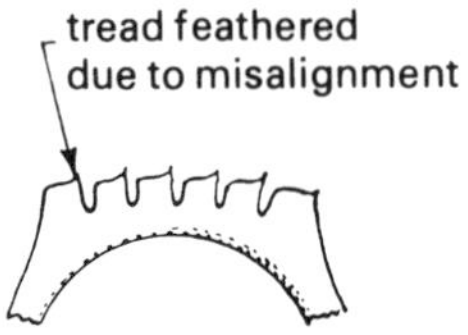


*(b) Section through tyre tread*

**Q** The diagram on the left is a plan drawing of a vehicle's front wheel alignment. Tyres wear only when the vehicle is travelling, so the settings when the vehicle is stationary might seem to be unusual: a technician will set the alignment so that it is not parallel. Why is this, and how does it differ between rear-wheel- and front-wheel-drive vehicles?

**E** Why is it important to adjust equally the track rods when setting the wheel alignment? Explain the effects and use a diagram to help to show your ideas.

## Steering system components

### Steering box

A steering box or gearbox provides the driver with a (ratio) lever system which enables a large force to be exerted at the road wheels (to steer the vehicle) with a minimum of driver effort. A steering gearbox should also allow the driver to control the direction of the vehicle accurately.

Steering boxes are often used in large vans, trucks and buses, although they were also the most common systems in light cars until the 1960s.

## Steering boxes

### Recirculating ball

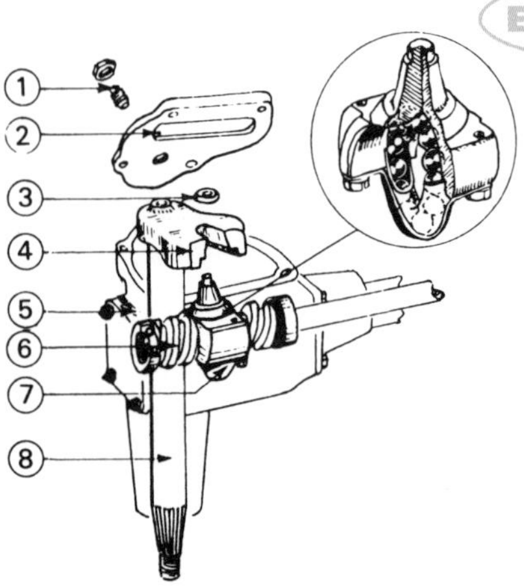


**E** Test your knowledge of steering boxes by naming the parts and following the drive path from the steering wheel down to the output. Arrange them in logical order.

Q Research the advantages a recirculating-ball type has over other types of steering box.

## Worm and roller

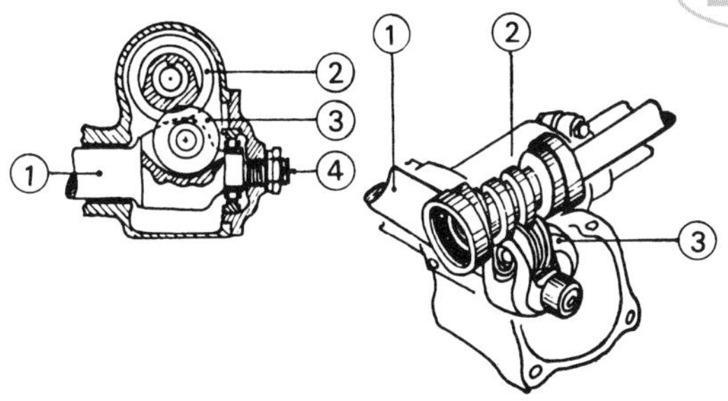


E Using the numbers in the diagram above, name the components in order of effort (or drive path) from the steering wheel.

### Steering box maintenance

Consult manufacturers' specifications. MOT regulations apply to steering systems and give set limits for free play at the circumference of the steering wheel.

Maintenance usually consists of checking and topping up the oil level. Repairs are usually limited to adjustment to reduce free play at the steering wheel.

## Rack and pinion

**discussion point** Test your knowledge by discussing with a partner the reasons why rack and pinion steering systems are most commonly fitted. Between you, create a drawing of this type of steering and label all the parts. Write down your ideas and present them to the rest of the group using drawings to help you.

**Variable ratio rack and pinion**

E

Research different types of collapsible steering column. Sketch them out and explain how each type works.

## Steering joints

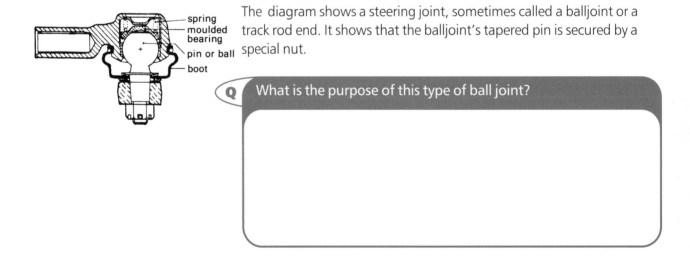

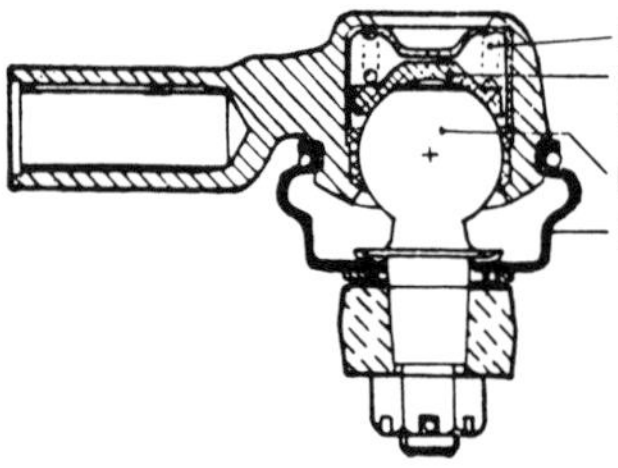


The diagram shows a steering joint, sometimes called a balljoint or a track rod end. It shows that the balljoint's tapered pin is secured by a special nut.

Q

What is the purpose of this type of ball joint?

## Front hubs

Front hub construction depends on whether the hub has to accommodate the driveshaft assembly and the hub bearings. Driven hubs are used for front-wheel drive vehicles or four-wheel drive vehicles.

Non-driving hubs are used for rear-wheel drive vehicles, where stub axles are used to locate the hubs and bearings.

E

Label the two diagrams and indicate which type, driving or non-driving, A and B are. Describe how you adjust bearing free play in type A.

**Type A**

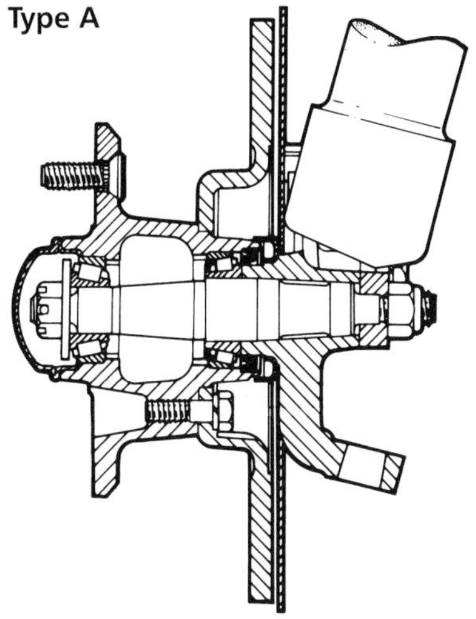

**Type B**

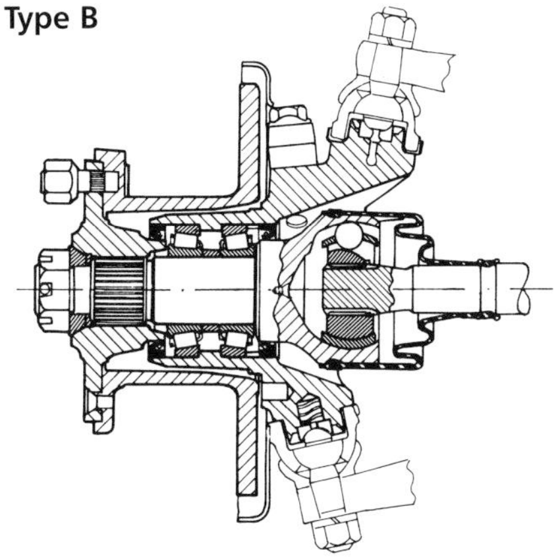

Q

Which of the following torque settings would you expect to use on type B?

a A nip b 20–30 Nm c Over 150 Nm d 40–50 Nm

**Note:** Always refer to the manufacturer's settings and procedures for tightening sequences and torques settings.

## Power-assisted steering

E

Using the missing words from the list below complete the statement to explain why power-assisted steering is a necessity in modern cars and how it improves driver comfort and safety.

With front-wheel drive, the additional weight of the powertrain assembly increases the __________ exerted on the __________ wheels. This, together with steering __________ design and wider section __________ to provide good road holding, means that a large __________ is required at the steering wheel to turn the steered wheels. The additional effort required makes the driver's job very tiring and difficult, especially while __________ the vehicle at __________ speeds.

effort load low manoeuvring steered tyres geometry

Q

What are the two main features that a power-assisted steering system should have?

E

Through research, sketch out and label the main components of a hydraulic power assisted steering system. Describe briefly how it works.

Q

Look at the schematic diagrams (right). Which diagram shows the steering in the straight ahead position?

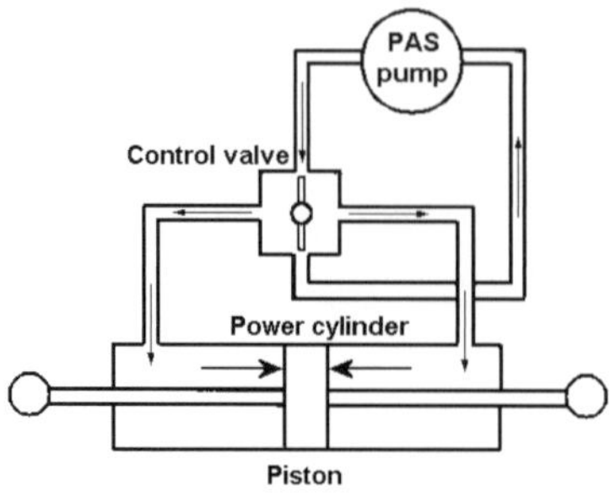


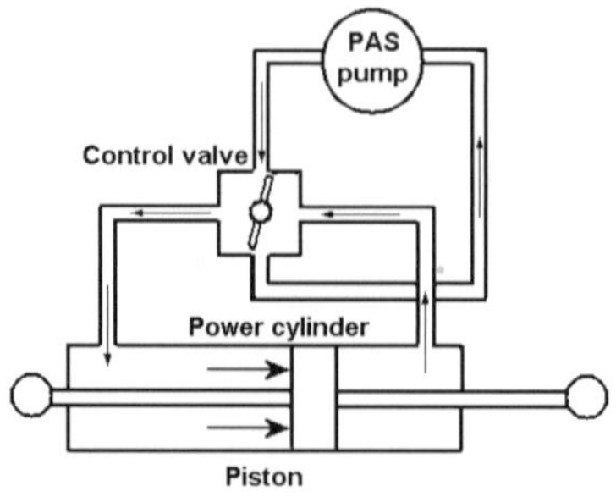

**discussion point**

If you were parking a car with power-assisted steering in a confined space, what could happen if the car was on full lock with the engine at tickover? What have manufacturers done to get over this problem? With a partner, write down your ideas, including any sketches that might be useful. Then discuss your conclusions with the rest of the group.

**discussion point**

Discuss with a partner why it is not always ideal to have engine-driven power assistance? Write down your ideas and be ready to present them to the rest of the group.

**Q** State two different methods of providing power assistance other than purely hydraulic.

**E** Look at the picture below. Arrow and label the parts clearly (a minimum of six) and state what type of steering this is.

**Q** What happens if a suspension bush is incorrectly fitted?

## Steering and wheel alignment

### Steering system maintenance

Q The steering system will be inspected during servicing and safety inspections, usually the MOT. Describe a procedure for servicing a steering system and the checks carried out in an MOT test?

E Complete the table below stating the key checks on the various components that should be made during servicing.

| |
|---|
| Steering wheel |
| Steering column |
| Steering gearbox |
| Steering (linkage) ball joints |

### Hydraulic power-assisted steering maintenance

Q What should be checked during normal routine servicing of a hydraulic power-assisted steering system? (It might be helpful to use a service schedule manual; state the make and model.)

Q What would be a good indication of an internal component failure or premature wear in a hydraulic power-assisted system?

## Wheel alignment

**Q** The alignment and geometry of the wheels are set during production. What can cause the settings to alter during the life of a vehicle?

Wheel alignment is often part of a major service, sometimes at extra cost if the customer requires it. Even if no excessive wear or damage can be found in the steering geometry, the front wheel toe settings can often be outside the manufacturer's limits.

**Q** What equipment would you use to check misalignment of the front toe (or tracking)?

**E** Describe, using bullet points, the procedure for checking the tracking on a vehicle. State why it is important to adjust the track evenly on both track rods.

### Four-wheel alignment

The handling, stability and steerability of a modern vehicle is dependent on the alignment of all four wheels. The alignment of each wheel will have an effect on the alignment of the remaining wheels.

## Road testing

After the checks and adjustments have been carried out, ideally the vehicle should be road tested to check handling and stability.

**discussion point**

**Discuss with a partner what checks should you, as the technician, carry out during the road test and why? Write down your list of checks, and be read present your ideas to the rest of the group.**

**Note:** A road test provides an ideal opportunity to a required for the next service and offer preventati customer.

# Suspension

## Introduction

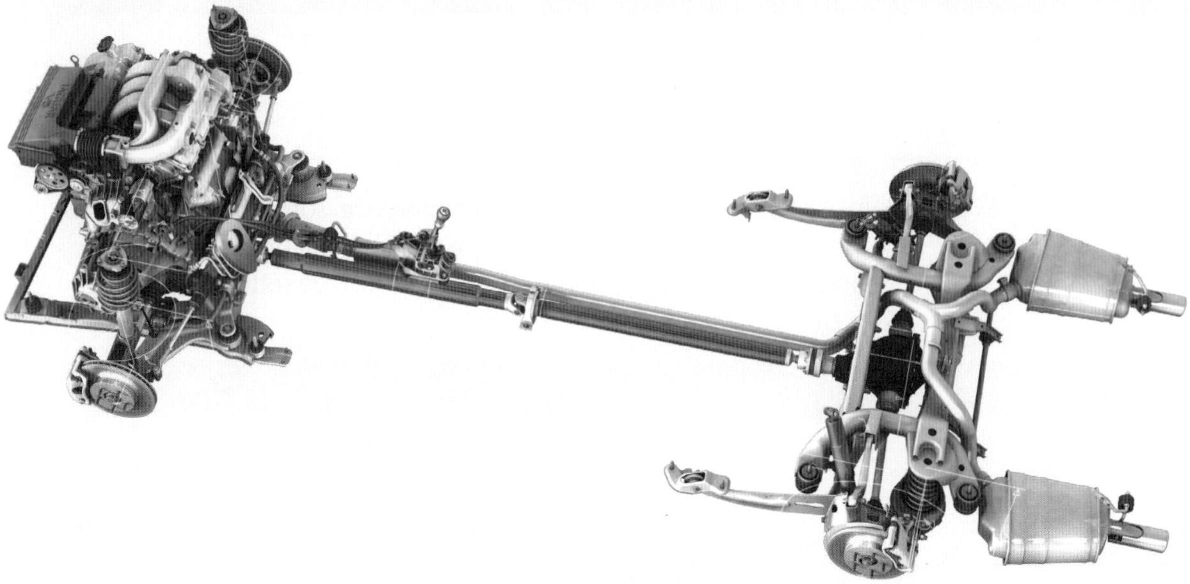

Vehicle suspension systems insulate the vehicle occupants against bumps and shocks from different road surfaces. They also provide stability on cornering and help maintain contact between the tyres and the road surface.

## Road springs, dampers and linkages

**Q** What is meant by sprung and unsprung weight and how can upsprung weight be reduced?

Forces exerted by body movement on sprung weight can be defined as pitching, rolling, bounce and yaw.

**E** Test your knowledge by matching the definitions with the following terms:

| | |
|---|---|
| Rolling | Vertical movement of the vehicle body |
| Pitching | Rotational movement of the vehicle body around the centre point |
| Yaw | Fore and aft movement of the vehicle body |
| Bounce | Side to side movement of the vehicle body |

**discussion point**

A customer has advised you that his car pitches excessively when going over a speed hump. This fault is accompanied by a clunking noise. Discuss this with a partner and decide:

- What questions would you ask the customer?
- What initial diagnostic checks would you carry out?
- What equipment could you use for diagnosis?
- What conclusions and outcomes would you expect to find from these symptoms?

Write down your answers to the above questions. You may be asked to present your ideas to the rest of the group.

## The requirements of a spring

### Helical springs

The most common type of spring used in modern cars is the helical (coil) type. These are compact enough to be used on all four corners of a vehicle and can provide independent suspension to the wheels.

E

Research different types of variable rate springs. Explain how each type you have identified achieves a variable rate using sketches to help you.

Q

How would increasing the diameter of the coil wire affect the suspension characteristics?

### Torsion bars

Torsion bars are used used in some passenger and light goods vehicles. They provide good load carrying capabilities and independent movement for the road wheels.

### Hydropneumatic suspension

Hydropneumatic suspension systems are similar to rubber and hydrolastic systems. They use the same materials, such as rubber and fluid, but they also use gas to provide suspension.

**Q** Which inert gas is generally used in this type of suspension?

**Q** If gas is used as a spring medium, what is used for damping?

**E** Research the Citroën hydropneumatic suspension. Sketch and label the layout and briefly describe its operation.

**Q** How are the fluid lines connected in some vehicles to interlink the suspension?

## Suspension dampers

The purpose of a damper is to control the oscillations created by the energy stored in the spring

### Hydraulic dampers

**E** Sketch a labelled diagram of a simple double acting damper and briefly describe its operation.

Research adjustable dampers. Explain how they are adjustable using sketches to help you. It may be interesting to look at performance cars in this respect.

**discussion point**

Discuss with a partner what inspection procedures might be used to determine whether a damper is serviceable or not. Write down your list of procedures, including any sketches that you think might help when you present your ideas to the rest of the group.

## Rigid axle suspension

### Construction

Older vehicles up to the middle of the twentieth century commonly used the rigid axle system. Rigid rear axles are still used in a number of vehicles today and can still be found in some light commercial vehicles.

## Stabiliser bars

**Q** To which type of suspension setup are stabiliser bars usually fitted, and why?

**Q** What is another name for a stabiliser bar?

E Using sketches to help you, explain how a stabiliser bar operates.

## Semi-trailing arm and coil spring system

E Label the diagram below and explain how this type of suspension offers 'compliance steer'. Include the benefits to vehicle handling that this effect provides.

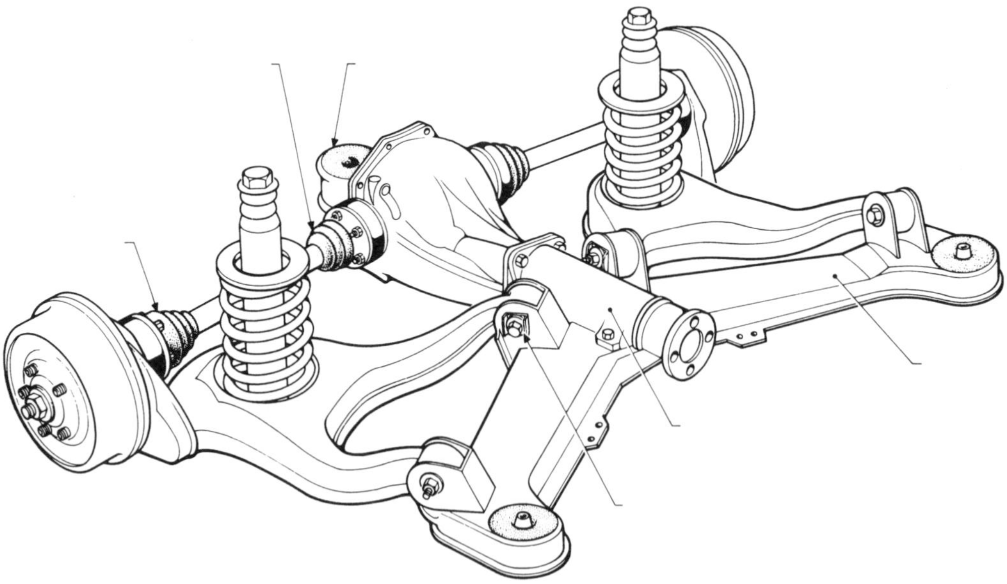

## Steering and suspension maintenance and diagnosis

**discussion point**

Discuss with a partner the aims and and objectives of carrying out a road test with regard to checking steering and steering serviceability. Set out a logical testing sequence, noting the components that will be checked. Be prepared to present your ideas to the group.

**discussion point**

Altering the suspension in a car in an attempt to improve its handling can sometimes have adverse effects on other systems. Discuss the possible effects of this with a partner. Note down your ideas, including any sketches that you think might help when you present your ideas to the rest of the group.

**mini projects**

Agree the following with your tutor:

- which projects to do and the order in which to do them
- the format and quantity of content
- the time frame for completion.

Research and report on how electronic control of suspension systems is becoming more popular. You should consider self-levelling types and other vehicle systems that interface with them, such as electronic stability control. Research into electronic systems in performance cars might be particularly interesting. Analyse the systems you find and state how they improve vehicle performance and safety.

## Practical activities

**practical activity 1**

Examine at least five different vehicles and identify and describe the suspension systems used in each. Carry out service checks and create a report for each.

| Vehicle | Suspension used |
|---|---|
| | |
| | |
| | |
| | |
| | |

**practical activity 2**

Find out and record the following manufacturer's data and carry out a service inspection of a steering system.

| Track rod lock-nut torque setting | Wheel alignment | Toe setting (Tracking) |
|---|---|---|
| | | |

Record your findings and create a report that would inform a customer of the condition of their steering system. Check and adjust wheel alignment (tracking) as necessary in line with the manufacturer's specifications.

# CHAPTER 4

# BRAKES

*Essential knowledge*

You will need to read and research vehicle technology covering the following:

- Hydraulic braking systems
- Power assistance
- Anti-lock braking systems (ABS) – an introduction

Note: some of this chapter refers to basic principles to ensure a full understanding.

## Hydraulic braking systems

### Benefits of hydraulic systems

E

Test your knowledge and complete the following description of a hydraulic system using the missing words below.

Among the advantages of hydraulic brakes are that they are fully __________ – they distribute even line __________ throughout the system.

The system is very __________ – the fluid can __________ without the resistances and frictions of a mechanical system. Fluid hoses allow movement in steering and suspension without the __________ of rods or cables in a __________ system.

Pressure can be controlled by the use of different sizes of __________ (manufacturer-set). The surface area of a __________ cylinder piston compared with the surface area of a __________ cylinder piston gives a __________. This applies to all hydraulic systems.

mechanical | flow | ratio | limitations | pistons | master | compensated | efficient | pressure | wheel

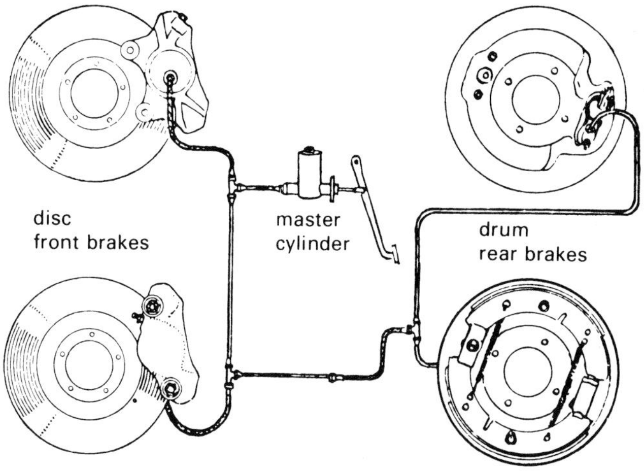


**Performance checks**

The diagram to the left shows a simple single line hydraulic system with disc brakes at the front and drum brakes at the rear.

A parking brake will be fitted at the rear of the system.

The parking brake is required to act on at least two wheels and, in the event of a hydraulic failure, to act as a secondary brake. There are set minimum performance percentage requirements for the main (foot) brake and secondary (hand) brake.

Q Where would you expect to see these performance checks carried out and what are the minimum performance figures?

E Research and find out at least two different methods of bleeding a hydraulic braking system. Explain each procedure and state why it is important not to have air in the system.

## The master cylinder

There are two types of brake master cylinder: the single cylinder and the dual cylinder (or tandem).

### Single-cylinder type

Although this type of master cylinder is no longer used in brake systems, its successor, the tandem cylinder, is the most commonly used system today for operating brakes.

The single-cylinder layout can be seen in the diagram below.

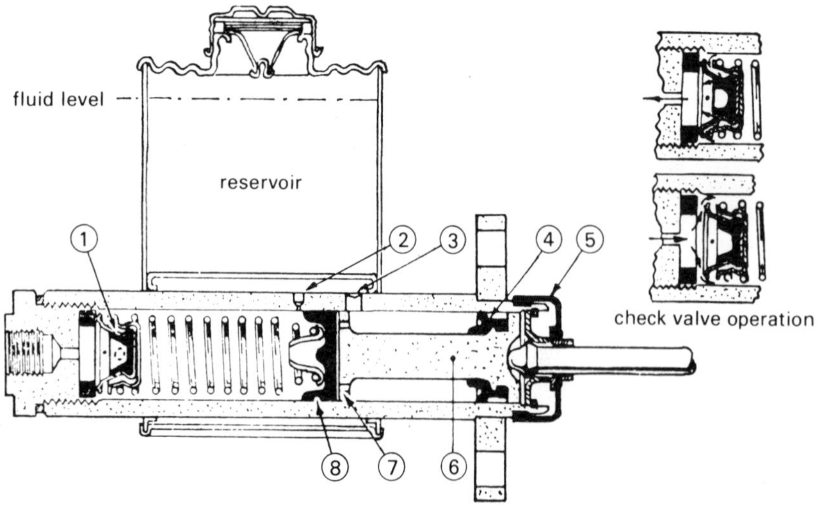


E Complete the numbered list below by naming the components of the master cylinder opposite.

1
2
3
4
5
6
7
8

**What is the purpose of the bypass port and check valve, and how could a fault in the master cylinder cause a brake binding problem?**

## Tandem (dual) cylinder type

**In the diagram below the top two schematic figures do not show the seals. In their simplest form draw the seals above the pistons, showing the direction that they need to be in to face the fluid pressure.**

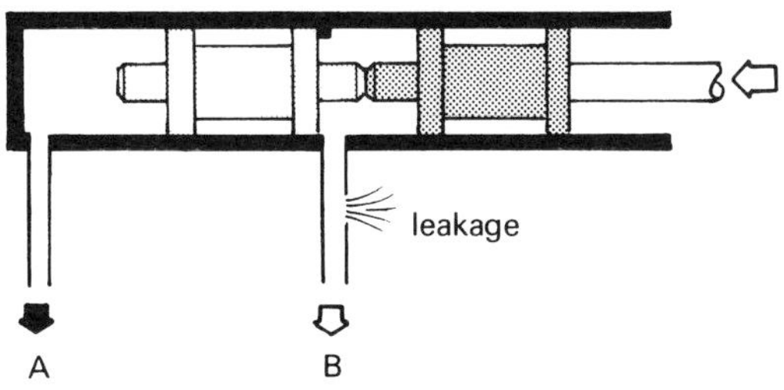


*failure in line B*

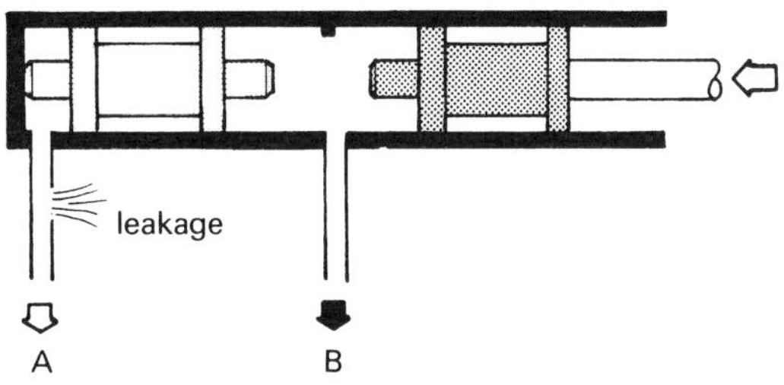


*failure in line A*

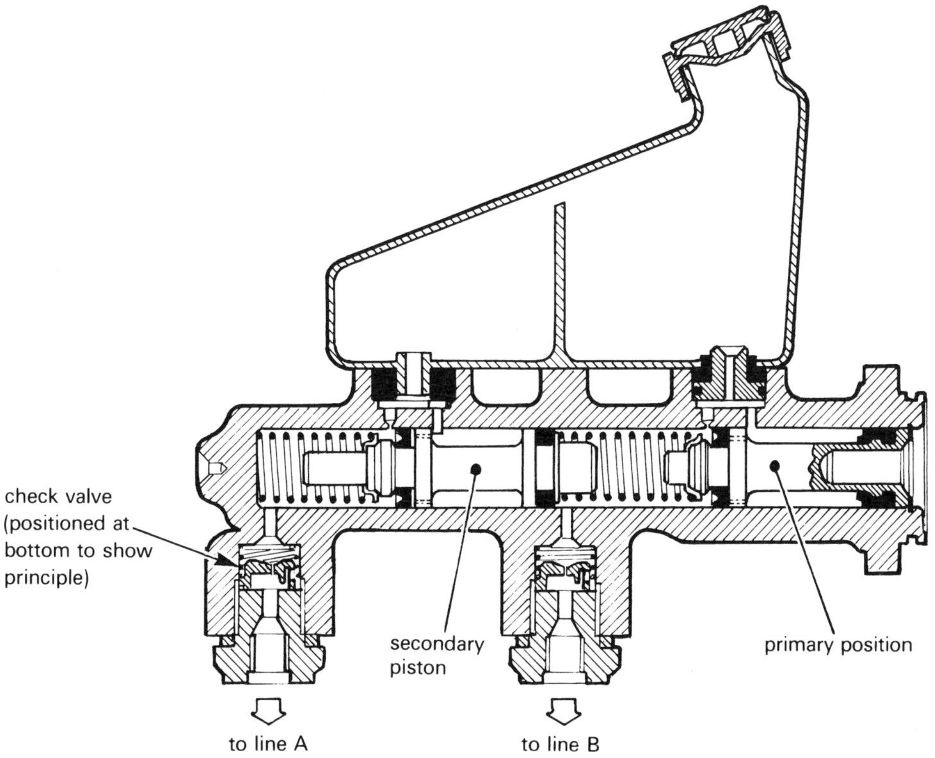


**Refer to the diagrams above to describe how a tandem master cylinder operates. Include an explanation of how it maintains braking even if a brake line fails causing fluid loss.**

**Q** Which features of the dual master cylinder make it suitable for a 'fail-safe' or split braking system?

A further research exercise towards the end of the chapter will encourage you to look more closely at different layouts for split braking systems

### The pressure-regulating valve

When a vehicle brakes, the inertia forces acting at the centre of gravity cause the load on the front wheels to increase and the load on the rear wheels to decrease.

The pressure-regulating valve regulates or restricts fluid pressure to the rear brakes under hard braking to avoid rear wheel lock-up.

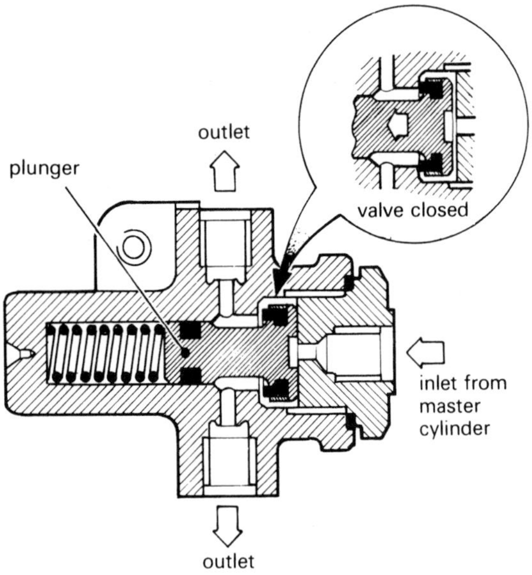


**E** Describe briefly how the pressure regulating valve shown in the diagram operates.

### Brake pressure control valve or inertia valve

The brake inertia valve is a development of the pressure-regulating valve.

The valve is particularly suited to overcoming the problem of the large load variations between the front and rear wheels of a front-wheel drive vehicle.

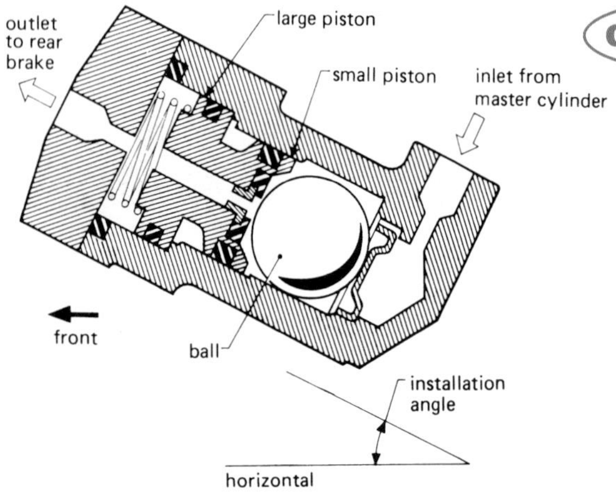


**Q** The inertia type control valve, as shown to the left, has two operating stages. What is the first stage?

Research and find a diagram of a pressure differential warning actuator. Make a sketch and describe its operation and purpose.

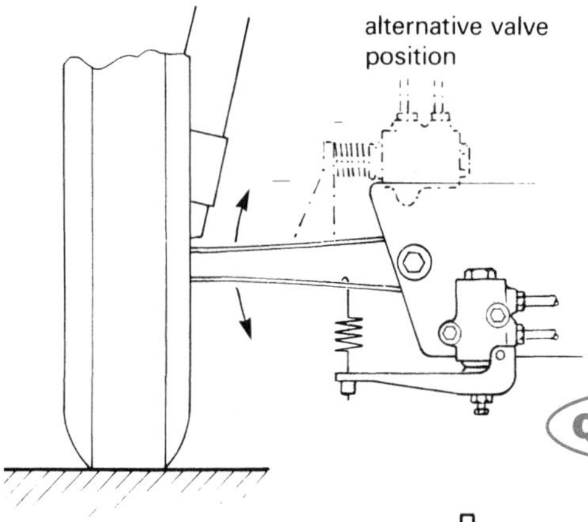


## Load-apportioning valves

The load-apportioning valve supplies, within specified limits, hydraulic pressure to the rear brakes in proportion to the load carried by the rear wheels.

The load-apportioning valve helps to reduce the risk of a rear wheel skid when the rear of the vehicle is lightly loaded.

Which type of vehicle would this valve ideally suit and why?

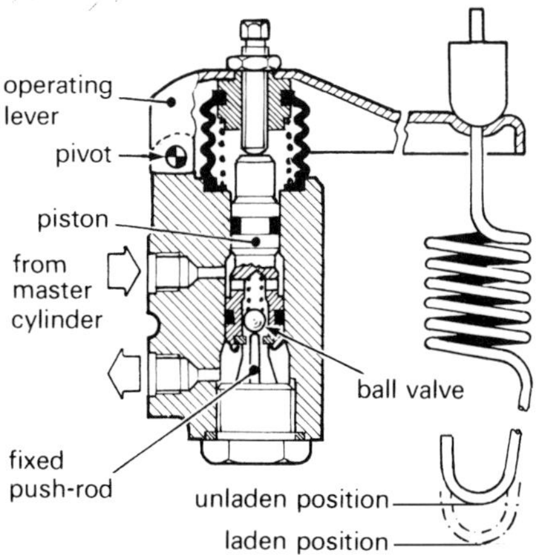


Underline the correct **component / term** to state how the load-apportioning valve knows what weight the vehicle is carrying.

The valve housing is fixed to the **body / suspension / brake line**; the spring connects the valve operating lever to a part of the **brake line / suspension / body** that moves proportionally to the load of the vehicle.

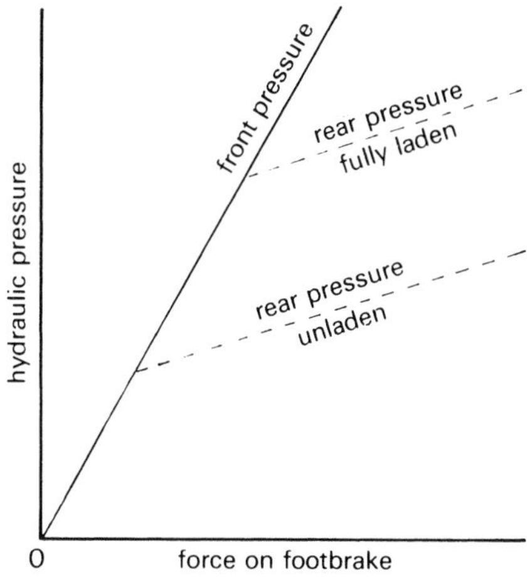


What can you learn from looking at the diagram on the left?

Safety Note: Always follow the manufacturer's specification for type and replacement intervals of brake fluid as well as following all safety procedures.

## Brake fluid

Brake fluid is a major component in a braking system and should be treated as such. Fluid of the wrong type (or specification), or that is old or contaminated, should be treated as a faulty part and be completely replaced.

**Q** What does SAE stand for?

**E** Complete the missing words in the following description of brake fluid properties.

Fluid for modern __________ systems needs to have many properties: a __________ freezing point, a __________ boiling point and a low viscosity. It must also be __________ and compatible with __________ hoses, seals and various materials manufacturers might use in hydraulic systems.

Brake fluid is hygroscopic. This means that it absorbs __________ out of the air. This is not __________ as an ingress of moisture will reduce the __________ point, raise the __________ point and make the brake fluid __________ to the system. One way that manufacturers reduce this problem is to completely __________ the fluid as part of the servicing of the vehicle, usually at 12 000 mile / 12 month to 24000 mile / 24 month intervals.

moisture | freezing | low | boiling | hydraulic | replace
corrosive | rubber | high | non-corrosive | beneficial

**discussion point**

A customer brings their car in for an annual service. You notice that the brake fluid is due to be changed on this service but the customer is reluctant to pay the extra cost. What hazards and risks would you advise the customer of if the brake fluid is not replaced? Discuss this with a partner and write down your conclusions, so that you can present your ideas to the rest of the group.

**Q** What is meant by the term 'wet boiling point'?

**E** Name three types of brake fluid and explain why they cannot be mixed.

**E** Describe the procedure for testing the serviceability of brake fluid.

**discussion point**

A vehicle is brought in on a recovery truck with the symptoms of the footbrake pedal fading when pressure is applied to it. An initial check shows that the brake fluid reservoir is full and that there is initially a firm pedal when pressure is applied. Discuss this with a partner and decide:

- What questions would you ask the customer?
- What initial diagnostic checks would you carry out?
- What equipment might you use for diagnosis?
- What conclusions and outcomes would you expect to reach from these symptoms?

Write down your list of conclusions and outcomes, including any sketches that you think might help when you present your ideas to the rest of the group.

## Power assistance

Before the introduction of power-assisted brakes drivers relied on their own strength to stop. In the past, assistance was provided by the self-servo action of leading brake shoes. Disc brakes have no self-servo action.

Drivers will feel safer and more comfortable if they have to apply only a moderate and controlled pressure to stop a vehicle.

**Q** What is the most common form of assistance in use on current vehicles?

**Q** What are the main functional requirements of a brake servo?

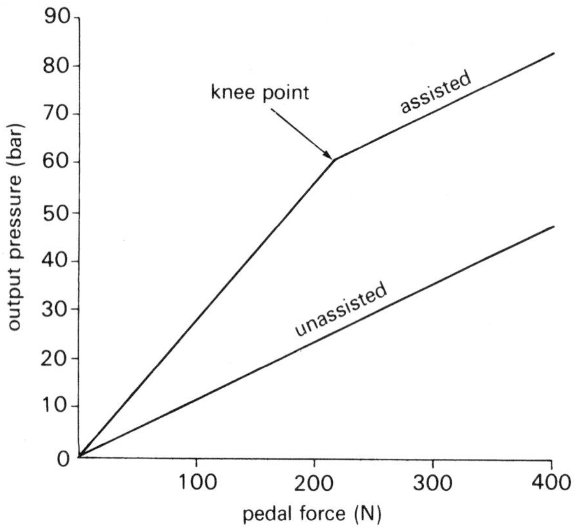


E The graph (left) shows the amount of assistance (pressure) given relative to pedal pressure. Explain what happens at the 'knee point' shown.

Q What does the term 'suspended vacuum' mean?

## Direct-acting servo

Q Most cars are fitted with a direct-acting suspended vacuum servo used with a tandem master cylinder. How does this get its name?

**discussion point**

Consider a vacuum supply. What does the term 'exhauster' mean, where is it usually found and why? Research and discuss this with a partner and write down your answers, including any sketches that you think might help when you present your ideas to the rest of the group.

E

In the diagram below (lower picture) draw in a brake pedal assembly connected to the servo. Mark the direction of operation with an arrow. Using the diagrams to help you, explain how this unit operates

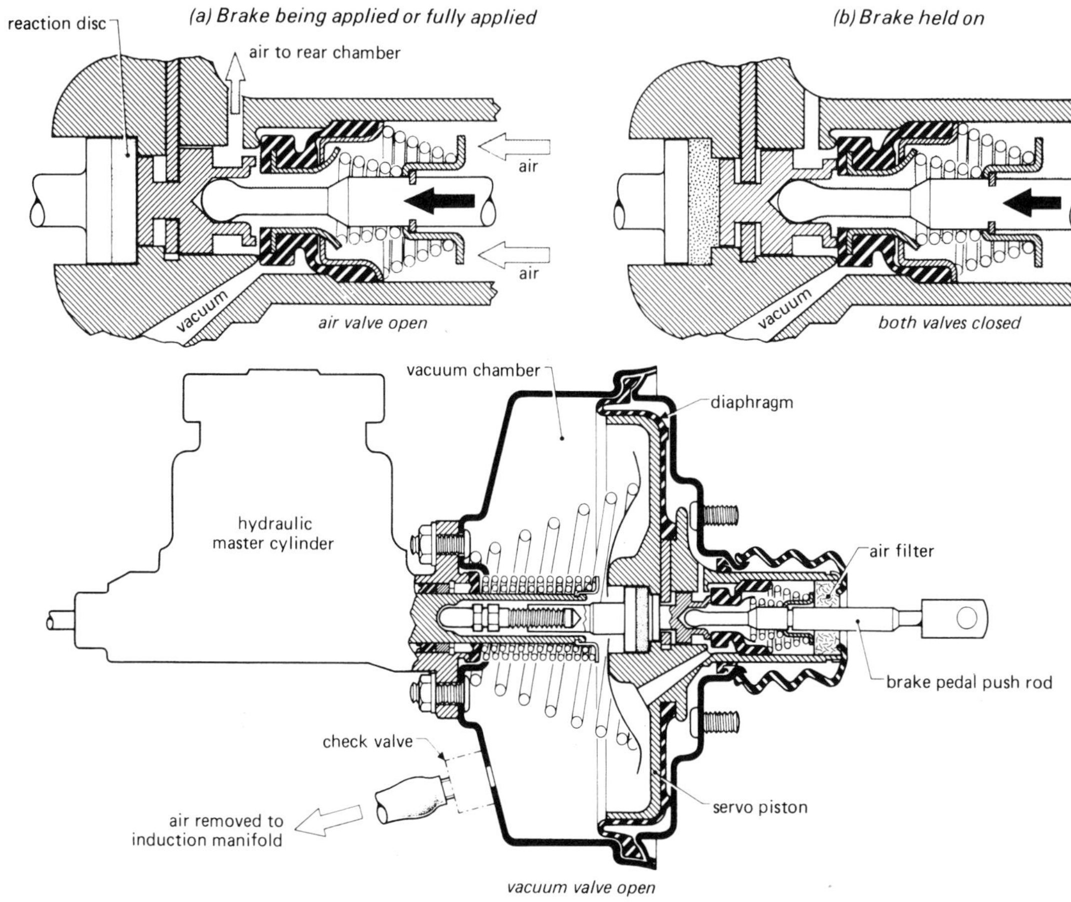


Q

How is the driver able to 'feel' the load applied to the pedal?

## Hydraulic assistance (power braking)

Heavy cars and light trucks often need greater braking assistance than the engine vacuum system could provide.

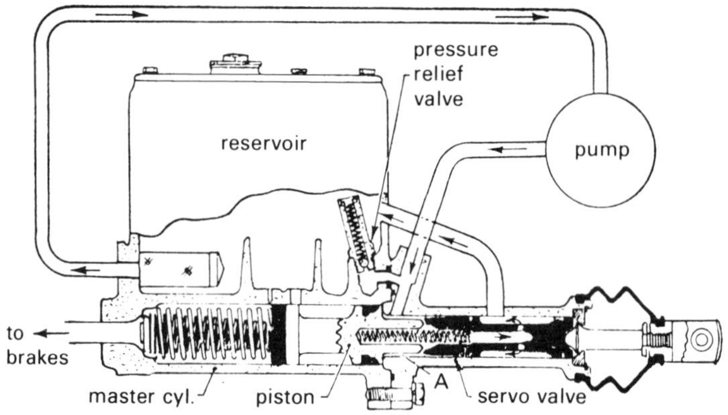


*(a) Continuous-flow system*

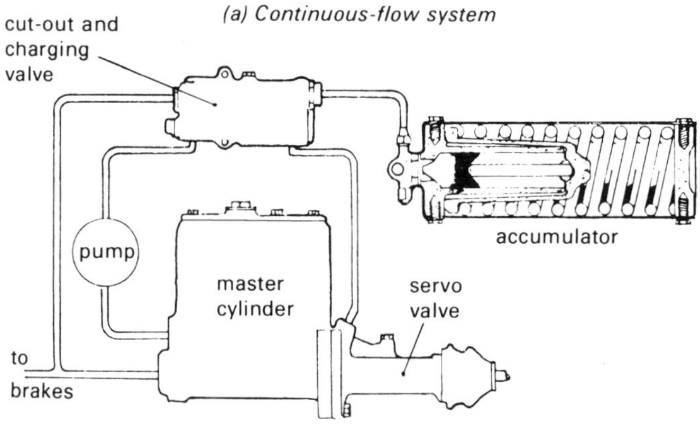


*(b) Continuous-flow system with accumulator*

E Referring to the diagrams explain in a logical sequence how this system operates. Include typical operating pressures and state what other vehicle systems can make use of this pressure.

*Safety Note:* ***It is essential that all hydraulic pressure is discharged from the accumulator. This is usually done by pumping the brake pedal with the pump off. If you are unsure, check the manufacturer's specifications and ask for your line manager's advice.***

Q Name two ways that hydraulic pressure can be produced?

## Antilock braking system (ABS) – an introduction

E Complete the following statement using the missing words from the list below.

With the increased number of road users and the increased demand for __________ vehicles, the ability to control a vehicle under __________ braking, to avoid skidding and __________ the wheels and still keep reasonable __________ of the vehicle is a very important step forward in safety.

Consider the effect of excessive brake pedal __________. The wheels are locked, __________ is generated between the road surface and the __________ of the tyre. Steering and __________ control is lost.

Now consider the effect of not enough brake pedal pressure. You still have __________ wheels and control of the steering but you may not __________ in time.

A point between too much pressure and too little is what is required. Unfortunately, with changing road conditions, snow, ice, grease, a loaded vehicle, etc., the parameters are constantly changing.

stop emergency footprint directional rotating
control pressure safer heat locking

E Draw a simple labelled diagram showing the main components of an ABS.

Q What effect might the driver notice when an ABS is operating?

Q What are the functional requirements of ABS?

Q What precautions must be taken when changing the brake fluid on a vehicle with ABS?

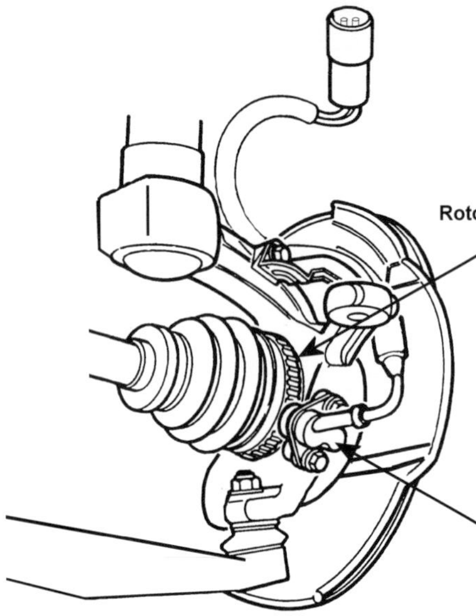

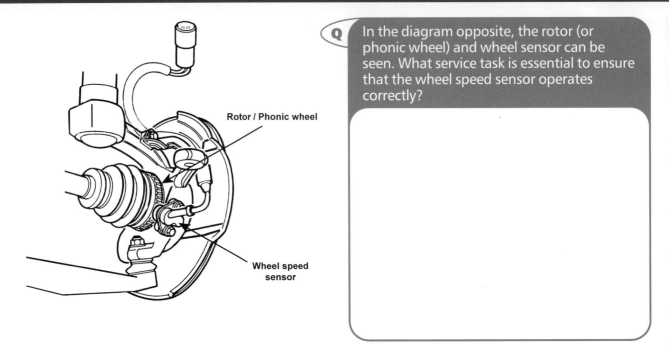

Q In the diagram opposite, the rotor (or phonic wheel) and wheel sensor can be seen. What service task is essential to ensure that the wheel speed sensor operates correctly?

## Traction control system (TCS)

The electronic sensing system used in ABS for the detection of road wheel speed and slip can be further utilised to control or limit the maximum tractive force applied to propel the vehicle.

E Complete the following description of how TCS works compared with ABS, using the missing words from the list below?

Wheel slip during __________ is opposite to that under braking. Under __________, the wheels slow down or stop. Under acceleration one wheel will __________ up. The __________ are making the same comparisons between all wheels and apply a braking __________ to the spinning wheel. Under braking the system would __________ the locking wheel.

sensors speed release braking force acceleration

Q Once a system has detected a spinning wheel, which two systems can the ECM control to rectify the problem?

### Electronic brake apportioning

Brake apportioning, which was previously done using mechanical brake apportioning valves, can also be carried out electronically via the ABS components.

Signals from the wheel sensors inform the ECM which wheels are about to lock. The ECM then apportions the brakes accordingly.

**Q** Via which component does the ECM limit or apportion brake pressure?

**Q** What feature does brake assist offer over a standard ABS?

### Electronic stability control

Developments in vehicle electronic technology and ABS have resulted in systems that can sense when a vehicle is being driven in a manner that would lead to instability and loss of control.

**Q** What are the main features of an electronic stability control system?

## Routine maintenance

### Safety

For obvious reasons, the braking system should be maintained to the highest levels at all times.

Brakes, like many vehicle systems, are partially fail-safe. It is rare to hear of a vehicle with total brake loss. However, there are regular articles in trade magazines on issues such as part system failures. This can often be attributed to human error on the part of the driver or technician, where manufacturer's instructions have been overlooked or disregarded. There are now considerable legal implications for yourself and the garage concerning vehicle safety and penalties if a court decides ignorance or negligence was to blame.

**mini projects**

Agree the following with your tutor:

- which projects to do and the order in which to do them
- the format and quantity of content
- the time frame for completion.

1 By researching a number of different manufacturers' braking systems identify at least two different ways in which a hydraulic braking system can be split for safety reasons. Create a report to include diagrams of the layouts and a comparison of any differences you can find. Analyse them and decide which one you feel is best.

2 Research and identify brake fluid classifications and ratings, and typical applications for the different types, including advanced types that overcome hygroscopic effects. In addition, choosing at least two different manufacturers' vehicles, identify and compare their recommended brake fluid change schedules.

3 Research and prepare a report on the symptoms a driver might experience if the following common faults were found in a hydraulic braking system:

a a seized caliper piston
b a split brake servo diaphragm
c a seized automatic brake adjuster
d a seized pressure limiting valve
e a seized handbrake compensator
f an excessive leak from one rear wheel cylinder
g no output from an ABS wheel speed sensor
h air in a hydraulic brake line.

Ideally set this information out in a file that you can build, over time, into your personal diagnostic manual for all vehicle systems.

## Practical activities

**practical activity 1**

Carry out a service inspection of the front brakes of a vehicle fitted with disc brakes.

Find out and record the following manufacturer's data for your chosen vehicle.

| Disc pad minimum thickness | Disc minimum thickness | Disc maximum runout | Wheel nut torque settings | Brake fluid type |
|---|---|---|---|---|
| | | | | |

1 Remove the disc pads.

2 Measure the runout of the brake discs and record your results.

3 Measure the thickness of the discs and pads and record your results.

| Measured disc pad thickness | Measured disc thickness | Disc maximum runout |
| --- | --- | --- |
| | | |

From your results, write down what advice you would give the customer on whether the brake system is serviceable and when future remedial work might be required?

**practical activity 2**

Using the correct equipment, carry out a brake fluid test on three vehicles and state your findings and recommendations below.

| Make and model | Results of test | Recommendations |
| --- | --- | --- |
| | | |
| | | |

If the equipment is available and with the assistance of your mentor or a senior member of staff, carry out a brake test using brake rollers or plates. List the results below and state any recommendations.

**Foot or service brake**

| Vehicle type | Make | Model | Weight |
| --- | --- | --- | --- |
| | | | |

Left front ________ Right front ________ Total effort/reading ________

Left rear ________ Right rear ________ Total effort/reading ________

Added total effort ________

$$\frac{\text{total effort}}{\text{weight of vehicle (kg)}} \times 100 = \_\_\_\_\_\_\_\_ \text{ Efficiency (\%)}$$

Balance or imbalance, front ________%

Balance or imbalance, rear ________%

**Park or secondary brake (handbrake)**

Left rear ________ Total effort/reading ________

Right rear ________ Total effort/reading ________

________ Add total effort ________

$$\frac{\text{total effort}}{\text{weight of vehicle (kg)}} \times 100 = \_\_\_\_\_\_\_\_ \text{ Efficiency (\%)}$$

Balance or imbalance park brake ________%

List below your findings and state what you would recommend. If no fault is found, suggest what might be the cause of a fault if, in the front brake balance test, you found that one side fluctuated excessively.

# CHAPTER 5

# COOLING, HEATING AND VENTILATION

*Essential knowledge*

You will need to read and research vehicle technology covering the following:

- The engine cooling system
- Heating and ventilation systems
- Air conditioning

Note: some of this chapter refers to basic principles to ensure a full understanding.

## The engine cooling system

### Function of a cooling system

**discussion point**

Test your knowledge by discussing with a partner the problems that can occur if an engine does not have an efficient cooling system. Write down your ideas, including any sketches that you think might help when you present your ideas to the rest of the group.

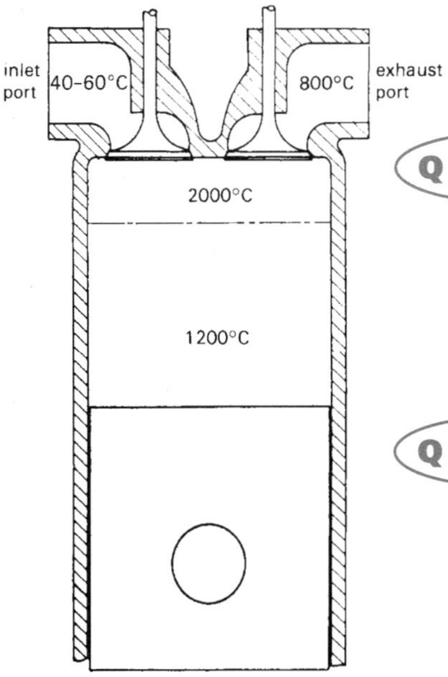


A cooling system is needed to maintain the operating temperatures of an internal combustion engine.

**Q** What is an approximate combustion temperature produced by the burning gases?

**Q** What is an approximate combustion gas temperature during the exhaust stroke?

**Q** What are the disadvantages of overcooling an engine?

**Q** Below what operating temperature is the cylinder head best kept in order to avoid overheating?

## Heat dissipation

E

Test your knowledge by describing three means of heat transfer used to dissipate the heat generated from an engine. Use diagrams to help you.

## Pump circulation systems

### The cooling pump

The diagram below shows a typical water pump.

E

Label the diagram of the cooling pump. State what the body of the pump can be made of. What type of bearings are commonly used?

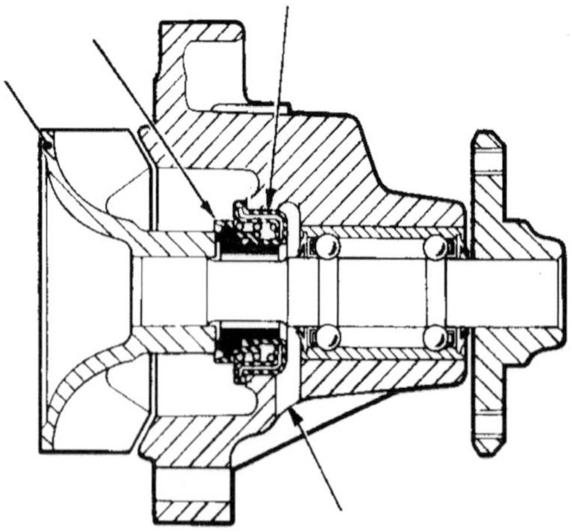

Q

How is the impeller secured onto the water pump?

E Name the various materials that can be used for an impeller and list the advantages and disadvantages of each of them.

Q How could a coolant leak from a water pump occur and how would it be noticeable?

E Make simple sketches showing two methods of driving a water pump.

## Radiators

Q What are the two common forms in which radiator cores are constructed?

### Tube and fin cores

Q From which material is a modern vehicle's radiator core generally constructed?

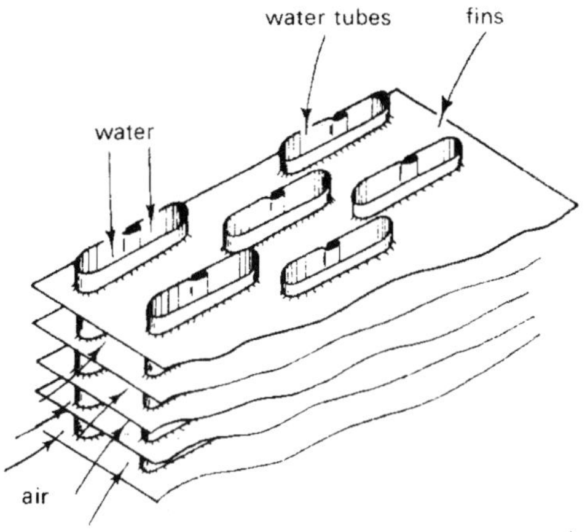

E Complete the following description of the construction of this type of radiator core using the missing words below.

The __________ through which the coolant flows are of a flattened __________ section and made of brass about 0.125 mm thick. They are arranged in three or four rows and pass through a series of thin __________ fins. The whole assembly is dipped in __________ to bond the tubes and __________ together.

copper | oval | fins | tubes | solder

### Flow direction through the radiator

Q Research and find out the two different flow directions used in radiators. Note which type is most common and why.

E Through research discover and describe two methods of checking for a blocked radiator.

## Temperature control of the cooling system

The cooling system must be capable of keeping the engine temperature within safe limits under the most arduous conditions, such as when climbing long, steep hills at full throttle in hot climates. Since these conditions represent a very small proportion of the running time for most vehicles, it is clear that the cooling system will overcool the engine most of the time unless there is some method of reducing its effectiveness when necessary.

### Thermostats

Q Which two main types of thermostat have been used in cooling systems?

E

Look at the diagram on the right. List the various components of a wax-element thermostat and describe their function by completing the following table.

| | |
|---|---|
| 1 | |
| 2 | |
| 3 | |
| 4 | |
| 5 | |
| 6 | |
| 7 | |
| 8 | |

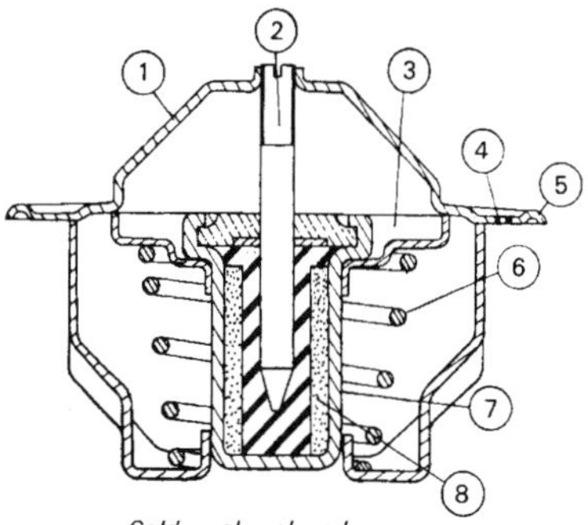


Cold – valve closed

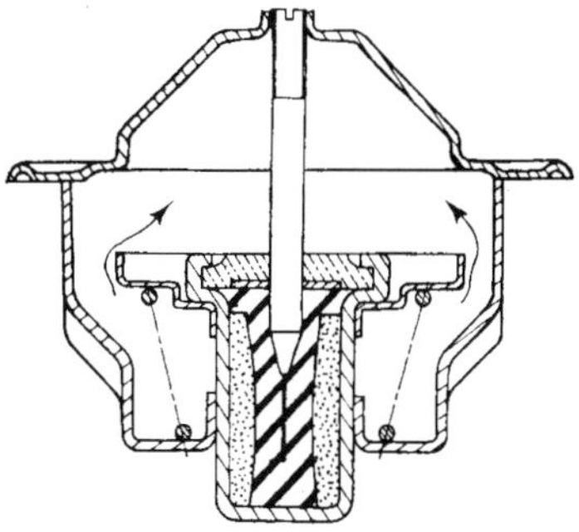

Hot – valve open

E

Referring to the diagrams and information above describe the operation of a wax-element thermostat. Include the main reason for using wax-element type thermostats in modern cooling systems.

Q

What would be the typical symptom if a thermostat were to fail? How would you diagnose this problem?

## Electric fan

**Q** What effect does the use of an electric fan have on energy savings and economy?

**E** Label the components and describe how this type of fan is constructed and how it operates. Include an explanation of how an engine management system controls the fan.

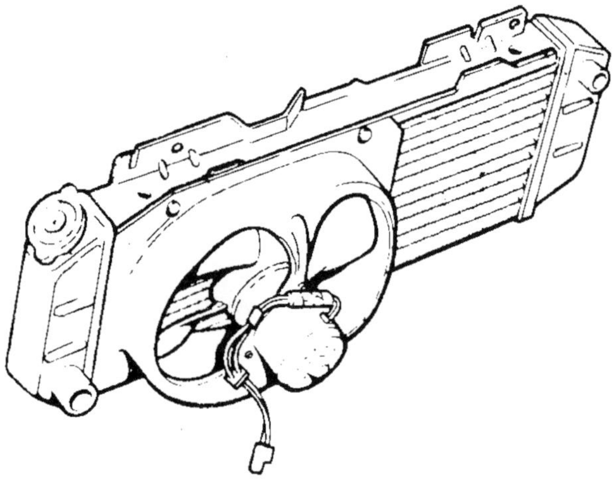

## Viscous fan

**E** Complete the following description of how a viscous fan is constructed and how it operates.

This type of drive has a __________ clutch plate that is placed in a container of __________ fluid. The viscous drag of the fluid, caused by its __________ to shear, provides a non-positive drive that is designed to slip at an __________ rate as the engine speed rises. A __________ disc is sandwiched between the two halves of the casing, which is fitted with __________ seals to prevent leakage of the silicone fluid.

resistance | silicone | increasing | disc-shaped | fluid | clutch

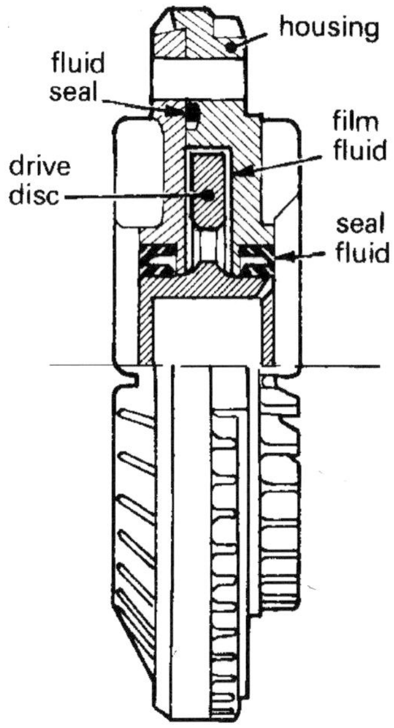


E

Research and discover two ways in which viscous drives are made. Describe their operation using sketches to help you.

Q

Which material is normally used for the disc and casing of a viscous drive and what are the material's advantages?

Q

What is the purpose of the fins on the outside of the casing?

## Pressurised cooling systems

**discussion point**

Referring to the graph below, discuss with a partner the advantages of pressurising a cooling system. When you have come to a conclusion, write down your ideas so that you can present them to the rest of the group. You may need to do some research to find all the advantages.

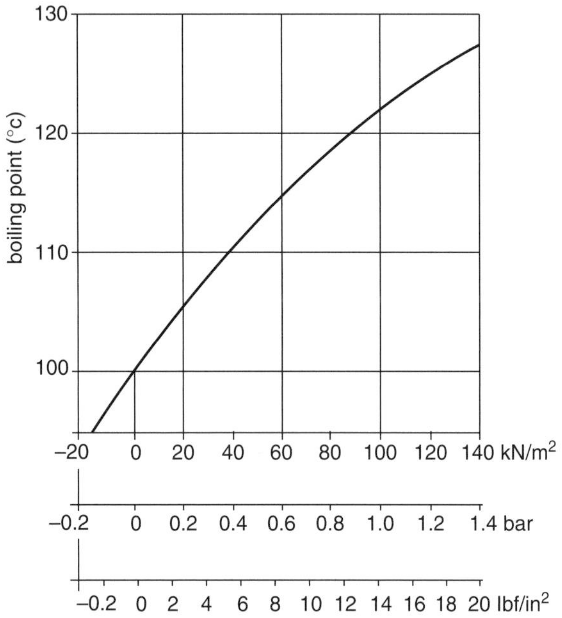


There is obviously a limit to the pressure that a radiator and rubber hoses can withstand, and a pressure relief valve incorporated within the pressure cap is needed.

E Label the components of the pressure cap.

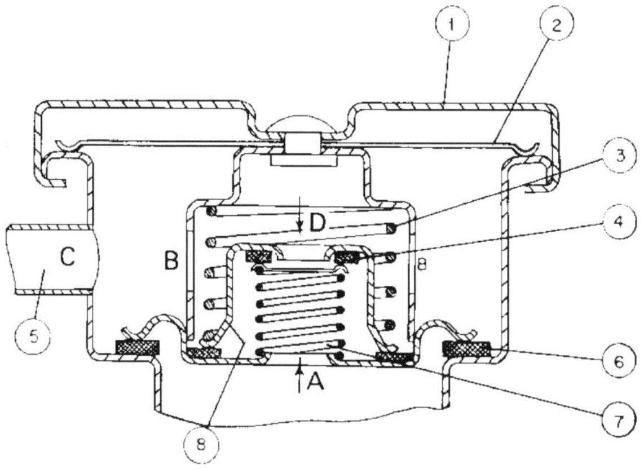

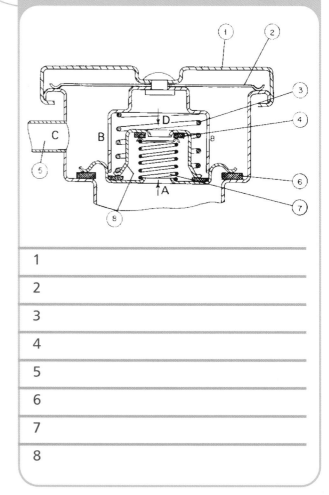

1

2

3

4

5

6

7

8

*Safety Note:* **Never remove the cap when the coolant temperature is above 100°C, since the release of pressure will cause the water to boil violently and the resulting jet of steam and water from the open filler can cause serious scalds. Always allow the engine to cool before re-opening the cap.**

Q Which part of the pressure cap controls the relief pressure?

Q What is a typical cooling system operating pressure?

Q What is the purpose of part number 4 in the diagram of the pressure cap?

## Sealed cooling systems

E Research and compare the differences between sealed and semi-sealed cooling systems. Sketch the layout and components of a sealed system and using arrows show the flow directions.

Q What are three advantages of using a sealed system?

## Use of antifreeze mixtures

**discussion point** Discuss with a partner what damage can occur when coolant freezes. Write down your ideas, including any sketches, and be ready to present your ideas to other members of the group.

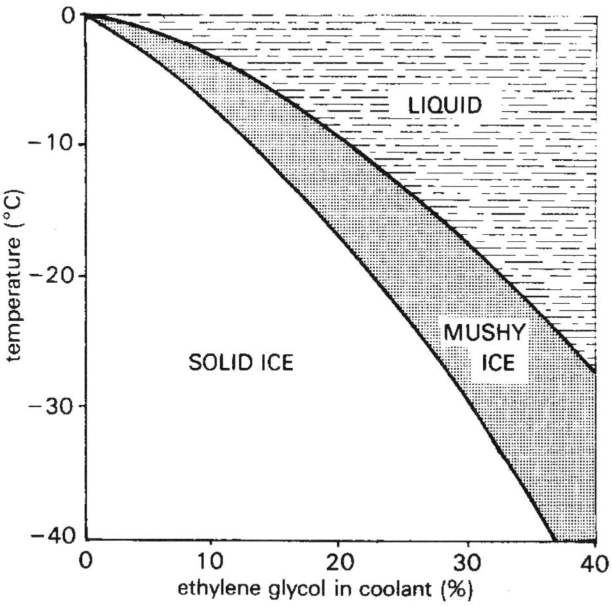


Q What is the function of core plugs?

The effect that ethylene glycol has in lowering the freezing point of the coolant is shown in the diagram here. This graph shows that the coolant passes through a 'mushy ice' stage before it reaches the solid state that causes structural damage.

*Safety Note:* ***Ethylene glycol is toxic and care should always be taken when handling such chemicals. Ensure that all antifreeze is disposed of after use in the correct manner.***

**Q** Why is it important to maintain the antifreeze strength all year round?

**Q** What is a typical proportion of antifreeze to water? What would you expect the temperature protection to be?

ENVIRONMENTAL NOTE

***Many manufacturers are now using different chemicals to make their antifreeze environmentally friendly. Some antifreeze solutions include propylene glycol because it is less toxic to humans and animals, while others are organic-based products, typically phosphate- and silicate-free.***

**Q** The use of ethylene glycol in coolant raises the coolant's boiling point. To what approximate temperature should a 25% solution raise the boiling point?

**Q** How would you check the antifreeze content in a cooling system?

## Heating and ventilation systems

For a long period in the history of vehicles it was not thought necessary to provide the occupants with any form of heating. Ventilation was abundant because there was no real bodywork around the passenger area. With the introduction of enclosed passenger compartments, vehicle manufacturers started to consider their customers' demands for basic creature comforts and associated safety aspects of demisted screens and warmth sufficient to allow the driver to concentrate on driving.

Q Look at this basic heating and ventilation system. What are the main places to which airflow is ducted?

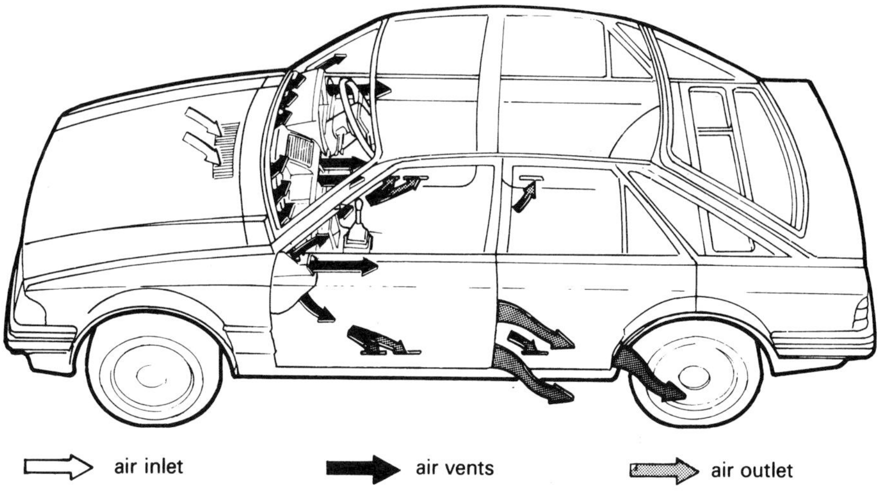


You can see from the diagram that unless air can pass through the passenger compartment and flow out again, the air inside the passenger compartment cannot change and would not be fresh.

Q Why is the air intake placed at the front of the vehicle?

### Airflow control

E In the diagram below, draw the direction of flow through the system and, using an arrow, indicate which is the heater box assembly.

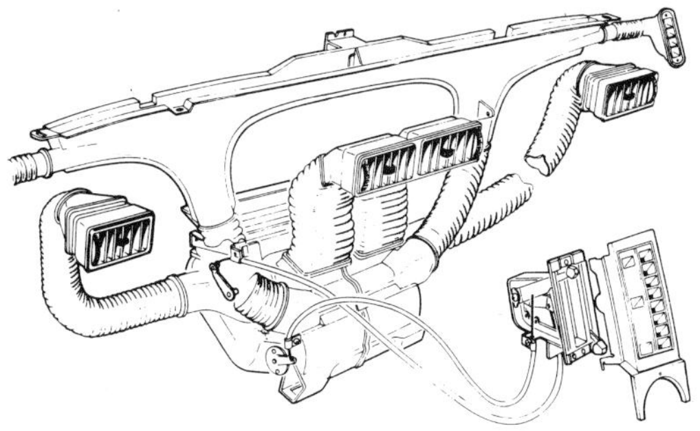

Q In the diagram above, how is airflow controlled and discharged at the various points?

### Temperature control

**Q** Which two areas of a vehicle can manufacturers use as a source of spare heat?

**E** **To give the driver and passengers control over their comfort, both temperature and airflow must be controlled. Complete the description of how this is done by using the missing words below.**

A coolant control __________ varies the flow of coolant to the __________

The preferred system is a __________ flow matrix where heat is mixed with the airflow via __________. If the flap directs all the __________ through the matrix the outflow of air will be hot; if the flap allows all the air to __________ the matrix the outlet air will be __________. The flap can vary the flow over the matrix or bypass it according to __________ requirements and consequently temperature control will be through a mix of __________ and cold air.

hot | temperature | valve | constant | bypass | flaps | cold | matrix | airflow

The diagram below shows the control flap above the heater matrix, which controls the intake temperature. It also shows a second flap assembly for windscreen demist and footwell control.

**E** **With an arrow, show where the fan assembly is located and draw the flaps in a position such that hot air would be directed to the windscreen only. To which engine components are the heater matrix pipes connected?**

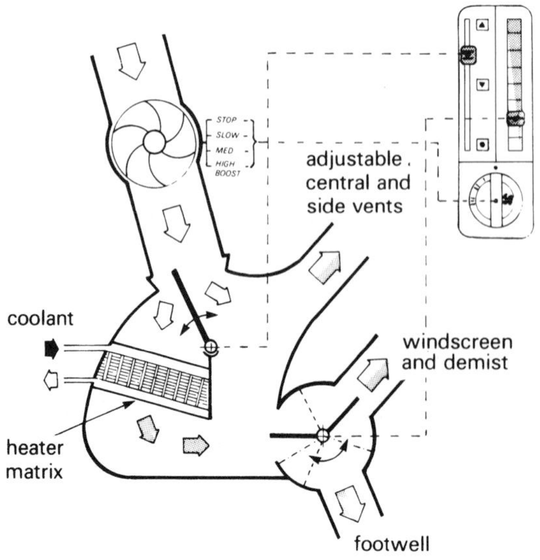

**discussion point**

Discuss the following scenario with a partner. A vehicle is brought to you with signs of water in the passenger footwell. You notice that the inside of the windscreen has a lot of condensation and there is a chemical smell inside the car. You have also found that the coolant reservoir is empty. Present your diagnosis of the fault to the group.

**Q** How is the speed of the fan or blower controlled?

**Q** To avoid outside air pollution and to work in conjunction with air conditioning, which additional feature do vehicle manufacturers include in their systems?

## Air conditioning

Air conditioning is now a standard fitment on many cars and an optional extra on others. For customers to want it, air conditioning must offer tangible features.

**discussion point**

Imagine you are going to buy a new car and you are offered air conditioning as an option. Write down three main benefits you could you expect from air conditioning. Discuss your ideas with the rest of your group.

**mini projects**

Agree the following with your tutor:

- the format and quantity of content
- the time frame for completion.

Research and report on the features, benefits and operating principles of a climate control system. Produce a diagram to show the layout of the main components.

## Practical activities

For these practical activities you will require the permission, guidance and supervision of your instructor. Document all aspects of health and safety that you will be observing in relation to all risks and hazards associated with the following tasks.

**practical activity 1**

Select a current vehicle. Complete the task below.

| Task | Brief description of task including any safety requirements | Sources of information and data |
|---|---|---|
| Test the current draw of an electric cooling fan. Test the fan switch to confirm it switches at the correct temperature. Record all your results. | | |

**practical activity 2**

Select a current vehicle. Complete the task below.

| Task | Brief description of task including any safety requirements | Sources of information and data |
|---|---|---|
| Pressure test the cooling system, including the pressure cap. Test the antifreeze content. Compile a report to inform the customer of the condition of the system. | | |

# CHAPTER 6

# VEHICLE ELECTRICAL SYSTEMS

### *Essential knowledge*

You will need to read and research vehicle technology covering the following:

- Basic principles of electricity
- Electrical circuits
- The battery
- Charging systems
- The starter system
- The lighting system
- Auxiliary lighting and equipment
- Routine maintenance of electrical systems

Note: some of this chapter refers to basic principles to ensure a full understanding.

From the very earliest examples to the most modern motor vehicles electrical power has always been needed to operate ancillary components. The designers of modern vehicles have included almost everything that anyone could want. For example, there are: entertainment systems, security systems, powered and heated seats with memories, climate control and numerous other features. Put together, these systems require substantial electrical power to operate them, so a much greater demand is placed on a vehicle's charging system.

**Main electrical circuits**

E

**All of the electrical circuits in a motor vehicle are connected to the battery. There are usually six main circuits. Match the circuits to the descriptions.**

| Circuit | Function |
|---|---|
| ___________ | Supplies the electrical energy for charging and maintaining the battery when the engine is running |
| ___________ | Provides a high voltage to the spark plug to ignite the air/fuel mixture in the engine cylinders (it might be integrated into the engine management system) |
| ___________ | Provides the necessary exterior/interior illumination and warning systems |
| ___________ | Enables the engine to be cranked over (rotated) at a speed sufficient for it to start, and keep running |
| ___________ | Includes various accessories, such as windscreen wipers and washers, horn, in-car entertainment, etc. Additional functions include computer-controlled systems such as ABS, climate control, electronically controlled transmission, etc. |
| ___________ | Controls the ignition and fuel systems, and the emission systems |
| ___________ | Provides the correct volume of fuel necessary to enable the engine to operate with the correct air/fuel mixture (it may be integrated into the engine management system) |

Charging | Starting | Ignition** | Fuel injection** | Engine management* | Lighting | Auxiliary

* later vehicles    ** earlier vehicles

# Basic principles of electricity

## Electricity – a fundamental part of the motor vehicle

Vehicle technicians need to understand thoroughly the electrical aspects of motor vehicles. A basic knowledge of electricity is essential before any fault finding is carried out on an electrical circuit using electrical test equipment, such as a multimeter or oscilloscope.

**discussion point**

Test your knowledge and discuss the following with a partner. What is electricity? Write down your ideas, including any sketches that you think might help when you discuss electricity with the rest of the group. Have a go at answering the questions below.

**Q** What are the three structural elements of an atom?

**Q** Which of the structural elements of an atom are:

a) negatively charged

b) positively charged?

**Q** What are electrons?

## Comparison of an electrical circuit to a water circuit

In many ways an electrical circuit behaves in a similar way to a water circuit. Electric cables are can be thought of as pipes and many electrical terms, expressions and components can be related to fluid flow. The difficulty in understanding electricity is that electricity cannot be seen passing through wires, whereas opening a water tap readily indicates the flow of the liquid.

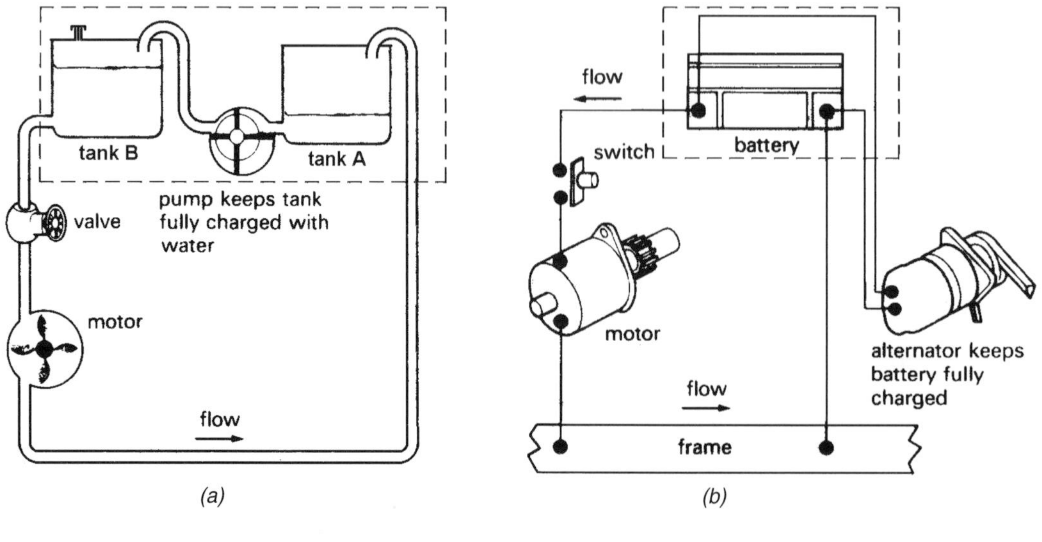

**discussion point**

Test your knowledge by working with a partner to explain how an electrical circuit works in comparison with a water circuit. Refer to the diagrams on the previous page and draft out your answer first. Write down your conclusions, including any sketches that you think might help when you present your ideas to the rest of the group.

**Q** For current to flow there has to be a pressure difference between the two battery terminals. In this case it would be 12 volts. What would the voltage be at the negative (–) terminal if the voltage at the positive (+) terminal was 12 V?

**Q** Which term can be used to describe the pressure difference between two points in an electrical circuit?

**Q** What is meant by the term polarity?

## Electromotive force (EMF)

**E** Complete the following statement about the principles of electromotive force by using the missing words below.

The __________ difference between the positive and __________ terminals exerts a __________ (in the same way as a pressure difference in a water circuit). This force is referred to as __________ force (emf), and is the force that drives the __________ current from one battery __________ to the other.

negative, force, electrical, pressure, terminal, electromotive

## Pressure/voltage measurements

**Q** What does a voltmeter measure and how would it be connected into a circuit?

### Electrical pressure measurement

Electrical potential is often referred to as voltage, which can be measured using a voltmeter. When voltage is measured, the voltmeter is in fact comparing the electrical 'pressure' difference between two points in the circuit. If one test probe of a voltmeter is connected to the positive terminal of a battery and the second test probe is connected to the negative terminal of the battery, the voltmeter would indicate 12 volts as the potential difference.

**Q** Multimeters are now usually digital. Name the other type of meter that can be used for electrical testing and state an advantage of its use.

## Electrical flow

### Electrical flow measurement

**Q** In an electrical circuit, when the switch is 'on', electricity flows in the circuit. There are two terms associated with this: conventional flow and electron flow. What is meant by each of these terms?

**Q** What is the term given to the rate of electrical flow through a circuit?

The amount of electricity flowing in a circuit depends on the voltage ('pressure') applied to the circuit, i.e. the pressure or potential difference between the positive and negative terminals. Additionally, the amount of electricity flowing will depend on any restrictions (called resistances) in the circuit.

**Q** How must an ammeter be connected into a circuit?

**Q** Which piece of equipment do you use to measure amperes or amps?

**Q** A multimeter is capable of testing only up to 10 A. What precautions would you take to ensure you will not damage the meter?

## Measuring resistance to flow

**Q** What must you ensure before connecting an ohmmeter into a circuit?

**discussion point** Discuss with a member of your group what might affect the flow of electricity in an electrical circuit. Put together your ideas and see how they compare with other members of your group.

**Q** What does the symbol 'Ω' mean?

**Q** If the number of ohms is greater, will the resistance be lower or higher?

Q In some circuits, resistances are deliberately included to control or restrict electrical flow. Give an example of a resistor that can be used to regulate the flow of electricity. How does it function?

E Research and find a colour coding chart for resistors. List the information below. Try to gain an understanding of this coding and keep the chart for future reference.

E Complete the following table defining volts, amps and ohms and their effect within an electrical circuit.

| Description | Effect |
|---|---|
| Volts | |
| Amps | |
| Ohms | |

**Note:** Bulbs, and any other electrical components, are usually designed to operate at a particular voltage, so they should be used only in a circuit that operates at this voltage. For example, if a 12 V bulb were fitted to a 24 V circuit, the current that the bulb would draw from the circuit would be twice as much as its design capacity, so the bulb filament would 'blow' (melt).

## Ohm's law – relationships between volts, ohms, amps

**Q** One volt is required to force a current of one ampere through a resistance of how many ohms?

**Q** Ohm's law is a formula used to calculate three electrical terms within an electrical circuit. Which three electrical terms are used in Ohm's law?

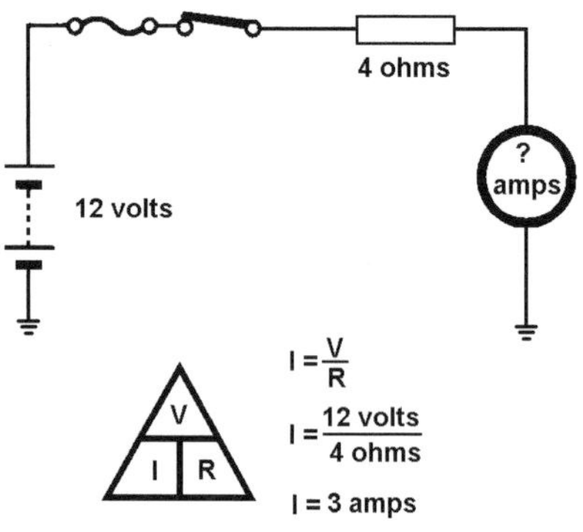


Assuming constant temperature and pressure, Ohm's law can be expressed by the following equation:

$$\text{Voltage} = \text{current} \times \text{resistance} \quad \text{or} \quad V = I \times R$$

$V$ = voltage (V)
$I$ = current in amperes (A)
$R$ = resistance in ohms ($\Omega$)

If two of the values are known, the third value can be calculated. The following exercises show how the third value can be calculated by using Ohm's law if two values are known. A useful aid is the Ohm's law triangle, which can be seen in the diagram on the left.

**E** Study the circuit diagram and by using Ohm's law, calculate the voltage (third value). Remember, two of the three electrical values are already shown in the diagram. Show your calculations in the answer box and fill in the triangle.

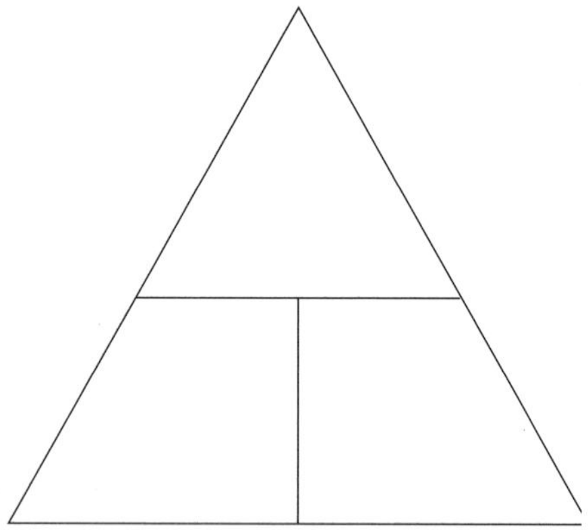

**Q** What is the unit of electrical power?

**E** In the same circuit as the previous exercise, the voltage applied to the circuit is 12 V and the current flowing is 3 A. Using Ohm's law, calculate the resistance of the circuit.

**E** In the same circuit again, the voltage applied to the circuit is 12 V and the resistance in the circuit is 4 $\Omega$. Using Ohm's law, calculate the current flow (*I* in amps) in the circuit.

Q A 12 V battery supplies a bulb with a resistance of 4 Ω. What is the current flow in the circuit?

Q A circuit has a current flow of 5 A and a potential difference of 12 V. What is the resistance of the bulb?

Q A bulb has a resistance of 6 Ω and a 4 A current flows in the circuit. What is the supply voltage?

## Calculating power (watts)

Q What is the definition of power?

Power can be calculated from the following expression, which is an extension of the basic Ohm's law formula:

Power (in watts) = voltage × current = volts × amperes

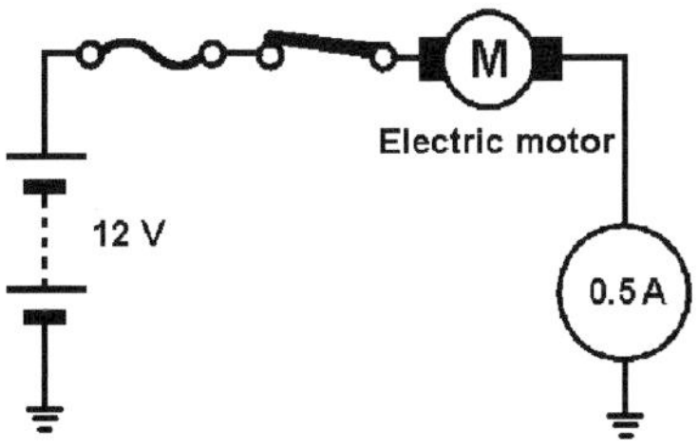


E The diagram (left) shows the voltage and current in a circuit. Calculate the motor's power.

## The effects of electrical energy

Q Which three effects can be produced by electricity passing through a conductor? Research and discover what they are and describe each briefly.

E

From the list below, place a tick in the correct column, to show which components are designed to work with the effects you discovered in the previous task. Insert the effects at the top of the table.

| Component | | | |
|---|---|---|---|
| Solenoid/relay | | | |
| LED | | | |
| Screen demister | | | |
| Injectors | | | |
| Ignition coil | | | |
| Light bulb | | | |
| Glow plug | | | |
| Alternator | | | |
| Neon tube | | | |
| Starter motor | | | |
| Cigarette lighter | | | |

**discussion point**

Through discussion with a member of your group and by research discover what things affect the strength of a magnetic field. Write down your findings and be prepared to present them to the rest of the group.

E

Through research find out and list several examples of vehicle components that use magnetism in their operation. Choose one of them and fully explain how it works, using diagrams to help you.

## Conductors and insulators

### Conductors

Q

What is a conductor?

Q

Which is the most common conductor used in motor vehicles and why?

**Q** Which other materials are used for conducting electricity in motor vehicles?

**Q** What effect does temperature increase have on the resistance of a conductor?

**E** Complete the description of how cables affect resistance and how temperature affects a conductor by using the missing words below.

The type of __________ used to connect electrical components together will affect the __________ within a circuit. The __________ area of the cable will affect the circuit resistance, as will the __________ of cable. In general terms, a __________ cable has a higher resistance than a __________ cable, just as a __________ pipe has a greater resistance to water flow than a __________ pipe.

The resistance of the wire also changes as the __________ of the wire changes. A change in temperature of the conductors that make up an electrical circuit affects the resistance in that circuit.

length | large | cross-sectional | small | thin | temperature | cable | resistance | thicker

## Insulators

**Q** What types of insulation material usually cover cables?

**Q** Which other materials can be used to insulate electrical current flowing within a circuit?

**E** Using the missing words from the list below, complete the statement describing an insulator and its function.

An insulator is a material that __________ or opposes the flow of __________. An insulator therefore has an extremely high __________ to the flow of electricity. If the __________ around a piece of wire comes in contact with another piece of bare __________, the insulator prevents the __________ energy from passing across to the other piece of wire.

electrical | insulator | wire | resistance | resists | electricity

**Q** When the insulation on a piece of wire fails, it can result in electricity flowing to a piece of metal which might provide a shorter path or circuit back to the battery's negative terminal. What is this condition called?

## Semiconductors

**Q** What is a semiconductor and how does it function?

**Q** When the materials used in semiconductors are in their pure state they will not conduct current. However, when they are mixed with very small amounts of impurities, their atomic structure changes and they allow current to pass through them. Name the two most widely used semiconductor materials.

**Q** A temperature sensor is an example of a semiconductor. How does a temperature sensor work and what is the name given to this type of sensor?

**E** Research and discover other uses of semiconductors in vehicle circuits. Explain briefly their function within the circuits.

## Electrical circuits

### Electrical circuits

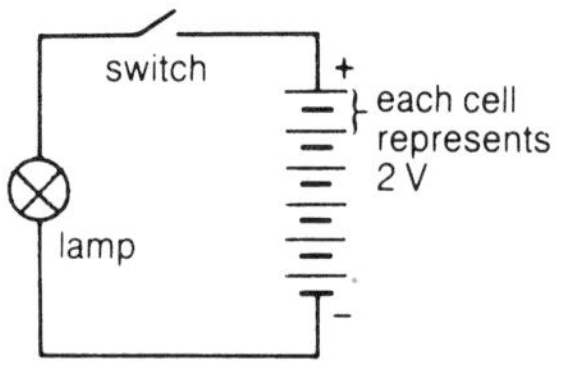


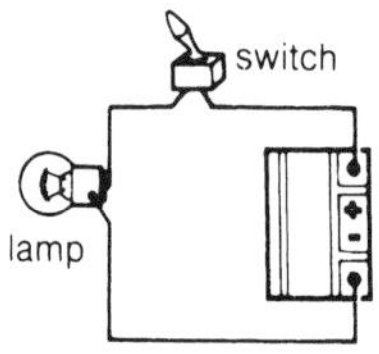


An electric current will not flow unless a complete circuit exists, as shown in the diagram on the left. The circuit is formed by connecting a lamp and switch to a battery. The diagram on the far left shows the same circuit, but it is illustrated with commonly used electrical symbols.

### Earth return

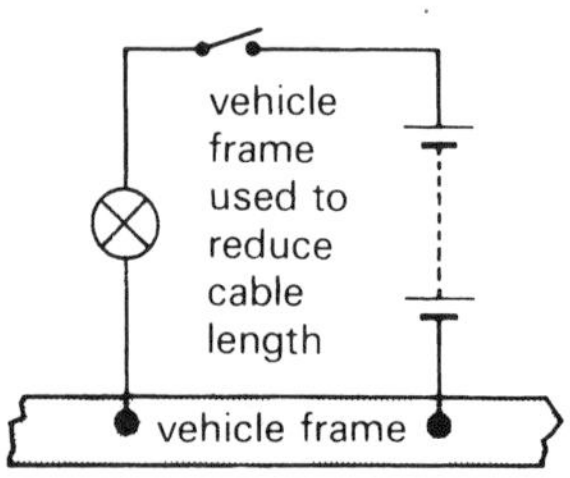


Nearly all vehicles use the metal body and frame of the vehicle as a part of the electrical circuit. By substituting the return cable with the body or frame of the vehicle, an 'earth return' system is formed, as shown in the diagram on the left.

**Q** When a lamp is connected to a battery by two cables, one cable is called the 'supply'. What is the other cable called?

**discussion point**

Discuss with a partner the advantages and disadvantages of using a vehicle chassis as an earth return. You may have to do some research to help you with your answer. Write down your thoughts and be ready to present your ideas to other members of your group.

### Types of circuit

**Q** Although simple electrical circuits might have only one resistance connected, many circuits have several. Multiple resistances can be connected in a circuit in different ways. What are the two main types of circuit known as?

## Series circuits

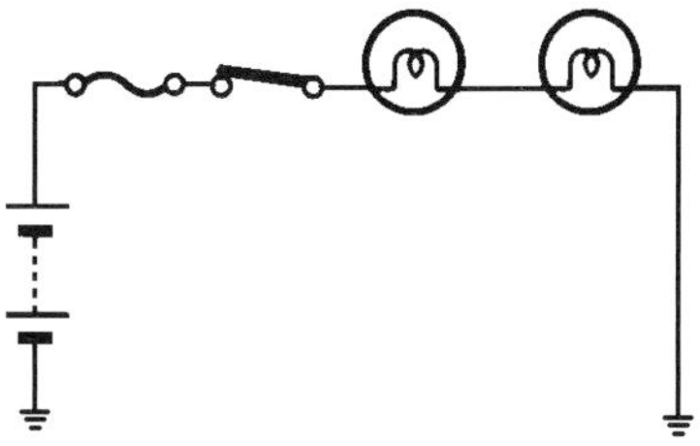

**Q** What is meant by a lighting circuit being in 'series'?

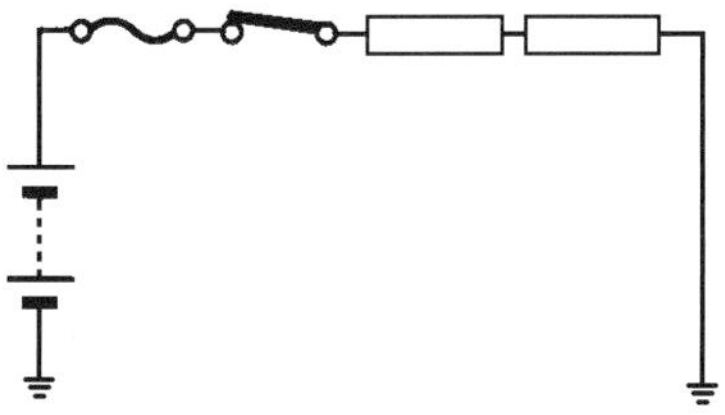

**Q** In the diagram, the circuit is fitted with two bulbs. What is the disadvantage with using this type of circuit?

## Parallel circuits

**E** Sketch a parallel circuit that includes a battery, a switch, two bulbs and two resistors.

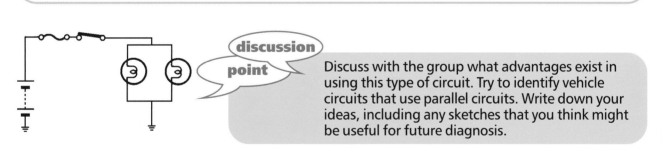

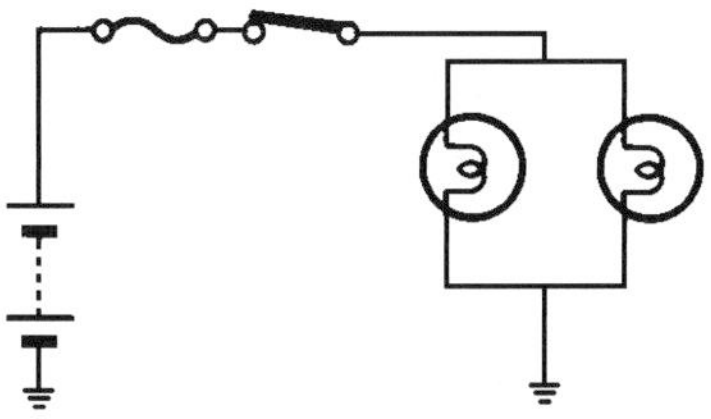

**discussion point**

Discuss with the group what advantages exist in using this type of circuit. Try to identify vehicle circuits that use parallel circuits. Write down your ideas, including any sketches that you think might be useful for future diagnosis.

**Q** Which electrical switch found on a motor vehicle operates by sensing temperature?

Three different types of switches generally used in electrical circuits are push-on/off, lever operated and the rotary type.

**E** Match the type of switch to the place where you would be most likely to find it in a motor vehicle.

| | |
|---|---|
| Push on/off | indicators |
| Lever-operated | ignition switch |
| Rotary | heated rear window |

## Voltage drop

E Complete the description of what is meant by voltage drop by using the words below.

When __________ flows in a circuit, a resistance causes the __________ (potential difference) to __________ as the current passes through the resistance.

So the voltage available at each side of a __________ will be different; the difference in the voltage is referred to as the 'voltage __________'.

current voltage fall resistance drop

Q Electrical connections can be tested for voltage drop. What reading would you expect on the voltmeter if the connection is good? What is an acceptable value for voltage drop?

## Open and short circuits

Q What are the two most common faults that can occur in a circuit?

### Open circuit

Q What does 'open circuit' mean?

Q Which electrical fault provides an open circuit?

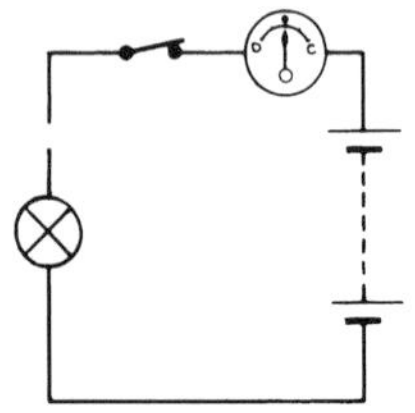

E Study the diagram on the left and describe the fault that is creating an open circuit. State the ammeter reading as a result of this fault.

### Short circuit

discussion point

Discuss with a partner what it means if a short circuit occurs. Write down your ideas, including any sketches that you think might help when you present your ideas to the rest of the group.

## Fuses and other circuit protectors

E

Mark which of the three fuse types (shown in the diagram) is most commonly used nowadays and explain how the different fuse ratings are identified.

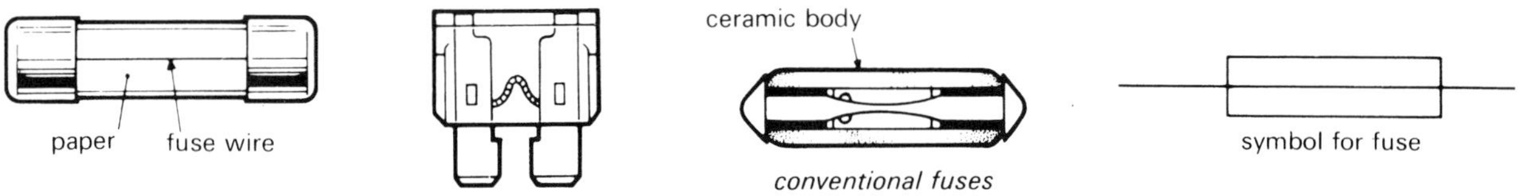


*conventional fuses*

Q

Where are the fuses normally located in a vehicle's electrical system?

E

Complete the following table by explaining how each of these components works to break an electrical circuit.

Fusible link

Circuit breaker

Switch

Q

What is the function of a fuse?

## Relays

**Q** What is the purpose of a relay?

The diagram shows a relay used to switch a headlight circuit which would carry a high current demand and load.

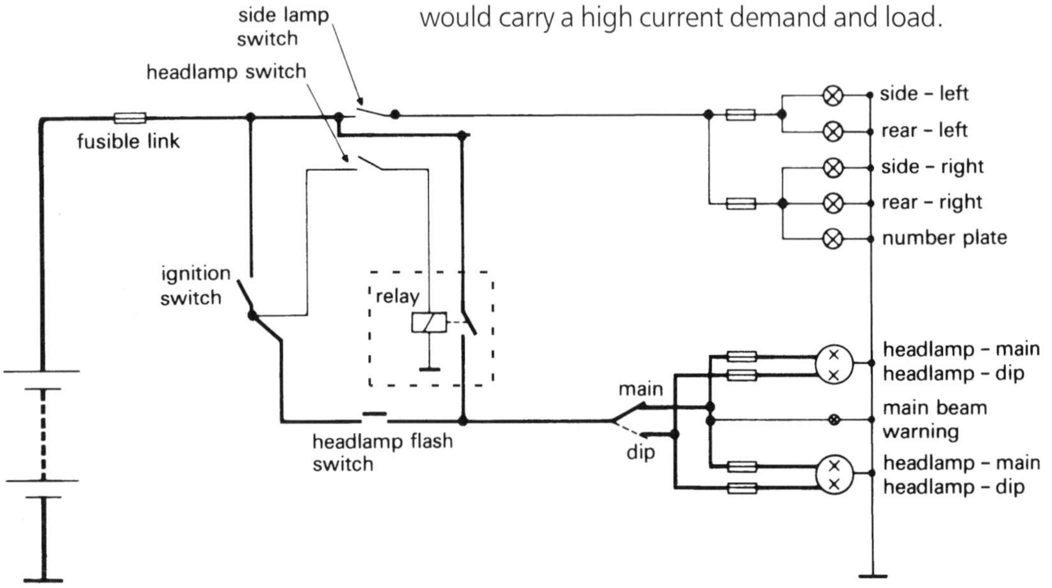


**discussion point** Working with a partner, research how a relay works. Discuss this between you and write down your ideas, including any sketches that you think might help when you present your ideas to the rest of the group.

**E** With reference to the diagram above, sketch a basic circuit diagram showing how the relay functions when the headlight switch is operated by the driver. Include the battery, relay, switch, fuse and bulb in your diagram.

**Q** What safety issue arises when a large current is passed through long lengths of wire?

## Cables

What is the term given to a group of cables taped together along a common route through a vehicle?

What could be the effect of fitting cable of too small a diameter to a circuit such as the starter circuit?

Describe the construction and materials used for the cables that connect the various vehicle electrical systems.

Various sizes of cable are used throughout a vehicle, depending on the current flow through a component. Identify the components that require a large diameter cable to function efficiently and those that require only a small diameter cable.

| Component | Large diameter cable (high current) | Small diameter cable (low current) |
| --- | --- | --- |
| Starter motor | | |
| Windscreen washer | | |
| Sidelight | | |
| Radio | | |
| Engine sensors/actuator | | |
| Alternator | | |
| Ignition switch wire | | |

### Cable colour coding and ratings

Research information about cable colour coding and rating. Compile a useful chart that you could use for future reference.

## Connectors

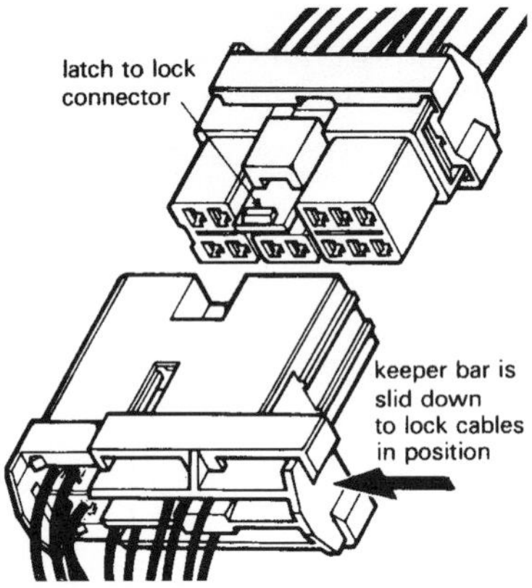


Most modern vehicles now use some form of plug-and-socket electrical connector to join a number of cables, as shown in the diagram on the left.

**Q** Why do some vehicle manufacturers use gold-plated terminal connections?

**E** Research and make sketches of the following types of connectors: Lucas, bullet, eyelet and fork. Also identify and sketch multi-connector types.

## Wiring diagrams

Wiring diagrams might show complete or partial vehicle circuits. For example, an old vehicle manual might have had only one or two pages to cover the whole of the electrical circuitry. Now, there are numerous pages of diagrams for each of the separate electrical circuits.

### Electrical symbols

A standard format to identify the components and the symbols is used in most vehicle manufacturers' circuit diagrams. What is the recommended standard for electrical symbols in wiring diagrams in the United Kingdom?

Look at the table below. Sketch the relevant symbols against the descriptions.

| | | |
|---|---|---|
| Direct current | Alternating current | Positive polarity |
| Current receding | Current approaching | Negative polarity |
| Earth – general | Earth – chassis frame | Battery, 12 V (Long line is positive) |
| Conductors crossing | Conductor – temporary | Conductor – permanent (Thickness denotes importance) |
| Junction – separable | Conductors joining | Without connecting |
| Variability: applied to other symbols | Plug and socket | Junction – inseparable |
| General winding (inductor, coil) | Resistor – variable | Resistor – fixed value |
| Diode, rectifying junction | Transformer | Winding with core |

E Look at the table below. Sketch the relevant symbols against the descriptions.

| | | |
|---|---|---|
| Diode | Zener/avalanche diode | Light emitting diode |
| Transistor – NPN | Transistor – PNP | Reverse blocking triode thyristor |
| Switch – 'make' contact, normally open | Fuse | Lamp |
| Switch – two-way | Switch – manually operated | Switch – 'break' contact, normally closed |
| Spark gap | Relay – thermal | Relay – single winding |
| Ammeter | Motor – DC | Generator – AC and DC |
| Capacitor – general symbol | Galvanometer | Voltmeter |
| Junction FET – N-type channel | Amplifier | Capacitor – polarised |
| Thyristor | Photodiode | Junction FET – P-type channel |

## The battery

### Introduction to the lead–acid battery

The purpose of a battery is to store the electrical energy needed to operate a vehicle's electrical systems. When the engine is not running or when the output from an alternator is low, the battery functions as the storage device. A battery stores energy by converting the electrical energy supplied to it by the generator (the alternator) into chemical energy. When an electrical current is required, the energy flow is then reversed, i.e. the chemical energy is converted back into electrical energy.

Whenever the battery supplies electrical energy to components, the energy consumed needs to be replaced. The electrical generator supplies further electrical energy, which the battery stores until required.

## Lead–acid battery ('wet-type' battery)

**Q** What are the three types of lead–acid batteries found on vehicles?

### Conventional lead–acid battery

**Q** Which materials are battery casings generally made from?

**Q** In a 12 volt battery, how many cells are there and how many volts does each cell generate?

**Q** What material is used for the cell plates and how are the plates arranged in the battery?

*Safety Note: It is essential that a battery is connected to a vehicle with the correct earth polarity. Extensive damage to electrical components will occur if the polarity is incorrect.*

**Q** How are the different battery connection terminals identified and why is it important to ensure that the terminals are clean and tight?

### Cell action

**Q** What happens to the specific gravity of the electrolyte when a battery is discharging?

**Q** How is the discharging action reversed and what is the resulting state of the electrolyte?

E

Research and discover what material battery plates are made from and explain what happens to the material as the battery charges and discharges. Explain what happens to the plates if the battery is left discharged for a period of time.

## Capacity

E

Using the missing words from the list below, complete the statement describing what is meant by reserve capacity.

Reserve __________ is an alternative method of expressing the capacity of a battery. This rating indicates the time in __________ for which a battery will deliver a __________ of 25 A at 25°C before the cell __________ drops to 1.75 V. A typical 40 Ah battery with a __________ capacity of 45 minutes should keep the vehicle operating for this length of time after the __________ system has failed, provided that the electrical __________ is normal.

reserve | minutes | voltage | charging | current | load | capacity

Q

A battery is rated at 38 A h, based on a 10 hour rate. Typically, what will be the current that it supplies?

## Maintenance of conventional batteries

discussion point

Discuss with a partner what important factors need to be determined before disconnecting a battery? Write down your ideas, and present your thoughts to the rest of the group.

*Safety Note: For safety reasons, the battery earth terminal should be disconnected before work is carried out on an engine or transmission, or any other components or vehicle systems that are likely to rotate or cause injury. The battery should also be disconnected before electric arc welding, since damage to electrical components can occur from the voltage induced by the welding equipment and welding process.*

## Electrolyte level

Q

At what level should the electrolyte be maintained in a battery?

Q

What possible fault would be indicated by a need for frequent topping up of the electrolyte?

## Terminal corrosion

Q

How would you neutralise battery terminal corrosion?

**Q** How would you deal with acid spillage on vehicle body parts?

## Use of jump leads

*Safety Note:* If a vehicle's battery is completely discharged, an engine can sometimes be started by using jump leads to connect temporarily another battery to the discharged battery. With jump leads, the two batteries are connected in parallel (positive to positive and negative to negative). After the engine has started and run for a few minutes, it must be allowed to run slowly before the jump leads are disconnected. When disconnecting the second battery make sure that the earth lead is removed first.

It is advisable to check the vehicle manufacturer's recommendations, since connecting and disconnecting jump leads has caused electronic component failure. 'Arcing' can occur when either of the jump leads is connected. In some cases this causes a small voltage surge or spike that can damage electronic components. Although most modern electronic components are protected against such problems, some vehicles may not have full protection.

## Battery hazards

*Safety Note:* A burn caused by battery acid should be treated immediately with sodium bicarbonate solution or, failing this, clean water. An eye that has had acid splashed into it should be bathed immediately in clean water and medical attention sought as soon as possible.

When batteries are refilled with acid, the acid supplied might need to be 'broken down' to weaken it before it is used. When diluting acid, add acid to water and not water to acid, and use a glass or earthenware container.

Acid splashes on clothes must be neutralised with an alkali, such as ammonia, to avoid holes. Gloves, goggles and an acid-proof apron should be worn when handling or pouring acid.

## Battery charging

**discussion point**

Discuss the following scenario with a partner. A customer has brought in a vehicle with a flat (discharged) battery. The customer tells you that the battery is only three days old and he needed a jump start to get the car to the garage.

- What questions would you ask the customer?
- What initial diagnostic checks would you carry out?
- Suggest the equipment you could use for diagnosis?
- What conclusions and outcomes would you expect to find from these symptoms?

Write down your questions, checks, list of equipment and conclusions, including any sketches that you think might help when you discuss your ideas with the rest of the group.

E

**Complete the following information on precautions that should be observed when charging a battery. Use the missing words below.**

- The battery __________ should be set at the correct level; add __________ water if the level is incorrect.
- Remove all __________ plugs from the battery. If the battery is being charged 'on the __________', disconnect the battery leads to prevent __________ to the vehicle's electronic components.
- Ensure that the battery __________ are clean before connecting the battery __________ leads; clean them if necessary.
- A quantity of explosive __________ gas is released from the cells when the battery is being charged. Always charge a battery in a __________ area. Ideally the vehicle workshop should have a specific area allocated for bench charging and provided with adequate ventilation.
- Never __________ the battery or you will damage it. Many battery chargers will regulate charging at the correct rate for the battery's condition. Refer to the battery charger instructions for the correct procedure. Ensure that the __________ of the electrolyte is below 45°C before and during charging; stop charging if the temperature is too high.
- There is a high risk of an __________ from the hydrogen when the terminals are being connected; take care to avoid a spark. Always switch off the battery charger main switch before __________ the charger leads from the battery.
- After the battery has been charged, it should be left to stand for a period of time before it is fitted to the vehicle, for hydrogen to disperse, since a vehicle __________ system (e.g. the central-locking door system) could cause the terminals to __________ as the battery is reconnected.

disconnecting | well ventilated | vehicle | damage | vent | over-charge | terminals

charger | electrical | hydrogen | electrolyte | spark | distilled | temperature | explosion

## Battery tests

### Hydrometer test

The specific gravity (or relative density) of an electrolyte is measured with a hydrometer; the readings indicate the state of charge.

**Note:** The value will change with changes in temperature.

E

**The numbers below are typical values expected when a battery is tested with a hydrometer. Write down alongside the numbers which of these is for a fully charged, half charged and fully discharged battery.**

1.150

1.280

1.200

### Electrical load test ('high-rate discharge' test or 'drop test')

E Although the car battery is described as being a 12 volt battery, this is not an accurate description. Find out what a typical fully charged battery voltage should be and record it below. Also, indicate what the maximum voltage will be when the battery could be described as discharged.

E State the typical values expected when an electrical load test is used to check a battery's state of charge. Sketch the piece of equipment used to carry out this test.

## Low-maintenance batteries

Traditionally, batteries would require periodical topping up of the cells with distilled water to replace losses caused by gassing. With improved materials and construction techniques, low-maintenance batteries have reduced the need to top up the cells.

Q How is the gassing process reduced in a low-maintenance battery?

## Maintenance-free batteries

A maintenance-free battery is sealed (except for a very small vent hole) and requires no service attention. It has a hydrometer which signals the battery condition by changing colour.

E Complete the table, matching the charge conditions and colour of the 'Magic Eye' hydrometer in a maintenance-free battery. The colours used are: green, green/black and light yellow.

| Condition of battery | Colour |
|---|---|
| Battery is charged and serviceable | |
| Recharging is required | |
| Internal fault is present (with this condition, do not recharge the battery or apply jump leads, since components might be damaged) | |

**Note:** If the battery is discharged to a point where it cannot crank the engine and the engine has to be started either by jump leads or by pushing the car, then it will be impossible for the vehicle's alternator to recharge the battery. When a battery is in this condition, it must be removed and bench charged. This is necessary because the voltage needed to recharge the battery is higher than that given by the charging system of the vehicle.

## Charging systems

Q What are the operating requirements of a charging system?

### Alternator operation and construction

E Referring to the diagram explain the basic operating principle of an alternator. You may need to discuss this with your tutor or carry out some research to find the information.

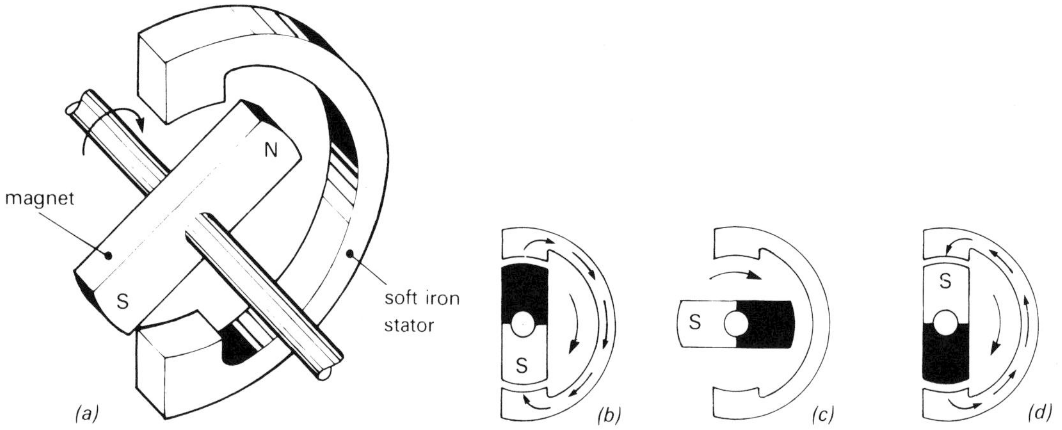


E Use the missing words from the list below to complete this information about alternators.

An alternator circuit has a ______________________ to signal to the driver when the system is not operating. When the ignition is ______________________, the small current needed to operate the warning lamp also passes through the ______________________ then through the regulator to earth.This current flow passing the rotor winding creates a ______________________ which is sufficient to enable the charging operation to begin, when the alternator ______________________.

Naturally this operation will not occur if there is an ______________________ because the bulb has 'blown'. When the alternator is operating, three ______________________ supply the field with a current as dictated by the regulator. As the engine speed ______________________, the output voltage at the field diodes also rises. The ______________________ reduces the current through the warning lamp circuit and causes the warning lamp to extinguish.

rises from stationary
switched on
increase in output voltage
rotor winding
weak magnetic field
charge-warning lamp
starts to rotate
field diodes
open circuit

Q

What component is an alternator equipped with to avoid damaging electronic components in the event of a high voltage surge?

## Construction of the alternator

E

Research and discover what is meant by the term 'regulated voltage'. Explain what this is and suggest a typical value for it. Describe the procedure and equipment used to test it.

E

The stator windings can be constructed in two ways. Produce sketches to show these forms and name them. Include one of them in a sketch of a rectifier circuit and briefly explain the rectifier's function.

E Label as many components as possible on the alternator in the diagram below.

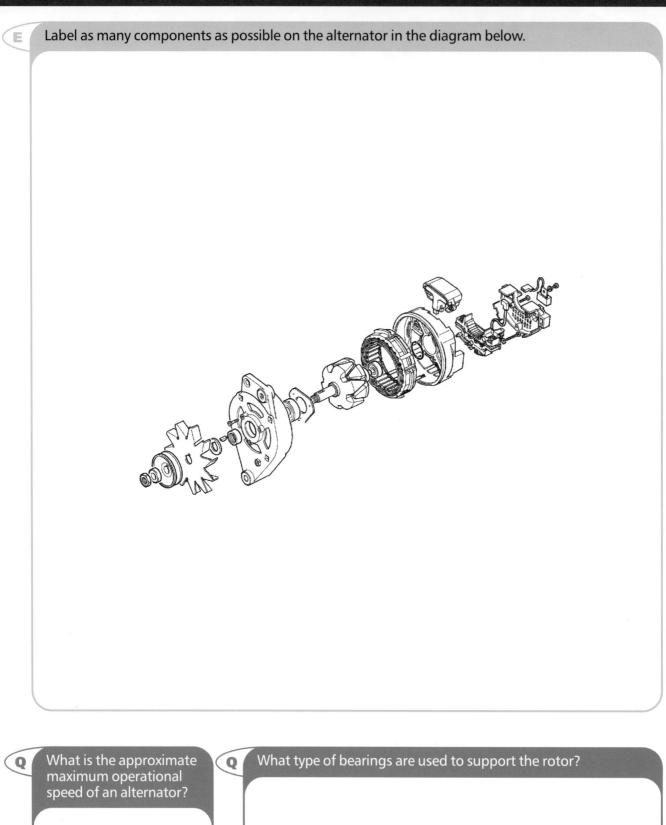

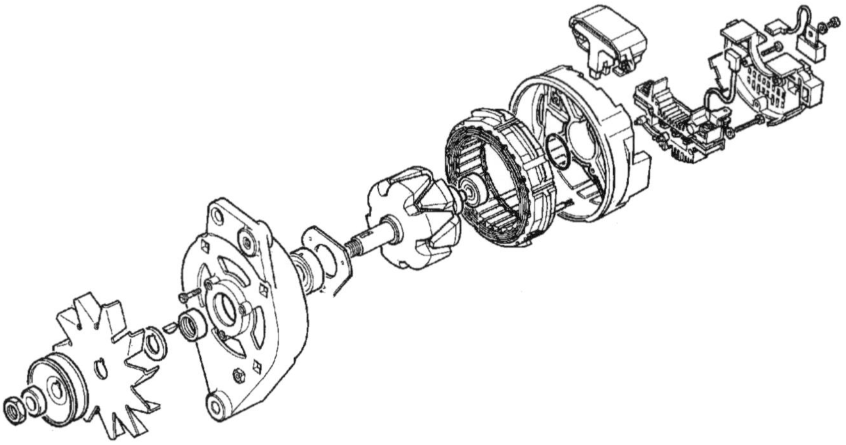

Q What is the approximate maximum operational speed of an alternator?

Q What type of bearings are used to support the rotor?

Q How is cool air circulated through an alternator?

# The starter system

## Introduction

**Q** At what speed does an engine need to be cranked (rotated) to enable the engine to be started?

**Q** A starter motor requires a considerable current to produce a high cranking torque. What would be an approximate current required to crank a light vehicle engine?

**Q** Sketch and label a starter motor circuit. Include the following components: battery, motor, solenoid, switch and chassis/frame.

## Operating principles of electric starter motors

**Q** Electrical energy supplied from the battery is converted by a starter motor into which other form of energy?

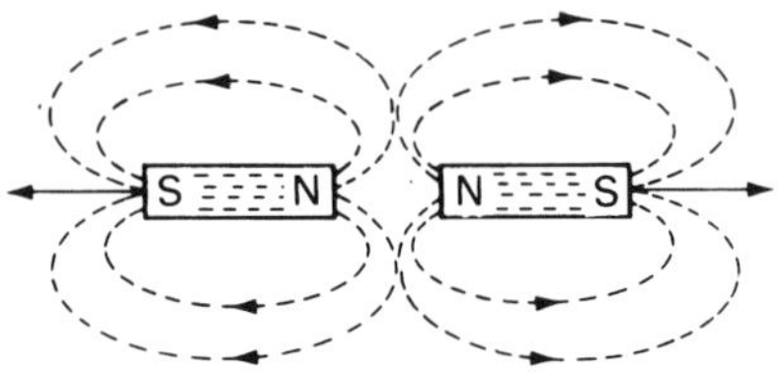


*like poles repel*

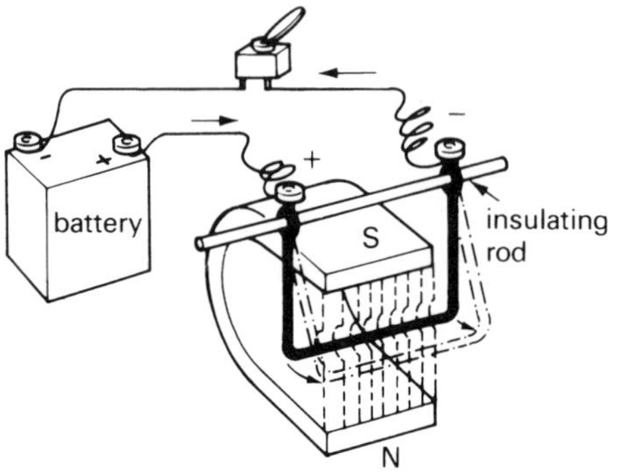


movement produced by magnetic action

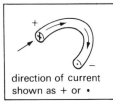

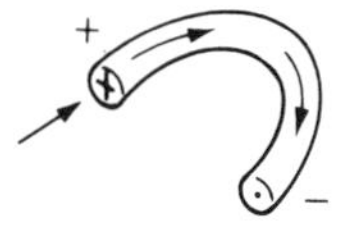


direction of current shown as + or •

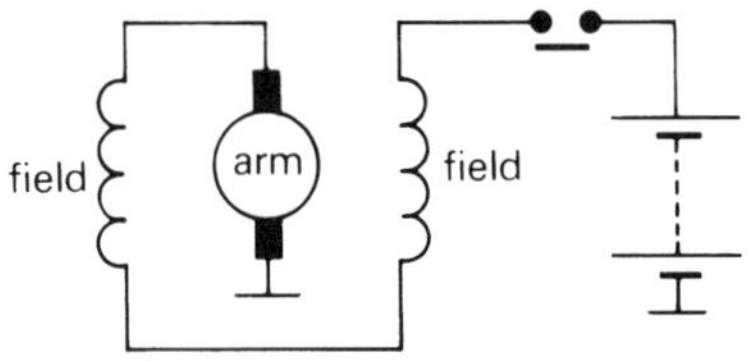


starter motor circuit

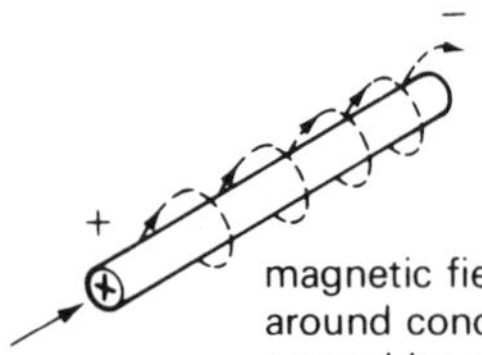


magnetic field around conductor caused by current flow

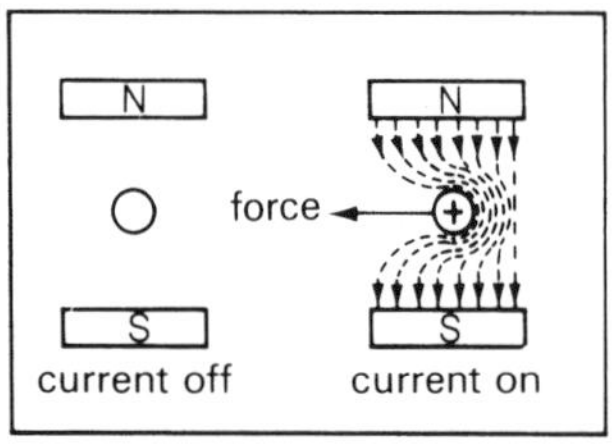


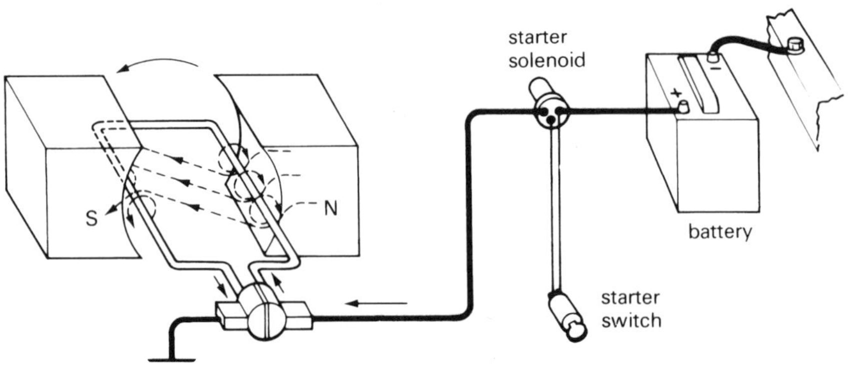

**discussion point**

Discuss the diagrams above with a partner. When you feel you fully understand these principles of starter motors, let your tutor know by giving them an explanation and completing the exercise on the next page.

Complete the following description of how starter motors work using the missing words below.

This is done by using an __________ principle similar to that used for the __________ of electrical energy. Although the principles used are the same as in the generator, they are __________: current is passed to the __________ which causes it to turn, whereas a generator is turned to create electric current. When the 'like' poles of two __________ are brought together, they __________ each other apart. Remember the expressions 'like poles repel' and 'unlike poles attract'. A motor uses the fact that like poles __________ to produce a force, which in turn produces __________.

magnets | repel | reversed | motor | generation | push | movement | electromagnetic

## Starter motor circuit and solenoid

What is the process that occurs in a starter motor electrical circuit when the starter/ignition switch is set to the 'start' position? Number the boxes to put the following statements in the correct sequence.

1 The small current is passed around a coil or winding within the solenoid, which creates a magnetic field, which then causes a metal plunger to move. ☐

2 When the starter/ignition switch is set to the 'start' position, a small current passes from the starter switch to the solenoid. ☐

3 The plunger is attached to the heavy-duty contacts, so that, when the plunger moves, it causes the contacts to close, thus connecting the battery supply to the starter motor. ☐

A solenoid is a type of relay. State its purpose in a starter circuit.

A solenoid is now an integral part of a starter motor assembly. It has a short power supply cable connecting it to the motor. Why is it best to keep this cable as short as possible?

What faults could be indicated by an audible clicking from the solenoid?

## Starter engagement with the engine

**discussion point**

Discuss the following with a partner. A low gear ratio between the starter motor and the engine enables sufficient torque to be developed to turn the crankshaft. How is this ratio obtained? Write down your explanation, including any sketches that you think might help when you discuss your ideas with the rest of the group.

**Q** What are two types of starter engagement used on light vehicles?

### Inertia engagement

Although the inertia starter motor is no longer commonly used in cars, you might still encounter one in your workplace.

**E** Briefly describe the inertia starter motor's operation, referring to the diagrams below.

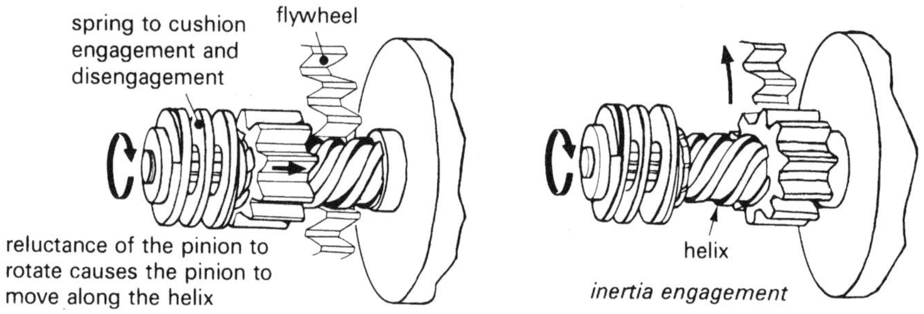


### Pre-engagement

**discussion point**

Discuss as a group the reasons for changing from using inertia drives to pre-engaged drives for starters. Record the reasons discussed.

## Operation of a pre-engaged starter motor

E Label the components on the pre-engaged starter motor in the diagram.

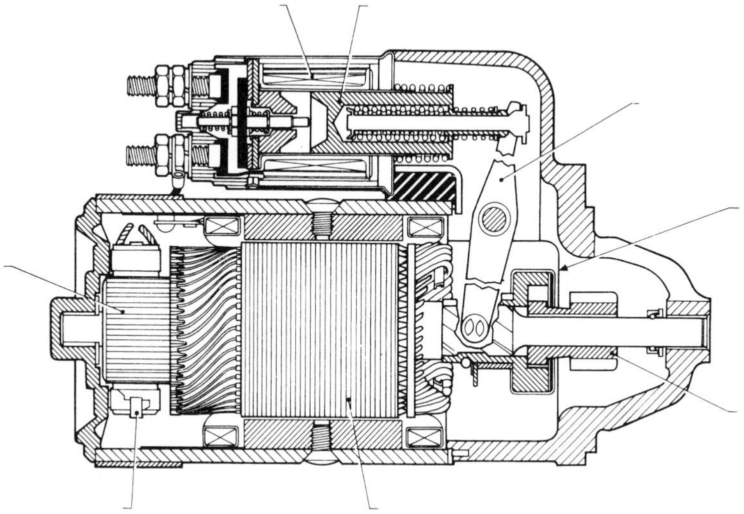

E Highlight the correct words to describe how the starter motor operates initially when the ignition switch is in the 'start' position.

When the **alternator / starter** switch is operated, the two-coil solenoid windings become energised and the plunger is **drawn / pushed** into the core. The **secondary / initial** movement of the solenoid causes the **lower / upper** end of the operating lever to move the guide ring and **pinion / flywheel** assembly towards the **flywheel / pinion** teeth. This movement, aided by the slight rotation of the pinion, normally provides full **disengagement / engagement** of the pinion and flywheel gears.

Q What happens after this initial action described above?

Q What is the function of the one-way clutch?

**Q** What happens to the pinion when the engine has started?

**E** Highlight the correct words to describe what happens when the ignition key is released from the 'start' position.

Release of the **starter / alternator** switch **energises / de-energises** the solenoid and allows the return spring to **close / open** the switch contacts. The **opening / closing** of the electrical contacts occurs **after / prior to** the disengagement of the pinion and so avoids over-speeding of the motor. Further movement of the solenoid plunger causes the operating lever to **engage / withdraw** the pinion fully from the flywheel.

### Reduction-type starter motor

**Q** By approximately how much do reduction gears reduce the speed of the pinion relative to the motor?

**discussion point** Working with a partner, research how the reduction-type starter motor is an improvement over the pre-engaged starter motor. Write down your ideas so that you can present them to the rest of the group.

## The lighting system

**E** Complete the following table describing the purpose of each of the different lights used on a typical modern passenger car. State the approximate wattage of each bulb.

| Lights | Wattage | Purpose |
|---|---|---|
| Side and rear lamps (marker lamps) | 5 W | |
| Headlamps | | |
| Rear fog lamp(s) | | |
| Auxiliary driving lamps | | |
| Reversing lamps | | |
| Brake lights | | |
| Directional indicators | | |
| Hazard warning lights | | |
| Instrument panel lights | | |

## Circuit arrangement

**Q** What is the advantage of connecting a lighting circuit in parallel?

**Q** How would the lamps be connected in a simple lighting circuit consisting of a battery, a single switch and several lamps?

**Q** How can the quantity of cable used in a lighting circuit be reduced?

**discussion point**

Working with a partner discuss the following scenario. If the earth connection points in a lighting circuit were in a poor condition, what would be the effect on the lamps? Write down your ideas, and discuss them with the rest of the group.

## Circuit diagrams

A compact schematic format is used by vehicle manufacturers to make wiring diagrams simpler to follow and understand.

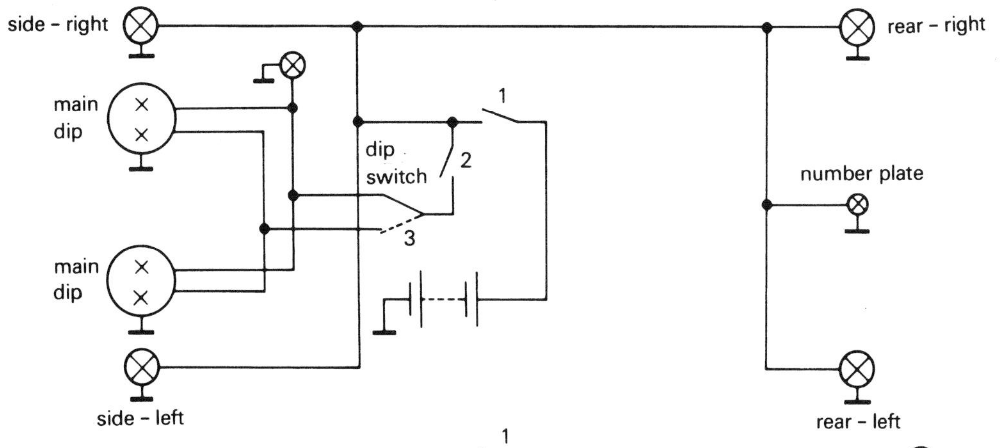


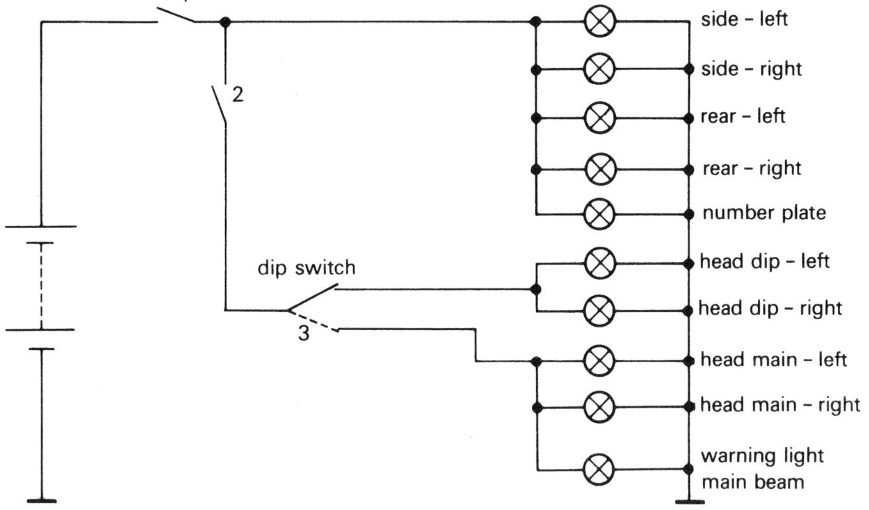

The diagram shows a simplified lighting circuit.

This parallel light circuit has lamps controlled by three switches, 1, 2 and 3

E

Number the switches 1, 2 and 3 in the table below to match the descriptions of how they function in a circuit.

| Switch number | Function |
|---|---|
| | Operates the side and rear lamps. It also supplies switch 2. |
| | Distributes the current to either the main beam or the dip-beam headlamp bulbs. |
| | Operates the headlamps and supplies switch 3. |

## Circuit protection

Q

Generally, a single fuse mounted in the main supply cable provides protection in the event of a short circuit. What problems could this create for the lighting circuit if the fuse were to blow?

Q

What precautions do vehicle manufacturers usually design into a lighting circuit to avoid this problem?

## Switch loading

Q

As vehicles have evolved in most areas, so too have the headlamps. Lamps generate greater illumination by using higher wattage bulbs, so the current flowing in the lighting circuit increases. What potential problems can this cause in the circuit?

Q

Which electrical component is used to relieve the main lighting circuit of the high current load and how does it do this?

## Filament lamps

### Side lamp bulbs

E

Using the missing words from the list below, complete the description of how a single centre contact (SCC) side lamp bulb is constructed and how it functions.

A single centre contact (SCC) side lamp bulb, has a helically wound tungsten filament enclosed in a __________ container. The filament is held by two support __________, one attached to an __________ contact in a brass cup (supply) and the other soldered to the cap to form an __________ connection. A low-__________ vacuum bulb has the air removed to reduce heat loss and prevent __________ of the filament. It is secured in its holder by a brass __________ cap (BC).

bayonet oxidation wires glass insulated wattage earth

E

Research some alternative methods of side lamp bulb fitment. Sketch and label the different types you have found.

## Headlamp bulbs

**Q** Which gas is typically used in a headlamp bulb?

**Q** How is heat loss from the filament due to gas movement reduced?

**Q** A headlamp bulb has two filaments to provide a main and a dip beam. How are the filaments connected?

## Tungsten–halogen bulbs

**Q** What is the alternative name for a tungsten–halogen bulb? Which materials are used and what are the benefits of this type of bulb?

**Q** What precautions do you need to take when replacing a tungsten–halogen bulb?

## Reflector

E Using the missing phrases from the list below, complete the description of how a reflector is designed and constructed to enhance illumination by the bulb.

A highly polished ____________________ with a ____________________ concentrates and directs the ____________________ in the required direction (i.e. dipped or main beam).

Positioning the main beam filament at the ____________________ of the reflector gives ____________________ and maximum illumination. This is achieved by positioning the ____________________ accurately. Some vehicles use a ____________________ reflector with several different ____________________ moulded together to form the light unit. These 'homofocular' plastic reflectors are ____________________, which allows them to blend in with the body contours.

focal point | focal lengths | parallel rays | very narrow | multi-segment

bulb filament | parabolic shape | aluminised reflector | light rays

## Lens

Q What are the headlamp regulations applicable to right-hand drive vehicles for beam deflection?

Q How is a glass lens designed and constructed to distribute the light produced from the bulb?

## The four-headlamp system

Q What are the benefits of a four-headlamp system?

## Newer headlamp technology

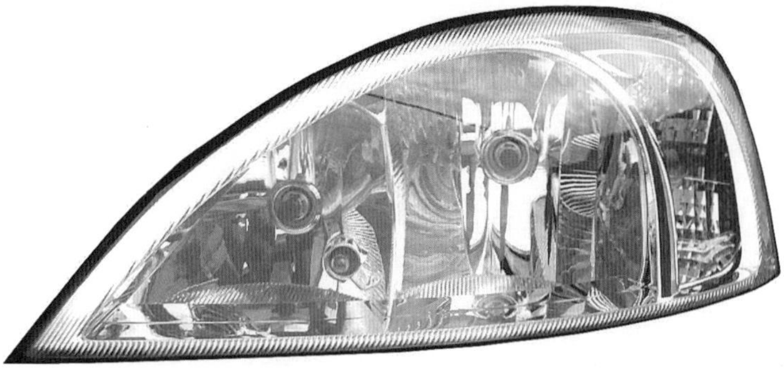

Modern headlamp with ergometric type reflector

**Q** Which part of the headlamp deflects the output from the bulb for the dipped beam?

**Q** What are the benefits of the type of headlamp cover shown in the diagram above?

**Q** What type of reflector does this headlamp have and what advantages does it offer over conventional headlamps?

### High intensity discharge headlamps (HIDs)

HID headlamps give a more intense light output, which is a vast improvement over conventional tungsten halogen bulbs; these in turn were a vast improvement over tungsten filament bulbs.

**Q** What are the benefits of an increased light output as far as road safety is concerned?

**Q** How do high intensity discharge (HID) headlamps work?

Q The voltage requirements of an HID headlamp are different from those of a tungsten–halogen bulb. How is the voltage supply maintained and controlled?

E Complete the table with how much voltage and current flow is required for the following examples.

| Example | Voltage | Current |
|---|---|---|
| Lighting system using a tungsten–halogen bulb | | |
| Arc initiation between the two capsule electrodes of an HID lamp | | |
| HID lamp once the arc is initiated | | |

Q How can you tell if a xenon capsule is beginning to fail?

*Safety Note:* ***To prevent personal injury being caused by the high voltages and currents in a HID system, you should always ensure that all necessary safety precautions, as detailed by the manufacturer, are taken before working on the system.***

Q State a disadvantage of the HID lighting system and describe the system used to overcome this disadvantage.

## Light emitting diode (LED) lamps

**discussion point**

You can probably find a few cars (new and modified) that have LED lamps fitted to the rear and elsewhere throughout the vehicle. But what are the benefits of using this type of light unit? Discuss this with the group and decide what benefits LED lamps might provide.

### Lamp marking

**Q** What identification mark is given to lamps that conform to EU standards for type approval?

## Auxiliary lighting and equipment

The main driveline electrical system (for the engine, transmission, etc.) consists of the primary circuits to enable the vehicle to be driven along the road. Additional electrical systems, known as auxiliary circuits, are responsible for powering the rest of a vehicle's electrical components.

**Q** Which auxiliary circuit components are statutory requirements for a modern vehicle?

**E** Complete the table by listing legal requirements for each item of auxiliary equipment. Look at a workshop manual or owner handbook and give the approximate fuse rating for each component.

| Equipment | Fuse rating | Legal requirements |
|---|---|---|
| Horn | 10 A | |
| Windscreen wipers | | |
| Windscreen washers | | |
| Directional indicators | | |
| Brake lamp | | |
| Reversing lamp | | |
| Instrumentation systems | | |

**Q** Compile a list of as many items of auxiliary electrical equipment as you can. It might help you to use a workshop manual for a high specification vehicle. Compare your list with those of others in your group.

## Directional indicators

Q Sketch a labelled diagram of an indicator/hazard lamp circuit. Explain what international standards this circuit has to meet.

Q What are the MOT/legal requirements for a flasher unit's operation?

Q What are the differences between a thermal flasher unit and an electronic flasher unit if one bulb fails?

### Thermal flasher unit

E Highlight the correct terms to describe the operation of a thermal flasher unit.

The vane or thermal flasher unit is a **complex / simple**, **high-cost / low-cost** unit which consist of a rectangular, snap-action, **cast iron / spring-steel** strip. Operation of the indicator switch instantly activates the signal lamps. The current passing through the metal strip **heats / cools** the strip, causing the strip to **contract / expand** and open a set of contacts. The indicator circuit is **made / broken** and the signal lights **extinguish / illuminate**. A short time after this action, the lack of current causes the strip to **heat / cool** and contract. The contacts then **close / open** again and the signal lights illuminate. The cycle is repeated until the indicator switch is turned **off / on**.

### Electronic flasher unit

**Q** Compare the differences in operation between an electronic flasher unit and a thermal type. Set out briefly the differences below.

## Routine maintenance of electrical systems

### Batteries

*Safety Note:* ***The electrolyte contains sulphuric acid. The acid can cause serious burns if it comes into contact with the body. If electrolyte contacts the skin, wash it off immediately using water. If acid contacts the eyes, wash the eyes thoroughly in water for several minutes and seek urgent medical assistance.***

The battery will need to be checked as part of a service or electrical system inspection to determine whether it is capable of storing and delivering electrical power to the vehicle's electrical system.

**discussion point** Discuss with a partner what checks are necessary when inspecting a battery during a service. Write down your list of checks, ready for discussion and comparison with the rest of the group.

**E** Using the missing words from the list below, complete the description of how to test and top up the electrolyte in a battery.

Always use __________ water to top up the electrolyte. Never use water from a tap (sink or similar). The impurities that ordinary tap water contains will contaminate the __________ and reduce the __________ of the battery. On those batteries where access to the cells is possible, the state of __________ can be checked with the aid of a __________. The hydrometer measures the specific gravity of the __________. A high specific __________ (1.290) indicates a fully charged battery, while a low __________ gravity (0.120) indicates a __________ battery. If the reading is low it will be necessary to __________ the battery and recheck the reading. Specific gravity cannot be checked immediately after charging a battery or __________ up a battery with distilled __________: allow the battery to stand for a short time before the check is carried out.

water | plates | topping | gravity | recharge | discharged | charge | electrolyte | hydrometer | performance | distilled | specific

### Disconnecting battery terminals

Q When you are disconnecting a battery, which terminal will you need to disconnect first?

Q When you are reconnecting a battery, which terminal will you need to reconnect last?

Q What could happen if the battery terminals were to be removed in the incorrect order?

## Starting systems

E Working with a partner set out a list of checks that can ensure the correct operation and security of the starting system.

## Charging systems

E Working with a partner set out a list of checks that can be carried out on a charging system to ensure its correct operation.

## Additional electrical systems

E Using a workshop manual or service schedule to help you, list the components that you would check when inspecting a lighting system for correct operation.

## Headlamp adjustment

Headlamps are now brighter than they have ever been before, so it is important to check their alignment as part of a service or MOT test.

This check ensures that, during night driving, the headlamps emit the best possible beam pattern to aid visibility and limit dazzle to oncoming vehicles.

E Research and discover how a headlamp alignment check is carried out. Why is it important to check the tyre pressures and to settle the suspension before carrying out the check? Record the procedure for future reference.

**mini projects**

Agree the following with your tutor:

- which projects to do and the order in which to do them
- the format and quantity of content
- the time frame for completion.

1 Identify through research a vehicle circuit that uses electronics in its operation. A good example might be the regulator circuit in an alternator. When you have found a suitable circuit explain how it works with the aid of labelled diagrams.

2 Using the Internet, research what the term 'telematics' means and identify vehicle components and systems that fall into this category. Create a piece of work that illustrates your findings and understanding of this term.

3 Through research try to gain an understanding of multiplexing. Gather information from the Internet to include circuit diagrams. Use other sources of information if necessary.

## Practical activities

**practical activity 1**

Circuit boards and bulbs provide a great way to understand how a circuit operates. Under supervision, assemble various electrical circuits . Using a multimeter, test the circuits and apply and prove Ohm's law.

**practical activity 2**

On a vehicle fitted with ABS, Use an oscilloscope to test the waveform of an ABS wheel-speed sensor. Draw the waveform produced, compare it with manufacturer's specifications and make recommendations about the system's serviceability.

**practical activity 3**

Using a good wiring diagram for a vehicle you have access to, locate the starter circuit. Sketch out and label the circuit to show it separately from other circuits. On the vehicle, locate the components shown on your diagram and state what type of starter motor is fitted. Note the cable sizes and record these, along with the colour codings.

**practical activity 4**

On a suitable vehicle test the supply voltage to the headlight and sidelight bulbs, and record your results. Test the earth (ground) connections and record the result. Make an assessment of the condition of the circuits tested and compile this into a report.

CHAPTER 7

# FUEL AND IGNITION SYSTEMS

### *Essential knowledge*

You will need to read and research vehicle technology covering the following:

- Engine management systems (EMS) – an introduction
- Fuel injection systems
- Ignition systems
- Diesel fuel systems

Note: some of this chapter refers to basic principles to ensure a full understanding.

## Engine management systems (EMS) – an introduction

**Requirements of an engine management system**

An engine management system (EMS) integrates both the fuel and ignition functions into one system, constantly monitoring all aspects of combustion, while ensuring optimum performance and driveability.

E Complete the diagram of an engine management system showing input and output components.

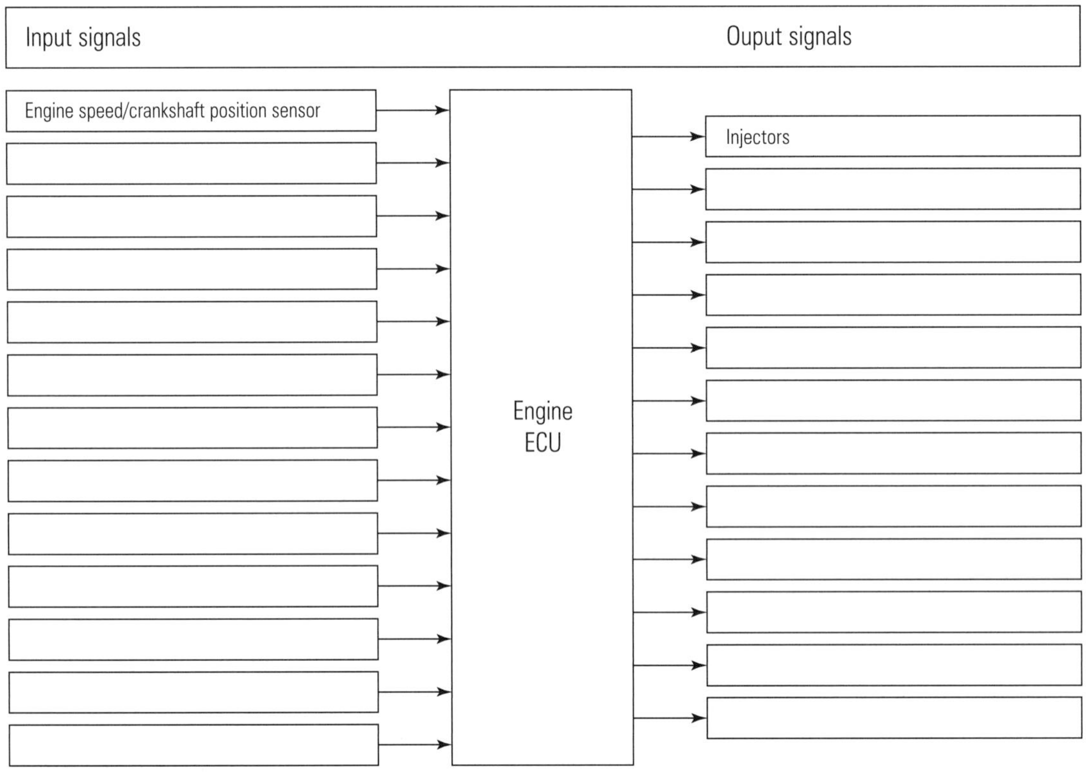

**Q** What are the two main input sensors that determine correct fuelling?

**Q** Which output actuator delivers the fuel into the engine?

**E** Give the meanings of these abbreviations for engine management components.

| Abbreviation | Meaning | Abbreviation | Meaning | Abbreviation | Meaning |
|---|---|---|---|---|---|
| AFM | Air flow meter (example) | EACV | | MAF | |
| ATS | | ECM | | MAP | |
| CANP | | EFI | | MIL | |
| CAS | | EGO | | MPI | |
| CFI | | EGR | | $NO_x$ | |
| CID | | EOBD | | $O_2$ | |
| CIS | | EVAP | | PCV | |
| CKP | | $H_2O$ | | PPM | |
| CO | | HC | | PTC | |
| $CO_2$ | | HT | | SEFI | |
| CTS | | ISC | | TPS | |
| DIS | | KS | | VSS | |

## System components – fuel systems

### Air flow sensing

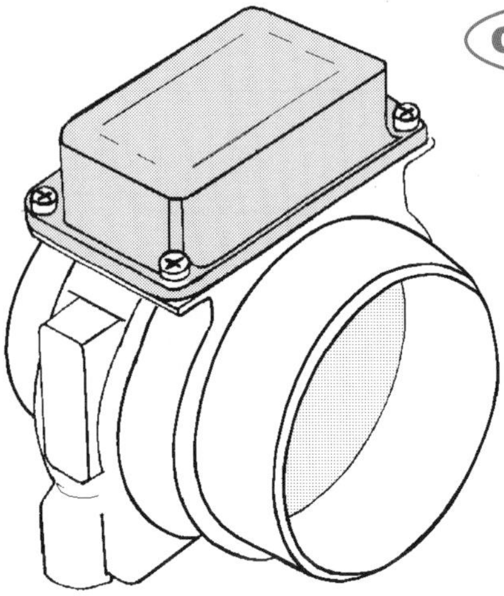

Q What is the function of an air flow sensor?

### Throttle position sensor

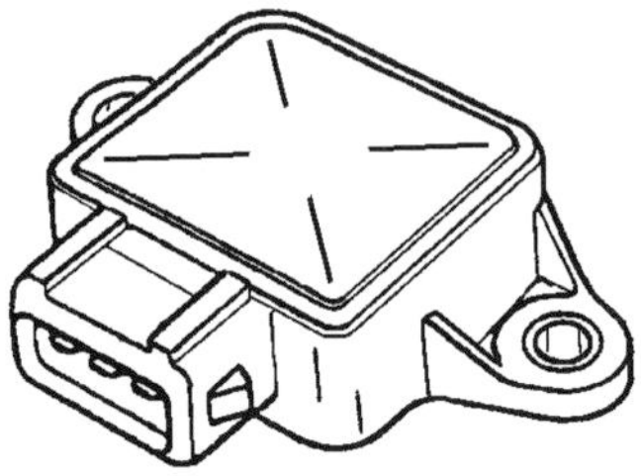

Q What is the function of a throttle position sensor and what type of sensor is it?

**discussion point**

Discuss with a partner the benefits of electronic control of the idle speed. Between you, research two different types of component that offer this control. Be prepared to discuss your findings with the rest of the group.

### Crankshaft and camshaft sensors

Q A crankshaft sensor usually measures engine speed. What does a camshaft sensor measure and what additional function may a crankshaft sensor have?

### Temperature sensor

Q It is important that the ECU monitors the temperature of the engine. Why is this?

### Combustion knock sensor

Q A knock sensor measures combustion knock in an engine. What setting does this sensor control?

## Catalytic converters and oxygen sensors

E Exhaust emissions are converted by a catalytic converter into less harmful ones. A three-way converter alters HC, CO and $NO_2$ into three other emissions. Complete the diagram to show these.

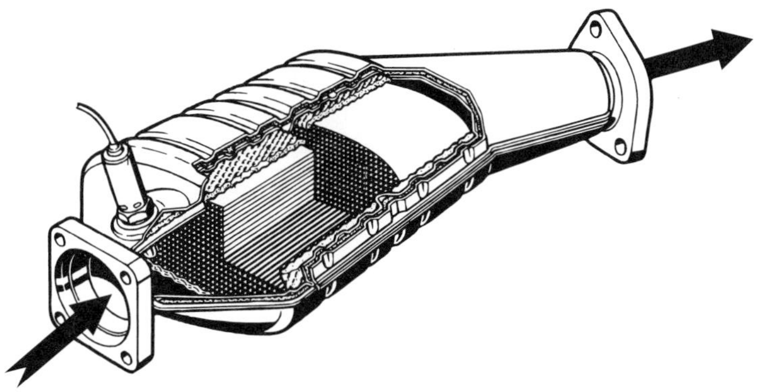

E A sensor is fitted into the catalytic converter in the diagram above. Name and explain the function of this sensor and label this component on the diagram.

Q A second oxygen sensor can be used to measure the correct operation and efficiency of which component?

## Other emission controls

**Q** It is no longer an acceptable practice to pollute the atmosphere with emissions, so fuel vapour (hydrocarbon) has to be kept in a recyclable closed circuit environment. What is this system known as?

**E** Add the corresponding numbers below to each part of the diagram showing the flow of vapours into an EVAP system.

1. Line from fuel tank to activated-charcoal canister
2. Activated charcoal canister
3. Fresh air
4. Canister-purge valve
5. Line to intake manifold
6. Throttle assembly with throttle valve

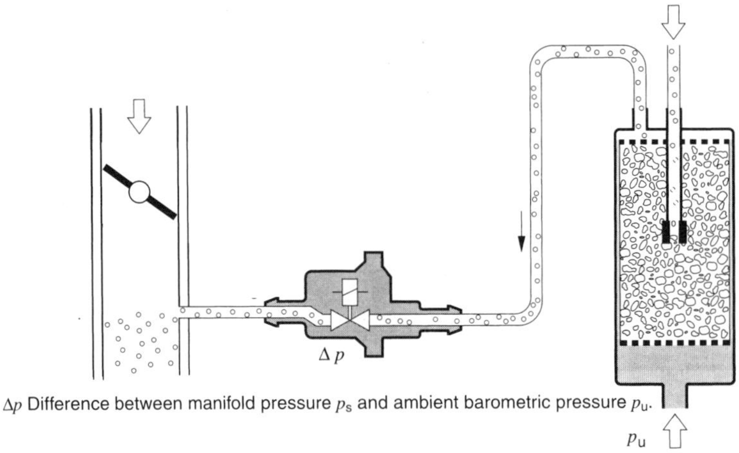


Δ*p* Difference between manifold pressure $p_s$ and ambient barometric pressure $p_u$.

**E** Research and discover the function and benefits of an EGR system.

# Fuel injection systems

## Electronic petrol injection

### Introduction

The term 'petrol injection' is used to describe a system in which pressurised fuel is forced out of a nozzle in an atomised state to mix with a supply of air.

Petrol injection systems were once mechanical, but almost all injection systems are now electronically controlled. Engine management systems provide electronic control of fuel and ignition.

**discussion point** Discuss as a group the reasons why fuel injection systems have been developed and have made carburettors obsolete.

**Injector positions**

The diagrams below show the two most commonly used types of petrol injection system.

E

How are the injectors positioned in each diagram below? Compare the differences and name each type, labelling the diagrams appropriately.

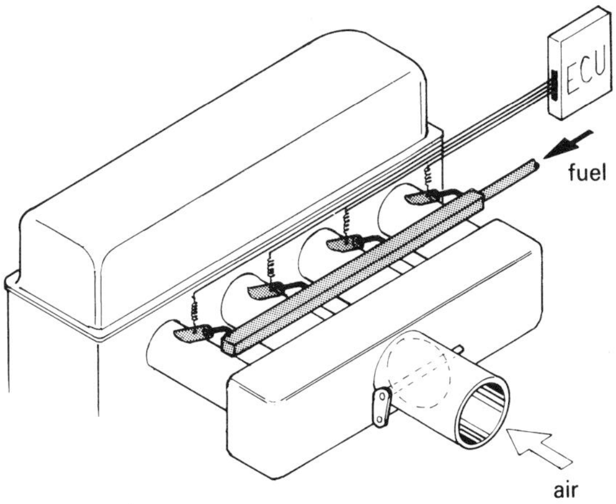


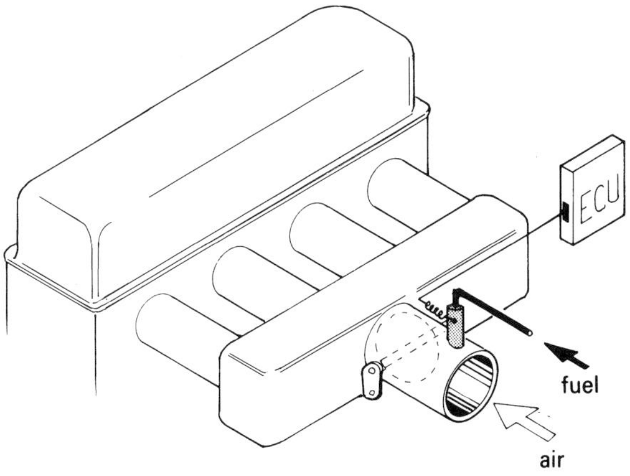

## Electronic petrol injection

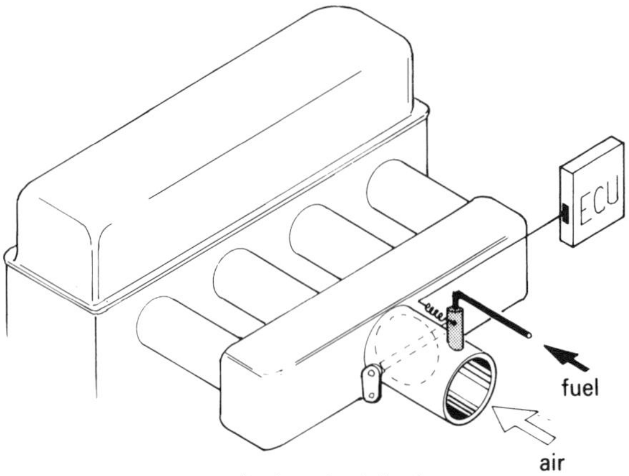

single-point injection

### Single-point injection

Single-point injection (SPI) is sometimes known as 'throttle body injection' (TBI) because it uses a single injector to deliver fuel into the induction.

Although single-point injection is an improvement over a carburettor, it does not have the good fuel distribution advantages of a multi-point injection system (MPI).

In general, single-point injection is used on smaller capacity engines and multi-point injection is used on larger capacity engines.

E

With a partner carry out some research to discover how a single-point injection system operates. Explain with the use of diagrams the basic operating principles of this system. Strengthen your understanding by completing the exercise on the next page.

E

Look at the diagram and number the list of components below. Then briefly explain their function.

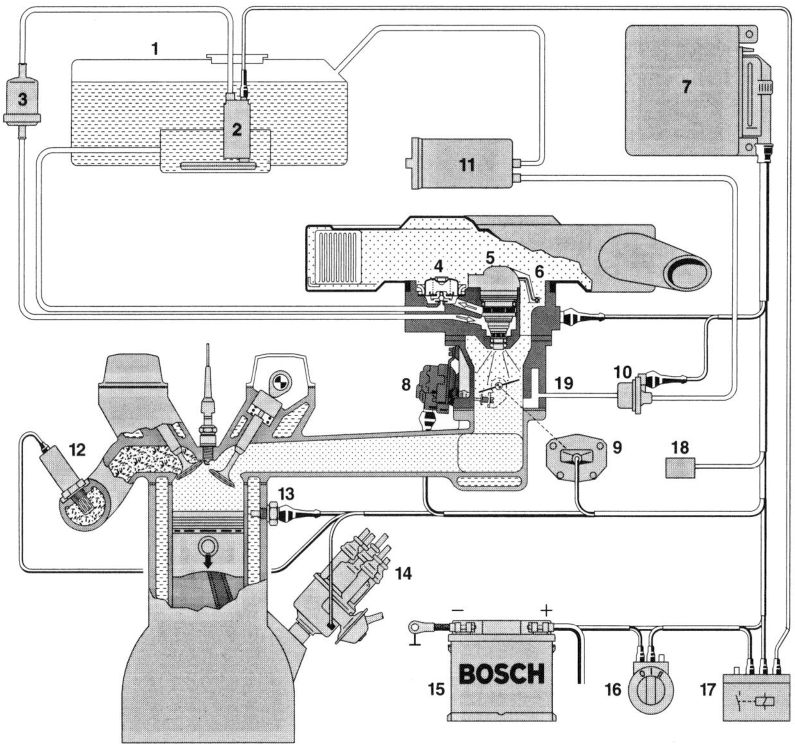


| Component | No | Function |
|---|---|---|
| Relay | | |
| Ignition distributor | | |
| Lambda oxygen sensor | | |
| ECU | | |
| Fuel pressure regulator | | |
| Air temperature sensor | | |
| Canister purge valve | | |
| Solenoid-operated fuel injector | | |
| Battery | | |
| Throttle valve potentiometer | | |
| Fuel tank | | |
| Ignition start switch | | |
| Fuel filter | | |
| Diagnosis connection | | |
| Electric fuel pump | | |
| Engine temperature sensor | | |

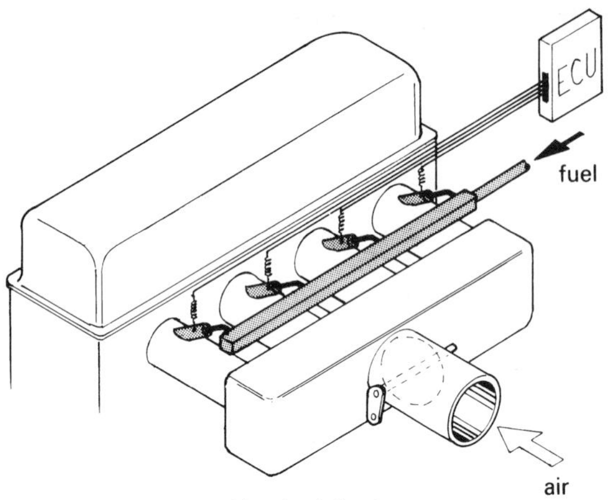

multi-point injection

## Multi-point injection

Multi-point injection systems have an injector for each cylinder. They inject fuel through each intake port, giving more precise fuel delivery, better fuel distribution and a faster response than single-point injection systems.

Multi-point injection is widely used, particularly on larger capacity engines.

E

**With a partner carry out some research to discover how a multi-point injection system operates. Explain with the use of diagrams the basic operating principles of this system. Strengthen your understanding by completing the exercise on the next page.**

E

Look at the diagram and number the list of components below. Then briefly explain their function.

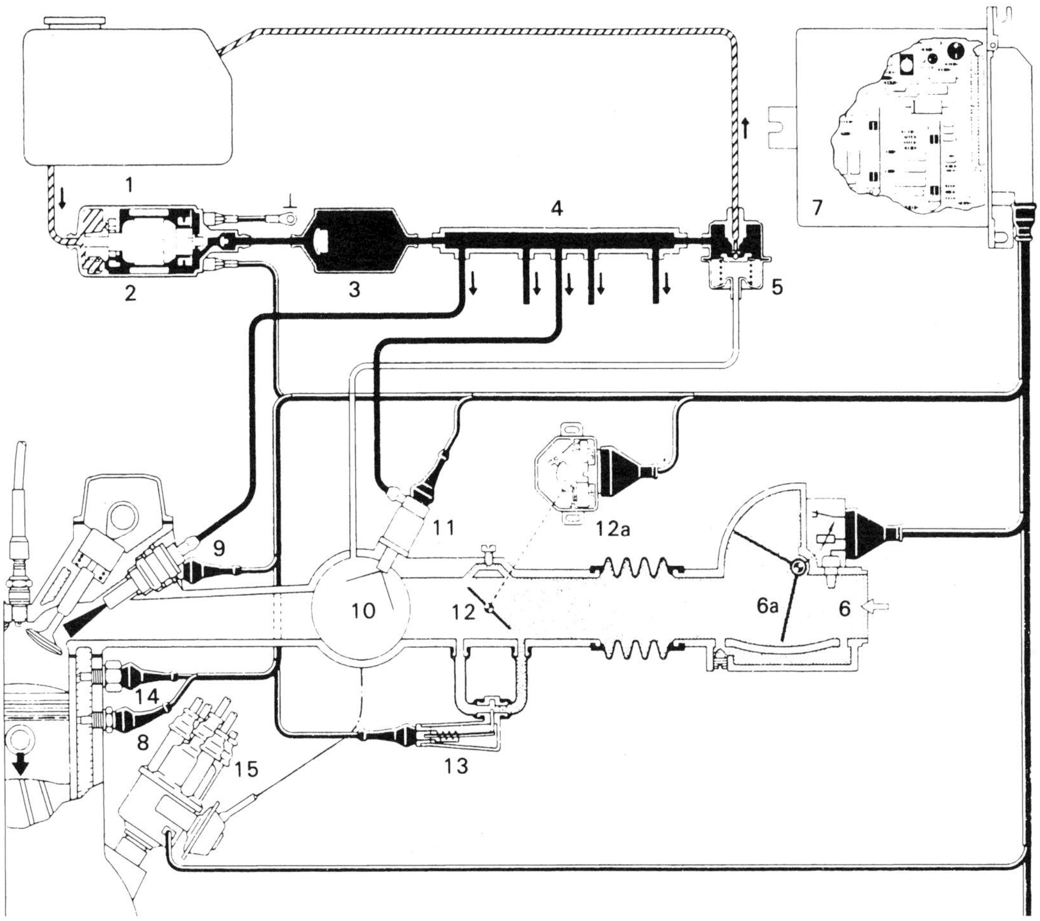


| Component | No | Function |
|---|---|---|
| Control unit | | |
| Intake manifold | | |
| Throttle valve with switch | | |
| Temperature sensor | | |
| Electric fuel pump | | |
| Thermo-time switch | | |
| Fuel distribution pipe | | |
| Ignition distributor | | |
| Pressure regulator | | |
| Fuel tank | | |
| Auxiliary air device | | |
| Injection valve | | |
| Air flow sensor with sensor flap | | |
| Fine filter | | |
| Start valve | | |

E Compare and explain the differences between single-point and multi-point injection systems.

discussion point

Discuss with a partner why manufacturers now produce vehicles with multi-point rather than single-point injection systems? Write down your ideas, including any sketches that you think might help when you discuss injection systems with the group.

## Fuel pump

E The diagram shows a typical fuel pump system. Label the parts of the pump and state what this type of pump is called. The fuel pump relay is a key part of the electrical circuit. Describe how the relay works to make the circuit function.

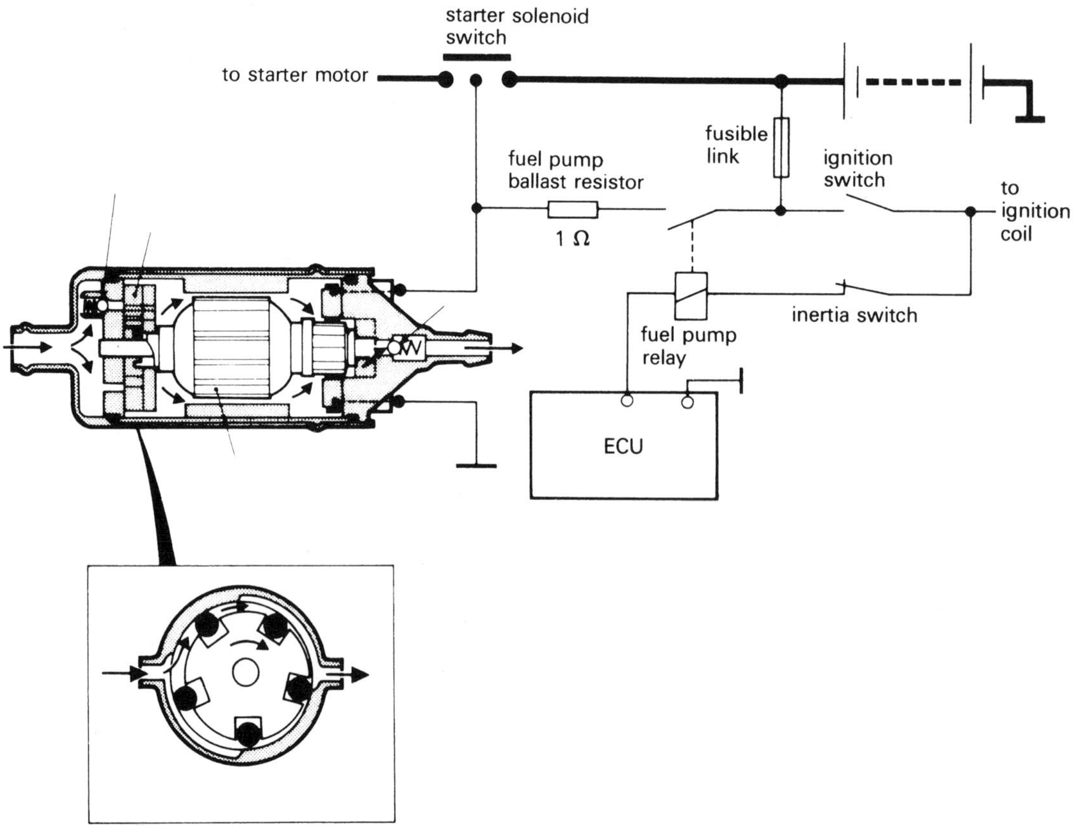

Q

What is the purpose of the inertia switch shown in the circuit on the previous page?

discussion point

Typically, fuel pumps are fitted inside the fuel tank and are immersed in the fuel. Discuss with a partner how you think an electrical component can work without causing an explosion. Think about safety issues when working on these pumps on the bench. Write down your ideas, including any sketches that you think might help when you present your ideas to other members of your group.

E

Using the missing words from the list below, complete the description of how this type of pump functions to deliver fuel.

Rotation of the __________ moves the rollers __________ and seals the spaces between the __________ and casing. As the __________ is carried around with the rotor, a combination of the rotor movement and the decrease in __________ of the pumping __________ causes an increase in __________. Operation of the fuel pump is controlled __________ by the system ECU. It is run for a brief period to __________ the system prior to starting the engine.

volume

pressure

electronically

pressurise

chamber

fuel

rotor

outwards

pump

E

Research and discover how a fuel gauge operates. Sketch a labelled diagram of the necessary components and briefly explain how it works.

## Fuel pressure regulator

E Label the diagram of a fuel pressure regulator.

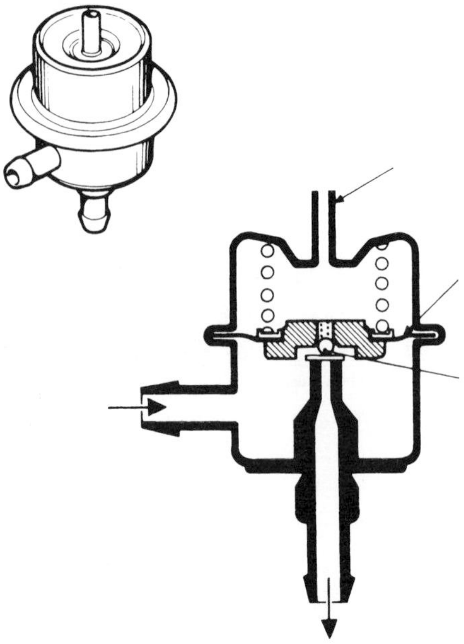

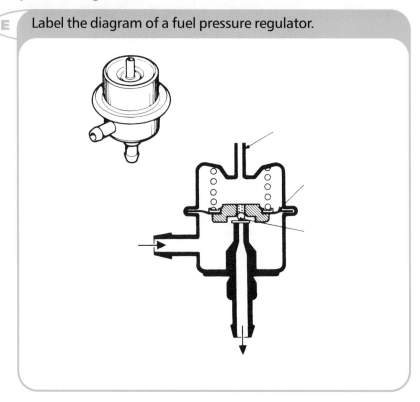

E Using the missing phrases from the list below, complete the description of the operation of a fuel pressure regulator.

__________ depends on __________ (e.g. engine load) so when the opening is small the __________ encourages more fuel to leave the injector. To compensate for this, the fuel system operating __________ when the manifold __________ (a high depression or high vacuum equals a low pressure). Lower fuel pressure is achieved by connecting one side of the regulator to the __________. When the engine is operating under a light load, the regulator valve is slightly opened and the __________ is reduced.

- pressure is lowered
- induction manifold
- fuel pressure
- depression is high
- throttle opening
- high depression
- manifold depression

E Complete the table below stating the typical fuel regulator control pressures.

| Engine condition | Manifold depression | Typical operating pressures |
|---|---|---|
| Idling | | |
| Full throttle | | |

**Note:** It is important to ensure that manifold depression is correct. For example, if the vacuum supply hose is split, the fuel pressure will not be correct.

## Injectors

**Q** The injector must vary the quantity of fuel to suit the engine's operating conditions. How is this done?

**E** Label the diagram of the injector to gain an understanding of the internal parts.

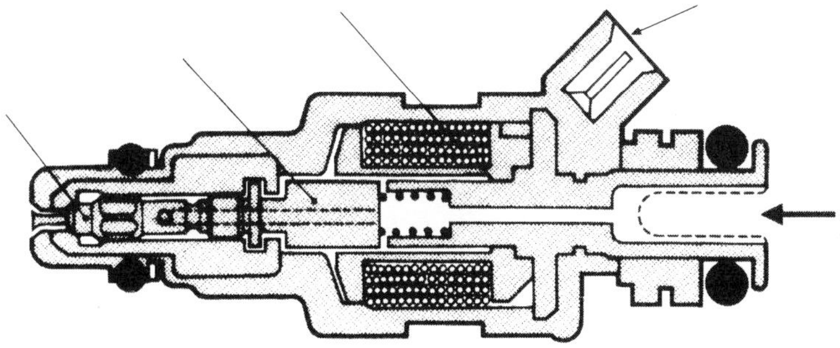

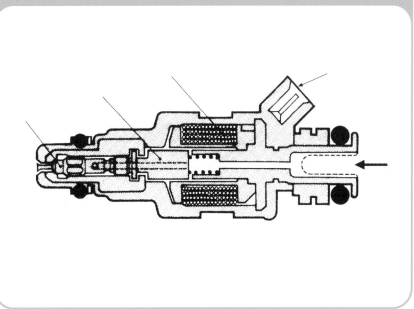

**E** Highlight the correct term to describe where the injector is located and the reason for this position.

The injector is located in the **inlet / outlet** manifold near to the cylinder **block / head** intake port. It is normally sealed in the **outlet / inlet** manifold with a rubber O-ring, held in position by means of a retaining clip.

The injector is positioned so the fuel spray is directed at the back of the closed **exhaust / inlet** valve. The **atomised / vapourised** fuel is then drawn into the cylinder with the air when the inlet valve **opens / closes**.

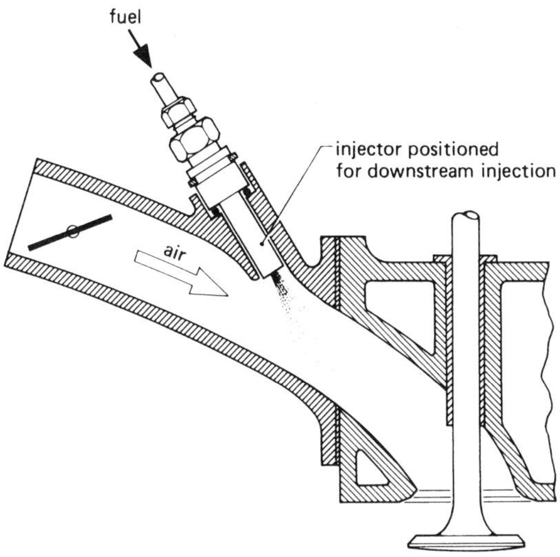


'Indirect' injection is generally used, although, with improving engine and electronic technology and stricter emission controls, some vehicle manufacturers are developing and fitting direct injection petrol systems.

**Q** In an indirect injection system, at what pressure does an injector usually operate?

**Q** Injectors deliver fuel into the engine at a predetermined rate according to engine loads and requirements. How is more fuel delivered when an engine is cold or under load?

**Q** Is the injector an electrical or electronic component?

**Q** What equipment would you use to test the winding in an injector?

## Ignition systems

Modern vehicles have to be designed with economy and performance in mind, but they also have to be designed to generate lower emissions. Therefore the ignition system has to generate a higher energy spark and have more variable timing conditions.

**E** Sketch the layouts of a programmed ignition system and a distributorless type used with engine management control. Compare the two systems and describe the function of each of the parts.

**discussion point**

Discuss as a group the advantages of electronic ignition systems over conventional types. This may require some research. Record all your findings.

## Coil-ignition systems

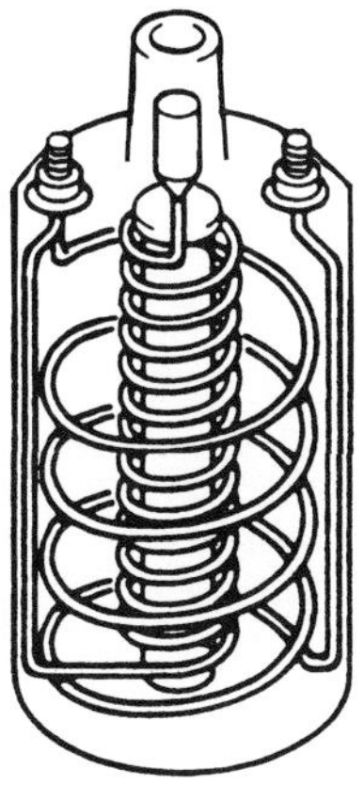

### Ignition coils

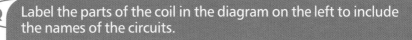

**Q** Label the parts of the coil in the diagram on the left to include the names of the circuits.

**Q** An ignition coil transforms the battery voltage into several thousand volts through mutual induction. Explain briefly what is meant by the term 'mutual induction' and how the coil uses this effect to produce a spark at the correct time in the engine cycle. Refer to any engine sensors that may be used.

E

The ignition coils in modern electronic systems are different in construction from older coils and are referred to as 'distributorless' types. Through discussion and research find out what different types there are. Sketch and label two of the types you have found (show cross sections if you can find suitable diagrams).

| Type 1 | Type 2 |
|---|---|
| | |

**discussion point**

Discuss with a member of your group why spark timing needs to be variable. You need to consider the four-stroke cycle as part of your discussion. Set out your ideas and be prepared to let the rest of the group know your conclusions.

Q

In relation to the engine cycle, when does the spark occur if it is 'advanced'?

Q

In relation to the engine cycle, when does the spark occur if it is 'retarded'?

**Q** To obtain a high power output from an engine, at approximately what position of the engine should the cylinder pressure be at a maximum?

## Production of high voltage

### Distributors

**Q** Electronic ignition system distributors are also know as 'pulse generators'. What are the names of the three main types?

**Q** What is the function of an amplifier module?

### High-tension lead

**Q** How is a high-tension lead constructed and why it is so heavily insulated?

## Sparking plugs

E

Sketch and describe the construction and function of a spark plug. Show on your sketches the differences between the heat paths of hot and cold spark plugs and suggest typical applications for each.

**discussion point**

Discuss with a partner the factors that affect the voltage required to produce a spark in a running engine. List the factors and discuss your list with the rest of the group.

Q

A spark plug has a gap of 0.6 mm (0.024 in). A voltage of about 600 V produces a spark across the gap in open air. What voltage would be needed to produce a spark in a cylinder under compression pressure?

*Safety Note:* ***The electrical spark in a modern ignition system has enough power to seriously injure a person. Always follow safety advice and guidelines***

Q

Which important factor has to be considered when testing the spark output from an ignition system?

## Diesel fuel systems

Diesel fuelled vehicles are becoming more popular than ever, mainly because of their high fuel efficiency. They also offer higher torque output than their petrol engined equivalents. All diesel fuel systems are now electronically controlled and mainly of the 'common rail' type. However, an understanding of basic diesel fuel system operation is important: it will help you gain a better understanding of electronic types. Electronically controlled systems will be looked at in detail in Workbook 3.

E Sketch and label the layout of a typical diesel fuel system, including all main components from the fuel tank through to the injectors.

discussion point

Diesel fuel needs to be extremely well filtered. Discuss this with a member of your group and decide why. Then see if you can decide what might be the purpose of a sedimenter fitted into the fuel line. Record your ideas and be prepared to let the rest of the group know what your thoughts are.

Q There are two types of mechanical injection pump. Which is most commonly used on light vehicles?

Q What are three main functions of a diesel fuel-injection pump?

E Label the main components on the diagram of a simple mechanical fuel delivery system below.

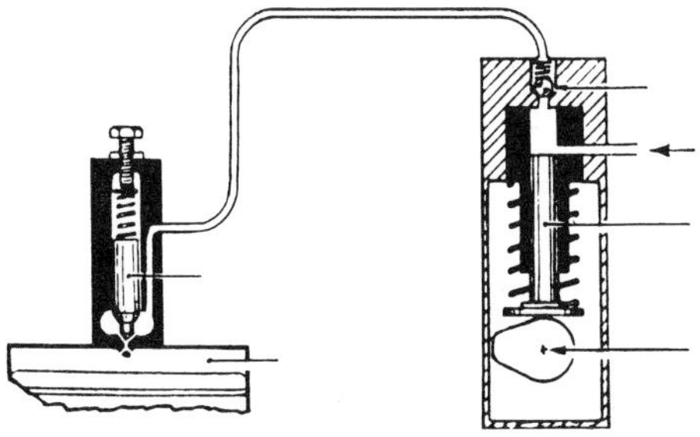

Q

Look at the diagram on the previous page. What is the basic operating principle of a mechanical system of fuel injection?

E

Label the components of the pumping element, typically found on in-line pumps, on the diagram.

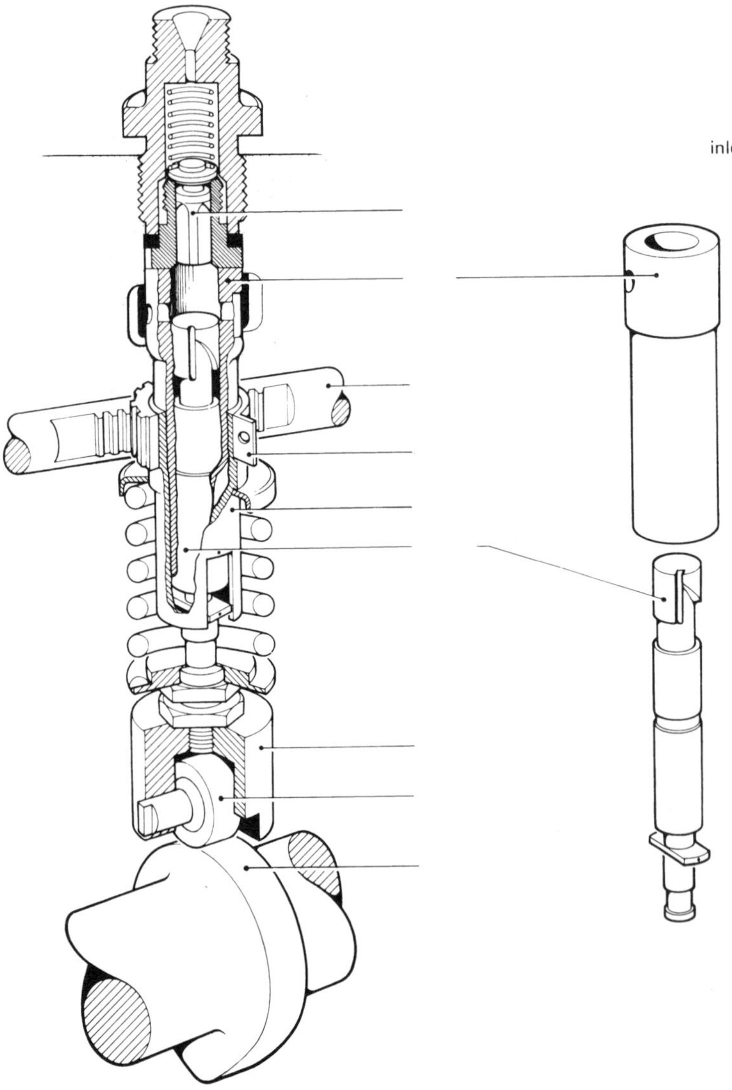

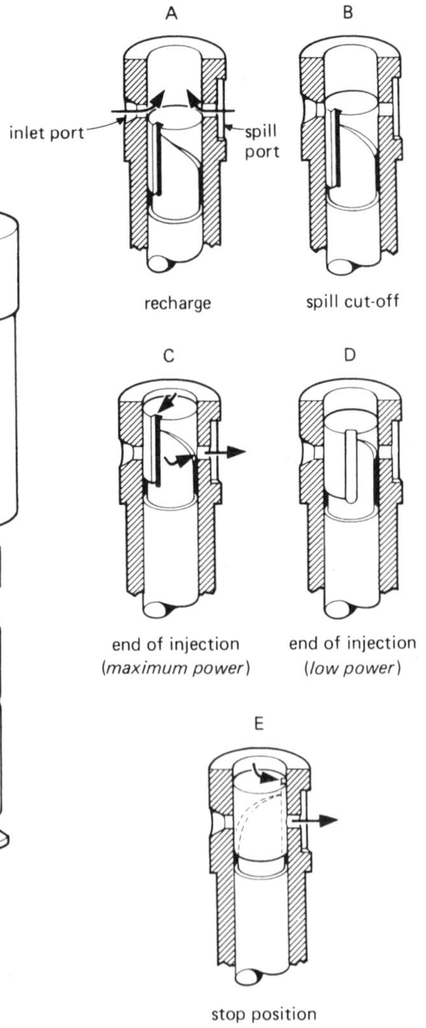

E

Describe the operation of the pumping element you have labelled above by filling in the missing words in the text below.

A When the __________ is at BDC the depression in the pump chamber causes fuel to enter both ports.

B This position, known as __________, is generally regarded as the theoretical point of injection. Both ports have been covered, and so the rising plunger raises the pressure of the fuel to produce injection.

C Injection stops when the edge of the __________ uncovers the __________. Pressure is relieved by fuel passing down the vertical groove, around the waist of the plunger and out of the __________.

D Rotation of the plunger causes the helix to __________ the __________ either earlier or later, to give less or more fuel, respectively.

E Moving the plunger to make the vertical groove __________ with the __________ means that the port will remain open; therefore no fuel will be delivered and the engine will stop.

line up

helix

spill cut off

uncover

plunger

spill port

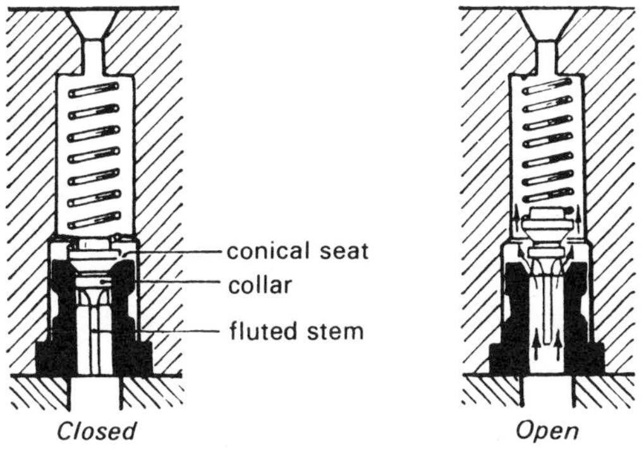


**Delivery valve**

Q

The delivery valve performs two duties. What are they?

Q

A governor is an important part of a fuel-injection pump. What is its purpose?

Q

What are the three types of governor?

There are several different types of injection pump which work on similar principles. The Bosch VE pumping unit is quite common on light vehicles and to simplify things this section refers to it.

E Label the main components on the diagram.

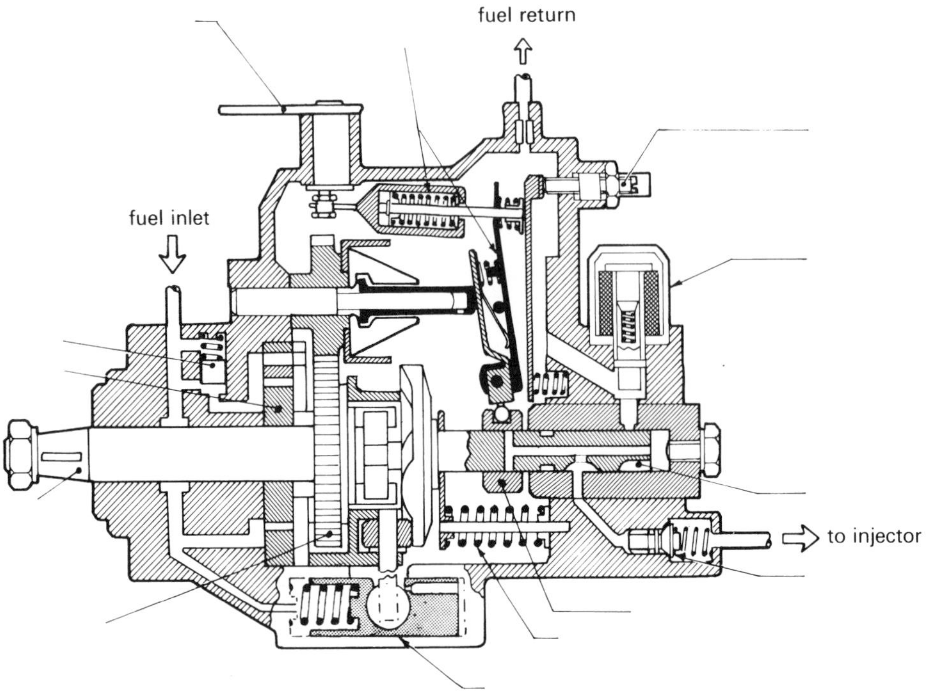


As with other rotary pumps, this pump has one pumping element and a number of high-pressure outlets, one for each cylinder. It can also have other features, such as a solenoid-operated fuel cut-off to give the driver key start/stop operation.

Q What is the purpose of the transfer pump?

Q At what speed in relation to the engine is the pump driven?

Q What three other add-on features might this pump have?

Label the diagrams of the Bosch VE pumping unit below.

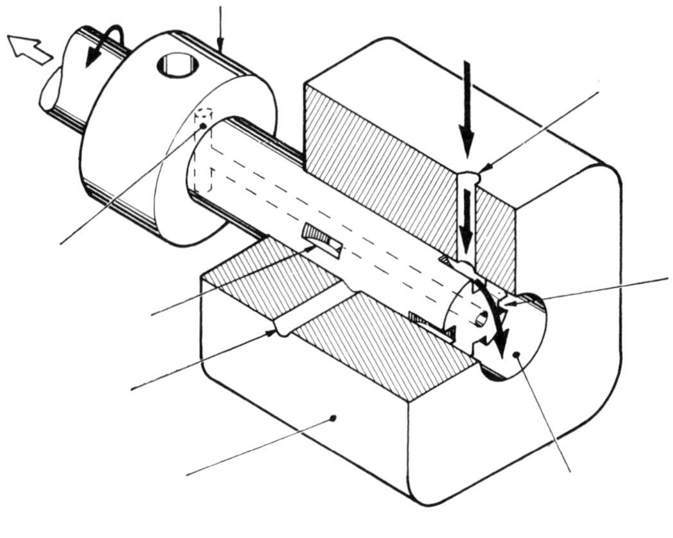

*(a) Fuel entry to pumping chamber*

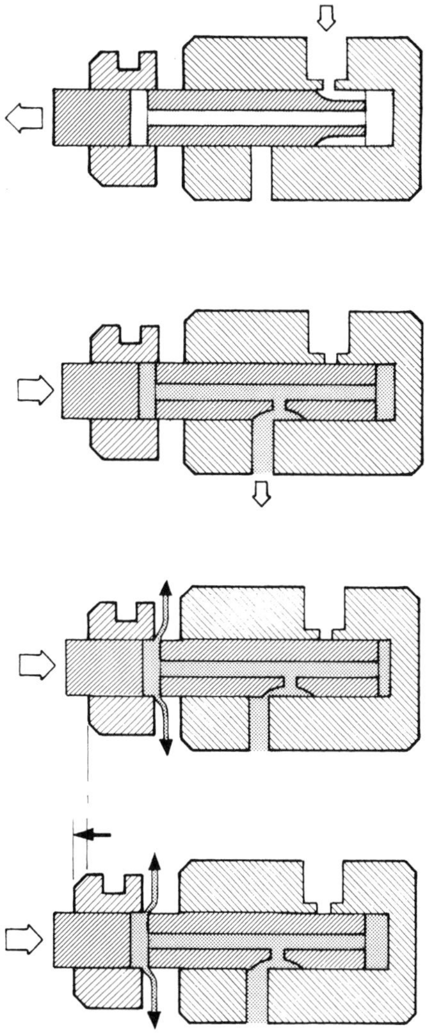

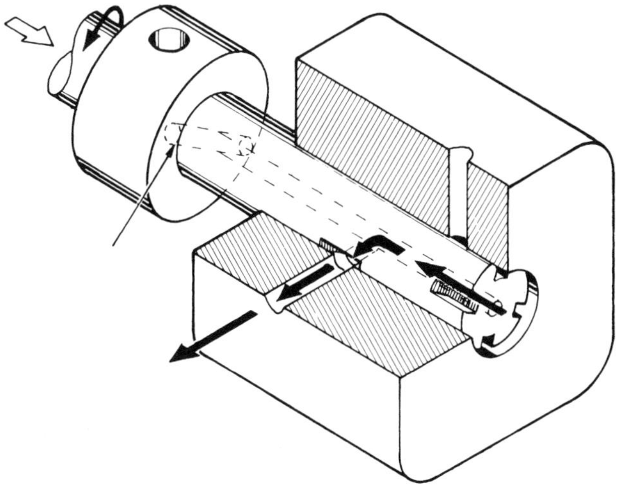

*(b) Pump at end of delivery*

Look at the diagrams above. How is the quantity of high-pressure fuel delivery controlled?

E Label the diagram of the plunger drive below.

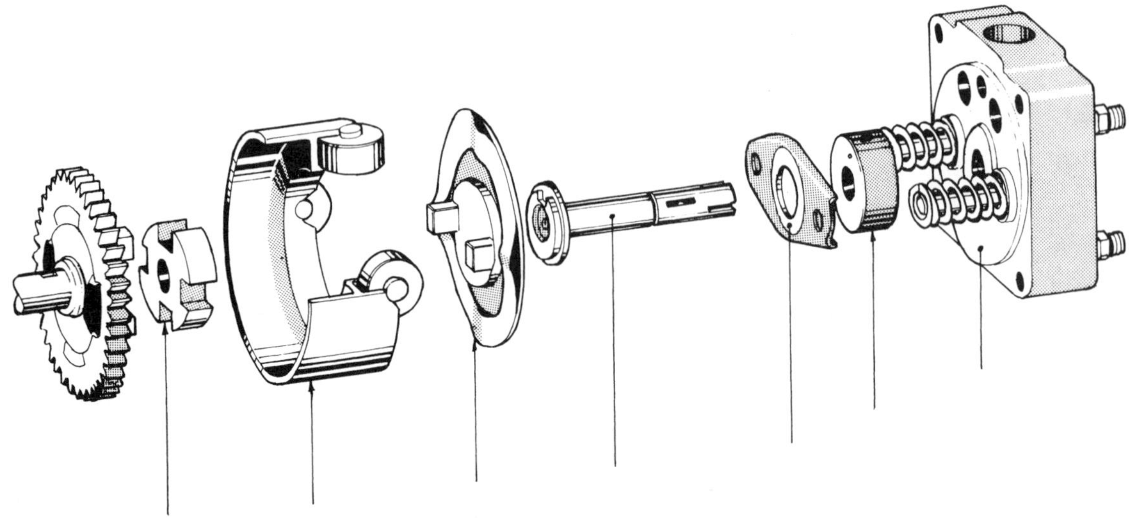

Q What are the two main things that the pump plunger must do during its operation?

To produce maximum power from the engine, the point of injection has to be advanced with increasing engine speed. The Bosch VE pump includes an automatic injection advance unit.

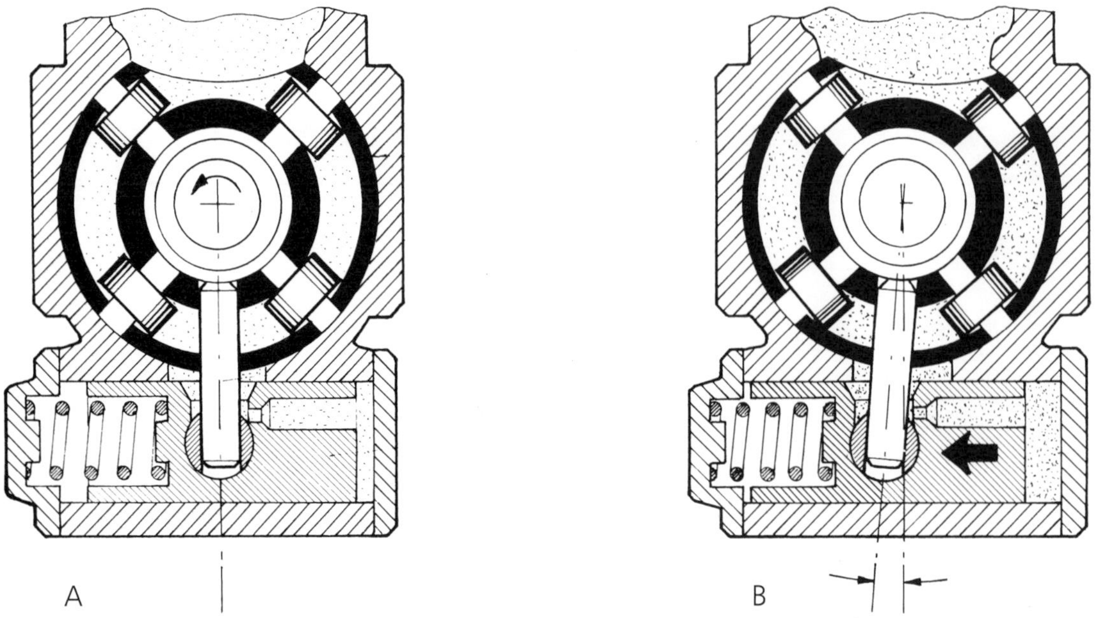

E Indicate which diagram on the previous page shows the unit in high engine speed position and low engine speed position, respectively. Briefly state how the unit moves to advance the point of injection in relation to engine speed.

The VE pump incorporates a two-speed governor. It controls the engine during the phases of idling and maximum speed operation.

Q Is the governor hydraulically operated or does it work through centrifugal force?

E Indicate which of the diagrams below show the governor position at idle and at maximum power.

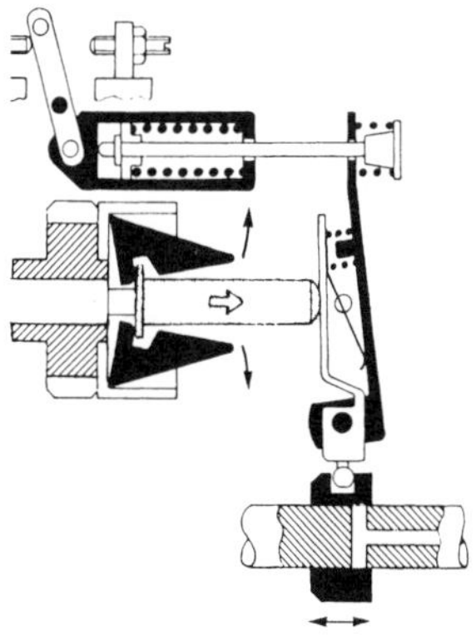

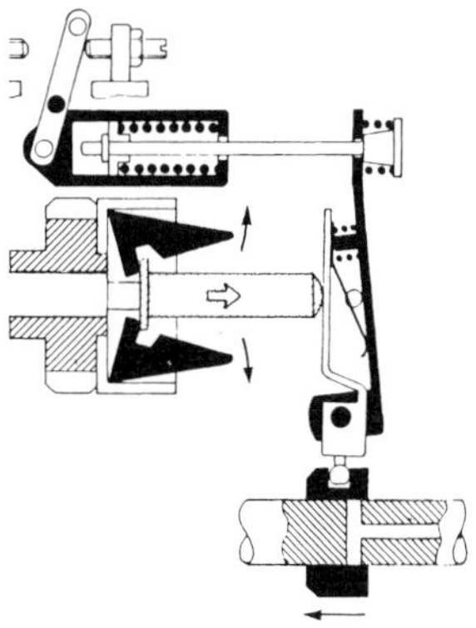

## Injectors

E Label the main components of the injector on the diagram below.

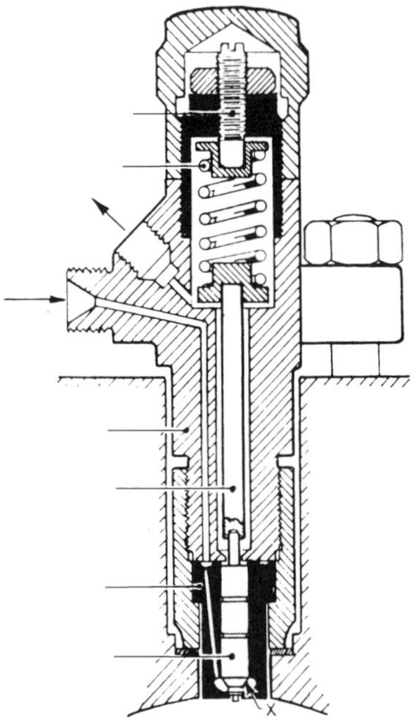


Q What is the purpose of a fuel injector?

Q What basic principle does an injector rely on to work?

**discussion point**

You have already learned about the diesel four-stroke cycle. See if you can remember or decide how the fuel is ignited in a diesel engine by discussing this with a member of your group. Record your ideas and be prepared to let the rest of the group know what your thoughts are.

The spray pattern delivered by an injector is designed to suit particular engine and combustion chamber designs.

Q The injector has a leak-off port. What is the purpose of this and what does it connect to?

E

**Sketch three main types of injector nozzle, label them and show the particular spray pattern that they deliver. Describe the features and operation of one of the nozzles you have drawn.**

mini projects

Agree the following with your tutor:

- Which projects to do in which order
- Format and quantity of content
- Time frame for completion.

1 Dwell angle, dwell time, dwell variation and advance and retard are all terms used in relation to ignition systems. Through research and discussion describe with the aid of sketches what these terms mean. Include in your explanation how spark timing varies according to vehicle speed and acceleration.

2 Research various spark plug manufacturers' sources of information to find out about different types of plugs, their applications and operating parameters. It might be interesting to find out what type of spark plugs are used in motorsport vehicles. Find some pictures that show, by their condition, spark plug faults. Use these illustrations for analysis when you next service the spark plugs on a vehicle.

3 Research the function and operation of the three main types of pulse generator found in electronic ignition systems. Describe, with the aid of a labelled diagram, the construction and operation of one of them.

4 Combustion processes and differing fuel ratios produce byproducts in the exhaust gas. Find out what these byproducts are when the air/fuel ratio is chemically correct, rich and weak. Include in your work a definition of 'stoichiometric ratio' and lambda 1. Research and explain the composition and terms used in relation to hydrocarbon fuels.

5 Using the Internet, have a look at various diagnostic equipment manufacturers' information to find out about the tools that are available to diagnose faults on engine management systems. Make a list of the most suitable pieces of equipment that would enable you best to diagnose a range of common symptoms and faults.

6 Mechanical diesel injection systems have been upgraded over the years to include some electronic control. Through research discover what electronic control can be found on these systems. Analyse and report on how this electronic control has improved the economy and performance of diesel vehicles.

7 Another type of diesel fuel-injection system, not mentioned previously, is the unit injector. Research and discover how these systems operate and what electronic control they have. Include diagrams to support your explanations. It might be useful to have a brief look at common rail types in particular: you need to take great care when working on these systems, since they operate at extremely high pressures.

## Practical activities

Carry out practical activity 1 on a suitable vehicle fitted with an engine management system and a catalytic converter.

Carry out practical activity 2 on a suitable vehicle fitted with a mechanical diesel fuel-injection system.

**Note:** Beware of the high operating pressures in this system.

**practical activity 1a**

1 Carefully connect an engine management diagnostic tool (scanner) to the vehicle's diagnostic socket.

2 Run through 'key on engine off' and 'engine running' or similar test sequences your equipment has, and record any fault codes and descriptions in the table below. Make an analysis of any faults and report on what action needs to be taken to repair them.

| Key on engine off | | Engine running | |
|---|---|---|---|
| Fault code | Fault description | Fault code | Fault description |
| | | | |

**practical activity 1b**

Find out and record the following manufacturers' data for the vehicle.

| Idle speed | CO% at idle | HC ppm at idle |
|---|---|---|
| | | |

1 Visually inspect the air cleaner element.

2 Visually and aurally inspect the exhaust system.

3 Connect the engine to some engine diagnostic equipment that has a tachometer and gas analyser.

4 Run the engine up to operating temperature and test the oil temperature to ensure the correct test conditions.

5 Compare the emission levels with manufacturer's specifications to determine whether the catalytic converter is working correctly and create a report to advise the customer.

**practical activity 2a**

1 Remove the fuel filter. Take care to prepare yourself in case of fuel spillage before you start.

2 Carefully note the positioning of all seals and then fit a new filter.

3 Bleed the system of any air, run the engine and check for leaks.

**practical activity 2b**

1 Record the manufacturer's data in the following table.

| Injector make | Injector type | Injector opening pressure | Torque setting |
|---|---|---|---|
| | | | |

2 Remove the fuel injectors. Take care not to bend the injector pipes.

3 If the equipment is available, test the opening pressures of your injectors and record them in the following chart.

| Injector 1 | Injector 2 | Injector 3 | Injector 4 |
|---|---|---|---|
| | | | |

4 Clean and carefully refit the injectors, noting the position of the sealing/heat protection washer and tighten them to the correct torque settings.

5 Bleed the system of any air, run the engine and check for leaks.

6 Make sure you record the test procedure and note what the injectors are tested for. This can then be used for future reference.

WITHDRAWN
153023